Smoking Privileges

Critical Issues in Health and Medicine

Edited by Rima D. Apple, University of Wisconsin–Madison, and Janet Golden, Rutgers University, Camden

Growing criticism of the US health care system is coming from consumers, politicians, the media, activists, and healthcare professionals. Critical Issues in Health and Medicine is a collection of books that explores these contemporary dilemmas from a variety of perspectives, among them political, legal, historical, sociological, and comparative, and with attention to crucial dimensions such as race, gender, ethnicity, sexuality, and culture.

For a list of titles in the series, see the last page of the book.

Smoking Privileges

Psychiatry, the Mentally Ill, and the Tobacco Industry in America

Laura D. Hirshbein

Rutgers University Press

New Brunswick, New Jersey, and London

Library of Congress Cataloging-in-Publication Data

Hirshbein, Laura D.
Smoking privileges : psychiatry, the mentally ill, and the tobacco industry in America /
Laura D.Hirshbein.
p. ; cm. —(Critical issues in health and medicine)
Includes bibliographical references and index.
ISBN 978-0-8135-6397-8 (hardcover : alk. paper) —ISBN 978-0-8135-6396-1 (pbk. : alk.
paper) —ISBN 978-0-8135-6398-5 (e-book)
I. Title. II. Series: Critical issues in health and medicine.
[DNLM: 1. Smoking—psychology. 2. Mentally Ill Persons. 3. Object Attachment. 4. To-
bacco Industry—ethics. 5. Tobacco Use Disorder—psychology. WM 290]
RC567
616.86'50651—dc23   2014017486

A British Cataloging-in-Publication record for this book is available from the British Library.

Visit our website: http://rutgerspress.rutgers.edu

Manufactured in the United States of America

For E.K. and his peers

Contents

Acknowledgments

This book began with a conversation with an individual with mental illness (E.K.) who I encountered in the course of my work as a psychiatrist, and I am grateful that he shared his thoughts and feelings so candidly. The information and perspective E.K. provided was further nurtured by the work of two exceptional scholars—Allan Brandt and Gregory Dalack. I had the good fortune of having a couple of conversations with Professor Brandt early in the process of formulating the book, and of course his own masterful work (*The Cigarette Century*) was an ongoing reference and source of inspiration. Dr. Dalack was one of the early researchers in the relationship between smoking and mental illness, and his humane approach toward the issue and toward patients is a model to all of us who are lucky enough know him as chair of the Department of Psychiatry at the University of Michigan.

I am also grateful for the wonderful communities of scholars and friends who were supportive, encouraging—and even excited—as I progressed through this project. At the University of Michigan, I have been very fortunate to enjoy a position that allows me both to see patients and write history. My colleagues in Psychiatric Emergency Services generously tolerated my impromptu talks on the connections between smoking and mental illness as we took care of patients. I have also enjoyed the support of scholars at the university, including Joel Howell and Alexandra Stern, and the passionate and engaged University of Michigan Tobacco Research Network, especially Cliff Douglas. The American Association for the History of Medicine has continued to provide a scholarly home away from home, and I remain grateful to everyone who listened, asked questions, and prodded for more detail, especially John Burnham, Gerald Grob, Howard Kushner, and Nancy Tomes. Rima Apple and Janet Golden are outstanding series editors with Rutgers University Press, with just the right combination of nudging and nurturing. Rima made extremely helpful comments to both the proposal and a complete draft. Martha Gardiner helped in numerous ways with suggestions for sources and an important reading of an early version of the manuscript. And Peter Mickulas at Rutgers Press has been an incredibly helpful and supportive editor.

The much-needed time for research and writing of this book was available thanks to a grant from the National Library of Medicine (1G13LM010186). I especially appreciate the helpful comments provided by two anonymous reviewers of the grant. An early version of the mental-health consumer perspective in this book was published as, "'We Mentally Ill Smoke a Lot': Identity, Smoking, and Mental Illness in America" (*Journal of Social History* 44 [2010]: 7–21). An early version of the tobacco industry perspective was published as, "Scientific Research and Corporate Influence: Smoking, Mental Illness, and the Tobacco Industry" (*Journal of the History of Medicine and Allied Sciences* 67 [2012]: 374–397). Many, many thanks to Nicole Triche, assistant professor of communication at Elon University, who created the cover photograph for the book.

Last but most certainly not least, I want to thank my friends and family who cheered me on and listened with good humor to what must have been interminable stories about the tobacco industry. My community in Ann Arbor has really been a family. And my family scattered elsewhere around the country has been extraordinarily supportive, especially Alison Davidow, who has always believed in me and who inspired and directed the cover photo, and Jessica Hirshbein, who was confident in my writing (even when I was not). Thank you to my husband Peretz for being my best sounding board and cheerleader, and a special thank you to Abigail for her research assistance and to Daniel for his encouragement and listening skills.

Smoking Privileges

Introduction

Smoking Privileges

When I first encountered E.K. in 2003, he was an inpatient on our psychiatric ward at the University of Michigan Hospital. He was thirty-five, but looked about sixty. E.K. had not had an easy life. He was diagnosed with schizophrenia in his teens, but no one knew if he really had the disease or if years of hard use of every illicit substance he could get his hands on had fried his brain. He had no social support—he had a chaotic relationship with his mother, his father was in and out of the picture (and in and out of prison for drugs), and his long-term girlfriend had borne him three children and put up with endless broken promises about him getting sober before she finally kicked him out. He was homeless with only a small monthly Social Security Disability check, and also had a genetic problem with his kidneys that had caused them to fail. He had been on three-times weekly dialysis because of his kidney failure for more than a decade. Dialysis requires patients to go to an outpatient center three times a week, sit for hours while their blood is cleansed by a large machine, and endure frequent exhaustion and weakness as a result. Not surprisingly, E.K. was not very good about making it to dialysis appointments.

E.K. had worked pretty hard to get into the hospital in 2003. When I met him, he had been hospitalized several times in previous weeks—and discharged several times in that same time period because of the very brief length of stay that has become typical for acute psychiatric units. For this particular hospitalization, E.K. had come to our emergency department five times in four days to tell staff that he was suicidal. The fact that his urine was always positive for drugs, and that his community mental-health case manager thought he was looking to get away from drug dealers, meant that he had been turned away four times. The fifth time, E.K. showed up with a knife, held it over his wrists, and started to cut before hospital security intervened and took it away from him. He succeeded in getting back into the hospital.

In our initial visit, E.K. was very irritable and expressed significant (and understandable) annoyance at the mental-health system that required him to work so hard to convince people that he needed help. He insisted that he was still suicidal and that he needed to stay in the hospital "for a long time" in order to straighten out all of his issues. Then with almost no pause, he said, "So Doc, you gotta let me go out for a smoke. I'm dying here. I promise I'll come back—I want treatment. I want help. I just need to smoke."

Our inpatient unit had gone smoke free four years before without major difficulties. After that time, patients routinely made requests to go outside and smoke and for a few years were occasionally taken out by staff (until that practice was banned). The unit is on the ninth floor of the hospital so it is not a small matter to take someone out for a smoke. It was certainly not routine in 2003 (and is unheard of now). Usually, by the time patients are psychiatrically stable enough to get a pass to go outside (with friends or family), they are ready for discharge. And in 2003 (or now) there is no way we would let a patient who was actively expressing thoughts of suicide leave our locked unit in order to smoke.

E.K.'s request was not honored. He was given nicotine replacement (which he didn't particularly like) and was eventually discharged to his chaotic existence where he resumed his two-pack-a-day smoking habit. But he and I developed a kind of relationship through our conversations about smoking that continued over years of recurrent encounters. A year or two later, he came to the emergency department on a day when I happened to be working and again was suicidal (and again worried about his safety because drug dealers were after him). He was more candid with me during that visit. He told me flat-out that he probably wasn't going to kill himself and that he was going to say what he needed to say to get into some kind of shelter. He also reminded me about his strong attachment to cigarettes and talked about how critical it was for him to smoke. He said that it was important to him that his providers understood this relationship and honored his expressed need to smoke. He knew—and I knew that he knew—that it was not good for his health, but he could not make a long-term investment in his health when his short-term, day-to-day existence was so hard.

That day, I didn't let E.K. go out and smoke (he was threatening suicide, after all). But over the next few years we developed a pattern when he came to the hospital—when he saw me, he resumed his conversation about cigarettes.

As long as he wasn't suicidal, I would let him leave briefly to go smoke. Our rapport—that started with his demand to smoke—got even better when he was able to get sober from other drugs for brief periods of time. He talked about how hard it had been to be on so many different psychiatric medications over the years and how much of a question it was to him and to his treatment providers whether he actually had schizophrenia. He talked about his children and wondered how they would do when they grew up. And he grieved when his mother passed away, though he was proud of himself that he had been able to be sober and at her bedside during her last months. He finally died a few years ago from complications around his kidney disease. He never quit smoking and never quit reminding us about how central cigarettes were to his life.

As I reflected on my relationship with E.K., it occurred to me that our dynamic around whether or not I would let him go and smoke when he came under my care put us both in difficult situations. From my perspective, I needed to weigh his psychiatric condition, his overall physical health, and my obligation to help as much as possible in the least restrictive way. Should I have said no to his requests to smoke because I was responsible for his health at those times? Or was it condescending of me to consider whether I should give him the opportunity to do what he was entitled to do as a citizen of the United States? From his point of view, he was doing the best he could to manage overwhelming social, economic, medical, and psychiatric issues. Smoking to him was not a problem—it represented a relationship and a way to cope. His attachment to his cigarettes was perhaps the most stable connection in his life.

In the end, our health system failed E.K. in many ways. We spent too much time arguing with him about what he needed. We couldn't help him out financially or get him off drugs. (When he finally got sober, it was due to his own determination, not any "treatment" we offered.) But I know that he valued being heard and having his feelings about smoking respected—even when we couldn't do what he wanted. And I appreciated the opportunity to learn from him about the strong attachment of many mentally ill individuals to their cigarettes.

E.K.'s story is not unique. Over the past couple of decades, it has become increasingly clear that individuals with mental illness smoke at very high rates.[1] As health management and policy expert Kenneth Warner has explained, the people who still smoke—despite decades of information about the health hazards—are "hard core" smokers. This group includes the mentally ill.[2] There are a number of ways to understand E.K. and his peers in their smoking behaviors. One factor is certainly addiction to cigarettes (and nicotine). Some have wondered also whether nicotine is doing something in the brains of mentally ill individuals—especially those with schizophrenia—that might mean that there is a biological connection between smoking and mental illness. But to frame smoking among the mentally ill only in terms of addiction or brain mechanisms misses how this behavior fits into the broader context of their lives, their relationships with other people and substances in general, as well as their encounters with mental-health providers and systems.

A historical approach can help illuminate some of the issues faced by mentally ill smokers. How have smoking behaviors shifted through major changes in mental-health settings? And what has happened to the mentally ill over the decades of increasing social restrictions on smoking? Thanks to the masterful work of historian Allan Brandt and others, we have a good understanding of the rise and fall of cigarettes in the last century, especially the growing awareness of the health consequences of smoking and the role of the tobacco industry and its efforts to deny them.[3] And through the foundation provided by Gerald Grob and others, we have a historical picture of the changes in mental-health care over the last two centuries, especially the appearance and disappearance of the mental hospital as the main location for psychiatric care and the shift to community systems in the last half-century.[4]

The intersection between these two important strands of history gives us a window into the lives of individuals with psychiatric diagnoses, the world of mental-health professionals, and a different view on the effects of health policy. Smoking involves a purchase of a consumer commodity (with an accompanying industry to market and sell it), a potentially dangerous encounter between fire and combustible materials, and meanings attached to both cigarettes and smokers that have changed over time. For mentally ill individuals, the relationship between their identities as patients and as consumers of products such as cigarettes has been complicated. The lurking danger of fire and the tensions between safety, autonomy, and normal social roles have been important aspects of the negotiation between patients and providers in mental-health settings. And for mentally ill smokers, the use of cigarettes has also involved meanings of smoking in psychiatric settings shifting from symbols of interpersonal interactions to signs of further marginalization in society.

This book explores the history of smoking among the mentally ill in order to understand power relationships in patient-provider encounters, the growing overlap between commercial entities (including tobacco and pharmaceutical industries) and mental-health researchers, changes in psychiatric professional self-definition and practice, and the unintended consequences of public-health policy. I look at the ways that cigarettes functioned in the old system of psychiatric care—the mental hospitals—both from the perspective of providers and patients. I also explore the actions of the tobacco industry and its recognition of the psychological factors in smoking, and the (relatively late) arrival of psychiatrists to the area of smoking problems. Two of the last four chapters examine the rise of neurobiological approaches toward this issue, particularly the role of nicotine, and the interests of both the tobacco and pharmaceutical industries. I look at the disconnect between the increasing intensity of the tobacco-control efforts and existing mental-health policy issues. I finally explore the result of the concentration of remaining smokers among those with mental illness in what has become the double marginalization of the mentally ill.

The history of smoking among the mentally ill highlights the complexity of what might seem to be a straightforward issue of public health. Over the last several decades, a growing and increasingly active group of experts in tobacco control, located in public-health organizations and in specialty health-advocacy programs, have developed policies and interventions to decrease the rate of smoking based on physical consequences of cigarette use.[5] In this book, I grapple with the question of whether it makes a difference whether people have emotional reasons to smoke and how social context affects their behavior.[6] Tobacco companies understood that stress and brain biology were important factors for some smokers, and mentally ill individuals were initially exempted from public-health pushes toward smoking cessation because of their psychiatric symptoms. More recently tobacco control advocates have dismissed the idea that there are emotional reasons to smoke, based partly on the desire to spread the benefits of smoking cessation among heavily smoking populations such as the mentally ill and also on a growing awareness of the nefarious practices of the tobacco industry to market their products. As a result, policies to reduce or eliminate smoking have increasingly affected mentally ill populations. But however well-meaning, tobacco control can have unintended consequences for the mentally ill by further stigmatizing them. And policy that centers on physical hazards of smoking can ignore many other issues faced by mentally ill smokers. By attending to the interaction between smoking and mental illness, we can see that public-health activities and initiatives can have disparate meanings and effects for different populations. Even a problem as apparently simple as smoking becomes more complicated when we include the perspective of the mentally ill.

There are some categories I use in this book that deserve clarification. The designation of "the mentally ill" has changed over time. The individuals we would now label with psychiatric diagnoses are not necessarily the same ones who would have been diagnosed (or labeled) in the past. And the locations in which people received treatment for serious mental illness changed over

the twentieth century. From the mid-nineteenth century, when American psychiatry was organized as a profession, to the 1970s and 1980s, when many of
the large psychiatric hospitals closed, state or local mental institutions were
the predominant locations for care for individuals with such severe emotional
and behavioral problems that they could not be contained within their homes
or communities.[7] In general, these people were the ones who were referred to
as mentally ill. The larger number of functional individuals who might have
received outpatient treatment (especially Freudian-inspired, psychoanalytic
office-based therapy) would not have considered themselves as mentally ill nor
would they have been counted as such by the few who looked at prevalence of
mental illness.[8]

By the 1980s, though, much of mental-health care had moved away from
long-term hospitals. In addition, the publication of the third edition of the
American Psychiatric Association's *Diagnostic and Statistical Manual* (1980),
the explosion of the use of medications for mental illness, and the rise of
psychiatric epidemiology shifted the picture of mental illness and the scope
of psychiatric intervention.[9] As a result, there was less of a clear distinction
between the seriously mentally ill, who remained within local community
mental-health systems (inpatient and outpatient) and people with other forms
of psychiatric distress that were labeled as mental illness and treated with
medication. It was after these shifts in psychiatric diagnosis that we began to
hear about the extraordinary prevalence of mental illness in the United States,
numbers that were derived from broad questionnaires (that included issues
such as substance abuse) given to the general population.[10]

As a result of these changes, it is difficult to talk about the mentally ill as a
single group. When seriously mentally ill patients spent long periods of time in
psychiatric hospitals earlier in the twentieth century, there was not much of an
emphasis on diagnosis. Now the focus in psychiatry is on diagnosis, but it has
less meaning when there are more than 350 diagnostic categories in the newest
edition of the *Diagnostic and Statistical Manual (DSM)*. For the purposes of
this book, I am using the designation of mentally ill to primarily include people
we would now consider as seriously and persistently ill, including those with
diagnoses such as schizophrenia, bipolar disorder, depression, and severe anxiety disorders (including post-traumatic stress disorder). It is among individuals
with these diagnoses that smoking is particularly prevalent.

As is clear throughout this book, the concept of "addiction" is also somewhat loose and does not have consistent meaning for health professionals or
the public. Historians of substance use have emphasized that patterns of drug
use over time have depended on many factors, including social context, legal

consequences, economic issues, as well as the biological drive to use. The inclusion of smoking among the other addictions makes sense in some ways (users of cigarettes are often unable to quit), but the other ramifications of addiction (such as social cost) does look different for smokers than for users of drugs such as heroin.[11] I do not make any attempt to define a transhistorical concept of addiction but rather attend to how the concept was used or contested in discussions about tobacco throughout the last half century.

Another important category is "patients." One theme in this book is power and how cigarettes have played into power dynamics in therapeutic environments. As the description of my interaction with E.K. indicates, the question of patients' smoking involves providers making decisions on their behalf and controlling the circumstances in which they can engage in some behaviors. Because I am interested in the way that power dynamics operate, I have chosen to use the term *patient*, rather than the perhaps more politically correct term *consumer* when I am specifically addressing the position of individuals within mental-health settings. The interactions between psychiatric providers and the people who were hospitalized (or treated as outpatients) were characterized by power. While it might be ideal to try to make the shift from thinking about a patient as the subject of an unequal power relationship to a client who is a partner in treatment, the reality is that the people who were hospitalized (and who experienced time as psychiatric patients in clinic settings) were very much affected by the staff-patient power dynamic. As observers commented in a 1954 exploration of the world of the mental hospital, "To describe the role of mental patient in the formal sense—as one complementary position in the doctor-nurse-patient triad within the broader mental hospital setting—is to run the risk of minimizing the vast amount of suffering the mental patient experiences, and to overlook the indefiniteness, complexity, and subtlety involved in 'being a mental patient.'"[12] In chapter 8, I address the issue of being a mental-health consumer and what that means for smoking and smoking cessation.

For better and for worse, patients were (and are) subject to the treatment decisions, rules, whims, and assumptions of treatment providers. Patients were not just passive victims of psychiatric power; their lives were controlled by the staff within institutions while they were there and by professional and economic forces outside their control in the community. Some of these power relationships were further structured by gender roles for both patients and providers.[13] They were undoubtedly also affected by race, though there are unfortunately virtually no sources to illuminate that issue. The point of attending to the power relationships is to validate individuals' experiences and concerns, which requires acceptance that the nature of mental illness put people into complicated relationships with care providers. As historian Nancy Tomes has pointed out, over the last few decades the mental-health consumer movement has had a profound effect on the relationship between providers and those who are the subject of care. Still, even with the recognition that consumers have rights, it is misleading to identify those who are prescribed medicine or controlled through economic measures or court orders as equal partners.[14] The use of the term *patients*, then, is not meant to denigrate but rather to reflect the reality on the ground.

I recognize that in using the category of "mentally ill," I am focusing on a group of people whose lives have many aspects other than their symptoms or their interactions with mental-health providers. Individuals with mental illness, like other groups of people who have disabilities, have insisted that they are people rather than diseases.[15] It is precisely this point that I am trying to make—that attention to smoking among individuals with psychiatric diagnosis needs to take into account the broader context of their lives. My goal is to look at the intersections between a behavior that has become a focus of public-health attention (with a population perspective centered on individual behaviors), a set of symptoms and diagnoses treated by mental-health providers (on a case by case basis), and experiences expressed by individuals who have been diagnosed with mental illness.[16] In the end, I want us to be able to engage in meaningful conversation with people who smoke and have to deal with mental illness.

This book would not have been possible without new sources that have come to light in the last few decades. Until the last twenty years, much of what the tobacco companies were doing—as with any private corporations—was hidden behind proprietary records and attorney-client privilege. As a result of the mass lawsuits of the tobacco industry in the 1990s, however, a large collection of documents from the industry became available for public use on websites maintained at a couple of academic centers. For this book, I have relied heavily on the Legacy Tobacco Documents Library maintained through the Legacy Foundation and physically housed at the University of California, San Francisco.[17] The documents in this library are searchable by key word. I began the project looking at the term *mental illness*, and uncovered a wide range of materials. I then pursued more specific search terms as I explored topics along the way.[18]

To put the tobacco documents into perspective and to understand the breadth of meanings in smoking encounters, I employed published literature in English that illuminated both mentally ill smokers and their care providers. I looked at hospital administration manuals, attendant handbooks, nursing texts, physician research articles and patient-authored narratives to understand each researcher, participant, patient, and tobacco-industry employee from the point of view of his or her own context. The bulk of these sources reflected ideas and practices in the United States, but some involved the United Kingdom, Canada, and Australia. Although those other countries' health-care systems vary, the trends around smoking in mental-health settings were similar, and researchers and investigators often reported on practices in other English-speaking countries.

E.K. asked me to try to understand his point of view about his attachment to cigarettes. By looking at the history of E.K.'s predecessors and the changes over time in their smoking behaviors in relationship to their illnesses and their care providers, we can see that smoking is more than a poor-choice behavior and that mental illness involves more than psychiatric symptoms. This book seeks to make sense of the behavior of E.K. and his peers, and put them in the context of changes in psychiatry, the tobacco industry, the pharmaceutical industry, and the mental illness experience over the last century. This is not an easy story of villains and heroes, perpetrators and victims. Nor is it just about addiction. Part of what makes this story so complicated is that it sits at the relationship between medicine and business, one that has become increasingly complex in the last several decades. Public-health policy directed toward mentally ill smokers needs to be shaped by the history that illustrates that smoking has played a complicated role in the lives of the mentally ill.[19]

Chapter 1

Ecology of Smoking in Mental Hospitals through the 1970s

In 1892, Illinois Eastern Hospital for the Insane superintendent Richard Dewey commented that tobacco had a powerful influence over patients in mental institutions. To get patients to cooperate with treatment, he suggested an inducement: "The privilege of a smoke or a bit of plug tobacco will bring a great many patients to the shop [occupational therapy] who would otherwise feel disinclined to go."[1] Like Dewey, psychiatrists and other mental-health care providers over the last century noticed that their patients had a strong relationship to tobacco and cigarette smoking. And for nearly a century, cigarettes played an important—and mostly unquestioned—role within such settings.

For decades there was little published psychiatric literature about smoking and its meaning for patients' mental or physical health. Early psychiatric hospital regulations about smoking focused on fire hazards to the buildings rather than on other issues for patients or staff. During the mid-twentieth-century-high prevalence of smoking in the general population, there were few limitations on smoking within psychiatric institutions. It was a behavior to be managed, a barometer for patient relationships with staff, a method for encouraging socialization, and a potential source of difficulty with certain patient populations.

Until the 1980s and 1990s, smoking was a fact of life in mental hospitals and among psychiatric patients. Recent critics have blamed the culture of mental-health settings for encouraging smoking over the decades. While it is true that the environment—and sometimes the staff—encouraged smoking, the ubiquity of cigarettes and smoking behaviors offer a window into the experiences of mentally ill individuals and their relationships with care providers. Mental-health professionals on the whole accepted that smoking was part of the illness experience, but practitioners within hospital health-care teams approached their patients' relationship with cigarettes using different management strategies. And individuals with mental illness saw and interpreted smoking and cigarette exchange as important aspects of their relationships with staff and one another. Patients' (and staff) use of cigarettes within mental hospitals and other locations of psychiatric treatment highlighted the slippery definitions of normal and abnormal behavior and the challenges of proscribed patient and caregiver roles.

Provider Roles and Smoking

The state-mental-hospital system was a key setting for care for seriously mentally ill patients in the first two-thirds of the twentieth century. There were also private psychiatric facilities and hospitals for alcohol or drug-abusing patients, as well as a system of hospital services for military veterans.[2] In all of these locations, cigarettes were a near universal part of the culture through most of the twentieth century. Some state hospitals grew and supplied tobacco for patients, and many included a tobacco allotment for patients as part of their basic board.[3] Mental hospitals located near tobacco companies often received donations of cigarettes to give to patients, and shortages of cigarettes for psychiatric patients could be reported as a newsworthy problem.[4]

But smoking was usually not raised as an issue. Hospital-administration guidelines at mid-century did not mention smoking, even though it was widespread.[5] Hospitals restricted patients' smoking patterns (either access to matches or lighters, or identifying specific acceptable indoor locations for smoking) in response to concerns about possible fires.[6] But beyond the basic safety issues, psychiatrists, nurses, attendants, and social workers encountered smoking in efforts to connect to patients, to control their behavior (both good and bad), and to effect a cure for their illness. All of these methods shifted over time, but for the most part providers accepted that their patients smoked and did not expect them to quit. Further, mental-health providers as a group tended to smoke and shared the culture of smoking with their patients.

The leader of the mental-health treatment team was the psychiatrist, the physician who was in charge of the mental hospital and who directed patients' treatment. As both medical professionals and leaders of a team, psychiatrists engaged on the topic of patient smoking on several levels, from understanding the role of tobacco for patients, to using tobacco to connect with patients, to directing smoking policy for the hospital. Physicians' approaches toward smoking among patients were shaped by their own smoking patterns, as well as their assumptions about who should smoke (or not) and why. Their interpretations of patients' smoking behaviors depended on their theoretical orientation. Psychoanalytically inspired psychiatrists could, for example, see smoking as displacement of libidinal energy.[7] And psychiatrists did not hesitate to use smoking to reinforce power dynamics with patients.

One of the issues for psychiatric patients was that they could not always communicate their thought processes or use words to express their distress, and psychiatrists used smoking as a barometer to gauge patients' internal states. In the 1920s, psychiatric pioneer Henry Stack Sullivan attended to the utterances of his patients and noted the frequency with which patients discussed their preoccupation with smoking.[8] During World War II, observers noted that smoking could be a marker of emotional distress due to combat-related anxiety: "Excessive smoking results in large areas of cigarette stain on the fingers. It seems that the patient is reluctant to toss his cigarette away, smoking it until it almost burns his fingers. One cigarette follows another."[9] Even without a conversation, psychiatrists could understand patients' mental condition by observing their relationship with cigarettes.

Physicians incorporated smoking behaviors as part of their assessment and evaluation of patients.[10] Sometimes patients did bizarre things with their cigarettes, and this became a management issue.[11] One patient at a Veterans Administration (VA) hospital in Virginia had been placed on a work assignment outside the hospital in the late 1940s. He did well, except that his supervisor was upset by his pattern of picking up cigarette butts and smoking them, especially since he had enough money to buy cigarettes. The patient's psychiatric team worked with the patient and noted as a mark of his progress that the patient eventually stopped picking up butts and began purchasing his cigarettes.[12] Patients also harmed themselves with cigarettes, either by extreme smoking behaviors or by burning themselves with cigarettes, accidentally or as part of their delusional systems.[13] Treatment-team leaders engaged with staff and patients to contain or stop these behaviors but often focused on changing circumstances to allow patients to smoke in a safer manner.

For some psychiatrists, the recognition of their patients' needs and desires to smoke reflected their benevolent intent. In 1933, Richard Dewey returned to the theme of tobacco helping patients adjust to hospital life in an address to the American Psychiatric Association (APA). He suggested that patients responded better when their staff displayed kindness: "A good humored attitude is hard to resist, a little refreshment, liquid or solid; even a cigarette; a little compliment would be well received and easy to give."[14] The offer of cigarettes seemed to be a benign and easy intervention. In 1938, New York psychiatrist Karl Bowman explained, "I would state unhesitatingly that it is better to give a patient one or two cigarettes at bed time than to dose him with barbiturates or other hypnotics. I believe that intelligent observation will indicate that the amount of hypnotics can be diminished by the judicious use of cigarettes at bedtime."[15] Psychiatrists understood cigarettes to be part of their armamentarium in dealing with potentially problematic patient behaviors and saw them to be more humane and less potentially harmful than medications.

Further, smoking allowed psychiatrists to connect with patients. One psychiatrist reported on his efforts to make contact with a psychotic Canadian Indian girl. The psychiatrist commented that he had been smoking, and so offered the girl a cigarette—which she accepted. This became the basis of a working relationship that, according to the psychiatrist, helped the girl recover.[16] Psychiatrists also used smoking to help patients relate to one another. One of the most frequently discussed deficits in schizophrenia, according to mental-health professionals, was difficulty with social interactions. Smoking was a ritualized behavior that allowed patients to engage with one another in a highly structured way. A Canadian psychiatrist experimented with using a variety of drugs in order to try to promote good social interactions with patients. In addition, "to make the atmosphere congenial, peanuts and cigarettes were provided freely."[17] Cigarette use smoothed the way to assess for other kinds of interventions.

Of course, one of the reasons for psychiatrists' awareness of patient smoking was probably their own smoking rates. Several University of Pennsylvania psychiatrists explored the behaviors of students at their medical school during times of stress and found that more than 60 percent smoked more while feeling nervous.[18] Popular cartoons in this time period illustrated psychiatrists smoking cigarettes as part of their patient interactions.[19] Even after other physicians began to focus on the health consequences of smoking, psychiatrists seemed to respond to a different set of priorities regarding their own smoking behaviors. Two psychiatrists in the 1970s speculated that since a psychiatrist had to sit and listen to patients instead of moving around during patient care, "he may thus experience an intense need to continue smoking as one of the few vehicles available to him for drive release and tension reduction." Further, since psychiatrists did not take care of patients with serious physical health problems, it might have been easier for them to ignore the health effects of smoking.[20]

While psychiatrists accepted patients' smoking behaviors (perhaps for their own reasons), other members of the mental-hospital team had different perspectives on the role of smoking in the hospital. Psychologists and social workers described the dynamics of smoking among staff members. Nurses recognized the power of smoking restrictions and privileges in the hospital.

And aides regularly interacted with patients around their smoking needs and were left to interpret and enforce any hospital rules or limitations on smoking. Because smoking was part of everyday life within hospitals, providers within the team interacted with—or attempted to manage—smoking behaviors at different levels.

Psychologists and social workers were active participants in psychiatric inpatient settings, though their roles were variable. Psychologists in the early twentieth century primarily focused on formal testing of patients, but by mid-century they became more established experts on social dynamics and interpretations of behavior.[21] Social workers in mental hospitals initially worked with families, though they also expanded their role to include more individual encounters with patients.[22] And they visited patients in their homes and were able to observe potential discrepancies between family reports and home environment. Members of both of these professions made efforts to understand and analyze patient behaviors, including smoking.[23]

For these practitioners, smoking was a behavioral manifestation of an emotional state rather than a determinant of health. In the 1920s, a psychologist interpreted patients' oral needs with regard to nutrition and psychological factors. While eschewing psychoanalytic connections between oral needs and sex, the psychologist argued that the mouth was an important site for learning and that the existence of smoking behavior at meals was a remnant of "infantile sucking projected into the medium of adult social intercourse."[24] Psychologists also observed behavior and interpreted the effects of interventions with patients. Two psychologists from a Pittsburgh VA hospital tried techniques to reduce anxiety in a chronic schizophrenic and could tell he was better because his cigarette smoking decreased.[25]

Other psychologists and social-work observers analyzed the social environment of psychiatric hospitals, including the role of smoking in interactions. Psychologist David Kantor, who did his dissertation on social relationships in a mental hospital, found that students who volunteered in the hospital often had difficulty relating to the patients. Smoking, though, helped the students to see the patients as people, such as when the male patients lit up cigarettes for the female volunteers.[26] Another social scientist observed a problematic dynamic on an inpatient unit in which a patient made excessive demands (especially for cigarettes) on hospital staff and divided them over the ideal approach to the problem. The investigator was able to present his observations about the patient and the group in a meeting, which resulted in an intervention to proactively provide the patient with a cigarette before she asked. The intervention helped the patient and the group.[27]

Social workers were particularly attentive to the group dynamics of hospital settings, and took on roles as facilitators and problem solvers. A 1955 social worker explained a situation in which there had been a conflict on a unit between a rigid, controlling nurse and a more permissive woman head psychiatrist. The psychiatrist instituted group work to be run by a social worker. Before they had the opportunity to engage in group interactions, the patients were apathetic and did not interact. With the introduction of group activity, the patients were much better groomed and more involved: "In the recreation room, some patients sat together smoking, talking, and playing games with the workers and each other while others danced to records."[28] In this case, smoking was a sign that patients were developing positive social connections. And the easing of restrictions, particularly around smoking, helped alleviate the conflict.

As the previous example illustrates, there were often clashes between the roles of different mental-health providers. Nurses were key members of the treatment group and functioned to direct the day-to-day activities of mental hospitals. And the fact that nursing was dominated by women shaped power dynamics. As a number of historians have pointed out, nurses had ongoing challenges in their relationships with their physician supervisors and in their efforts to become more autonomous professionals.[29] This tension was visible around smoking. While physicians were often more permissive regarding smoking, the task of supervising the patients' daily living environment fell to the nurses. On the disturbed ward of the Chestnut Lodge Hospital in Maryland, for example, the nurses had a long list of rules, including many restrictions on patients' smoking behaviors.[30] In textbooks, educators warned nurses to be ever vigilant about the potential safety risks in smoking, particularly when patients were brought cigarettes, lighters, and matches by visitors.[31] Nurses expressed discomfort over the conflict between their mission of allowing patient autonomy and their professional ethos of helping patients. One troubled nurse gave an example of dealing with a patient who kept burning her fingers because she would fall asleep with a lit cigarette. What should have been done when the rules were that the patient should not be denied her cigarettes, but the nurses did not want to neglect her physical well-being and allow her to get hurt?[32]

At the same time that they had to enforce the rules, nurses were also in a position to interact with patients in a more informal and potentially meaningful fashion than physicians or psychologists. Many of them worked on their relationships with patients in shared smoking time, and they were thoughtful about how to balance rapport with limits. Instructions for nurses and attendants included advice about when, how, and with what restrictions to smoke with patients. Nurses often understood the importance of smoking to patients and were able to use patients' smoking as a way to engage with them. One nursing textbook explained that the opportunity to smoke could be part of the plan for patients who became agitated: "It is well for the doctor or the nurse to remain with the patient while this technic [*sic*] is being used, not only to avoid accidents, but also to reemphasize to other patients that what is being done is treatment and not favoritism."[33] Nurses could combine surveillance with companionship, all around smoking. But relationships to patients around smoking highlighted a tension for psychiatric nurses—were they were medical authorities who helped to manage physical health (which would suggest more emphasis on safety and restrictions on cigarettes) or were they were companions to patients who could relate through shared experiences? And how did gender roles affect this tension?

Psychiatric nurses often interpreted their work with patients as modeling normal social interactions. Smoking was very much a part of this through the 1970s. But as historians have pointed out, social norms shifted from the early twentieth century when women's smoking was not acceptable to mid-century when women smoked cigarettes more openly. And smoking could be seen as a sign of power, an assertion of equality with men in social settings.[34] Cigarettes helped to symbolize a shift in psychiatric nursing responsibility to a more active therapeutic role, though nursing professionals commented that some did not understand the potential of this kind of interaction with patients: "Many nurses are reluctant to accept the psychiatric nurse because she is not giving physical care to the patients. They observe the nurse on the psychiatric unit sitting down and talking with patients, even having a cigarette with them."[35] The psychiatric nursing literature celebrated the many ways in which nurses were able to connect with patients, including shared smoking experiences. The direct connection with patients did risk leveling the power disparity between nurses and patients. But psychiatric nurses compensated for this by insisting that their professional role included intensive interactions with patients, and they asserted their power around smoking to establish authority in clinical settings.

Within the growing subfield of psychiatric nursing, smoking as a way of therapeutically interacting with patients was an important part of professional identity. Some suggested that nurses could appropriately understand patients' complaints that they wanted something (such as medication) as really being about a desire to connect—over a cigarette.[36] Smoking gave patients and providers a shared language. A nursing instructor gave an example in the 1970s of a hypothetical patient interaction in which a nurse used her feelings to help an agitated patient, framed around a smoking interaction: "Observe your own behavior: 'When I was lighting my cigarette just now, I noticed my hand shaking.

I am feeling tense. I wonder what is going with you and me right now.'"[37] When patients smoked with their providers, the connection helped strengthen the therapeutic relationship. Smoking could also help hospital staff get patients through their aggressive or agitated behavior to more constructive interactions. For example, a 1964 nursing educator relayed a story of an agitated patient who had cut her wrist while smashing a window. The patient's nurse knew her well and lit her a cigarette and asked her to sit down and explain what had happened. The patient immediately calmed down and used words instead of aggression to express herself.[38]

While negotiations around smoking highlighted role complications for psychiatric nurses, issues around access to cigarettes illustrated the class interactions that characterized patients' relationship to attendants or aides, the final main participants in mental-health treatment teams. These individuals had the least education and training as a group, yet spent the most time with patients.[39] And, as might be expected, they had extensive interactions with patients around smoking. Attendants or aides were often the ones to dole out cigarettes and lights. Like other members of the mental-health team, attendants who smoked with patients temporarily leveled the power differential between them. But cigarette access also showed ways in which patients' social status outside the hospital might have been superior to that of the attendant—it was only in the hospital that the attendant had power. Educational literature designed to raise the level of professionalism among aides and attendants stressed the importance of standards and consistency in patient interactions, including maintenance of appropriate boundaries and avoidance of favoritism (a problematic behavior often symbolized by allowing some patients special access to cigarettes).[40]

Attendants were particularly responsible for helping with safety in the hospitals. But hospital staffs were aware that safety issues also involved an element of control, and their ability to manage patient behavior depended on presenting safety in a positive light. For example, a training program for psychiatric aides outlined multiple-choice questions meant to help them learn how to talk appropriately to patients. One of the questions involved an interaction around smoking: "Mrs. Jones does not understand why she cannot smoke in her own room. You might explain, A. 'There is danger of falling asleep with a lighted cigarette.' B. 'You can only smoke when an aide is with you.' C. 'Some patients try to set fires, so we cannot have smoking in bed.' D. 'The rules say you can only smoke in the dayroom.' E. 'Smoke in the bedroom bothers some patients.'"[41] The correct answer was A, a response that attempted to rationalize the restriction. Yet the other possible responses—all plausible—speak to the control inherent (and perhaps necessary) in this environment.

In practice, attendants used their instincts and their feelings to guide them in their interactions with patients. One attendant interviewed for a 1961 book on mental hospitals explained, "Most attendants feel if you treat the patient right, he'll do what you tell him to do. We try to be kind to them. A man gets up at night upset and he wants a smoke—and it's against the rules—but what the hell, it'll do him good. The doctors and nurses are pretty highhanded with us about a lot of things, but to tell you the truth, I think sometimes we can do the patients a lot more good than they can."[42] A University of Michigan graduate student interviewed attendants at the Ypsilanti State Psychiatric Hospital in the early 1960s to find out how often attendants broke rules with patients, including rules about smoking. He found that the key factor was not the attendant's experience or education, but rather how well the attendant felt he knew the patient.[43] And attendants built on their relationships with patients—often developed or reinforced over smoking—to define their role in helping patients recover. As one textbook for psychiatric aides explained, for patients at the end of the day, "if sleep is impossible, there is someone to talk to, someone to give them a cigarette. That someone is the aide."[44] Both patients and attendants identified compassion in aides based on whether they would bend rules as needed to provide patients with opportunities (and materials) needed to smoke.[45]

Attendants' roles with patients—including their ability to connect with patients by facilitating their smoking behaviors—was built on by other members of the treatment team to help patients' overall progress in the hospital. But sometimes descriptions of smoking issues revealed problems. For example, attendants were the ones who were responsible for physical management—including restraint—of difficult patients. A mental-health team in the late 1950s, however, tried to show that attendants could use smoking interactions instead of force to help patients get in control. At the Central Islip State Hospital in Long Island, attendants were "being retrained by the doctors who go up to the ward, pick two or three noisy, deteriorated patients at random and take them to the nurse's office along with the attendants and they all sit down with coffee and cigarettes. The doctor listens and the patients can talk, stay quiet, walk about or shout as they wish. Within a few minutes the noisiest, most delusional patient calms down."[46] But while attendants needed to be told at times that they should treat patients as people (with whom they could smoke) rather than management problems, they were also at risk for another abuse of power, that of taking materials from patients. A social scientist in 1954 examined mental-health treatment at the private hospital Chestnut Lodge and uncovered only one type of unethical behavior—the frequent "borrowing" of patient cigarettes by attendant staff.[47]

Like the physicians who worked in mental-health settings, nurses and attendants were probably attuned to smoking issues because of their own smoking. Psychiatric nurses seemed to smoke at higher rates than their peers in other specialties.[48] Attendants also viewed their jobs as quite stressful, and not surprisingly they smoked at high rates as well. As a former state hospital attendant wrote to cigarette company R.J. Reynolds in 1937, "my work handling Mental Patients is pretty risky and you can never tell when one will turn on you, rest assured we must do some quick thinking at times and believe me I'm plenty glad to get a camel [sic] after I go off duty."[49] Psychiatric hospitals were perceived as intense places to stay and work, and cigarettes were part of the culture. And cigarettes and smoking helped members of the treatment team manage their own feelings as well as the behavior of their charges in the hospital.[50]

Mental hospitals both reflected external social norms and highlighted the abnormality of power structures within an institution. The role of smoking exposed this dichotomy. For example, in response to critics who complained that psychiatric hospitals were merely warehousing patients, Boston psychiatrists in the 1950s described ways to make their environment more therapeutic and less custodial. As part of that initiative, they helped patients learn how to socialize and enjoy mealtimes. Instead of rushing patients away from the table, staff "made meals more leisurely and social, added radio music for dinner, encouraged smoking by distributing cigarettes and ash trays. The efficiency motif gave way to the social motif which proclaimed the right of every person to 'dawdle' after meals and enjoy conversation."[51] In this context, smoking was a part of normal human interactions, and it was important to encourage such behavior in patients whose social interactions had become disrupted. Cigarette smoking, then, became a means to an end—the goal of improved social interactions. But at the same time, it was a parody of free and normal social behavior because the patients were only permitted to smoke when provided with materials from the staff.

Smoking was not a problem for mental-hospital staff through the 1980s, it was a fact of life. Providers expected that patients, like individuals within the broader population, would want to smoke. This did not change, even in the 1960s and 1970s when the health risks of cigarettes were widely discussed in the medical literature and the media. But in mental hospitals, staff enacted power relationships around cigarettes based on status, expectation, and gender. While providers used cigarettes to both connect to and control patients, the patients had their own relationship to their smoking. And while staff generally intended for their interactions with patients to be therapeutic and safe, patients did not always experience them that way, as we can see from their point of view.

Perspective from the Other Side

In 1987, psychiatrist Carol North published her autobiography in which she recalled her unique experience as both a physician and an individual with schizophrenia. North commented on an aspect of mental-hospital life that for decades affected both patients and practitioners: the overwhelming presence of cigarettes. As a student on her psychiatric-ward rotation, she "dutifully followed the orderly down the hallway, parting the thick cloud of cigarette smoke suspended in the air. Almost every patient had a cigarette hanging out the side of his or her mouth, or burning long-forgotten between charred fingertips." When she was hospitalized herself and interviewed in front of the whole staff, she noted, "Most were smoking, and their cigarette smoke hung in the room in a dense cloud." She was aware that later they were going to discuss her case over cups of coffee and more cigarettes.[52] As North outlined, cigarettes were embedded in the culture of mental hospitals for both patients and staff.

North was uniquely positioned to have both the perspective of a mental-health provider and a patient within the same system. But most individuals who experienced mental illness had a different relationship with the power structures of psychiatric-care settings. And their impressions around smoking highlighted both those power structures and the differences in their experience of smoking. The provider point of view on smoking among psychiatric patients until the last few decades was that it was a behavior that needed to be managed. In this same time period, individual accounts by people who experienced mental illness illustrated the importance of cigarettes for mental-hospital culture, as well as the power struggles for people with mental illness when they battled hospital staff over their smoking. Smoking was often a part of being mentally ill.[53]

Patients' perspectives on smoking is harder to access than the opinions of mental-health providers, but a significant number of individuals wrote and published first-person accounts of their experiences with mental illness and their treatment in psychiatric hospitals in the United States and in several other English-speaking countries.[54] While these narratives are certainly not representative—and the authors often had an axe to grind against practitioners they encountered in hospitals—the role of cigarettes and smoking helps us understand more about their experiences as they struggled with mental illness.[55] Several of the narratives were made into films, and their representations of smoking (sometimes in contrast to the primary sources) further highlight the issues involved in dealing with an illness without visible manifestations.

Cigarettes were ubiquitous in first-person narratives of individuals with mental illness from the early twentieth century when individuals tended to roll their own cigarettes (with tobacco supplied by or grown at the hospital), to mid-century when everyone inside and outside the hospital seemed to smoke, to the last thirty years when their smoking behaviors set the mentally ill apart from others. Patients keenly observed the structure of smoking opportunities and the ways that cigarettes affected their relationships with staff and other patients. But interactions over cigarettes also highlighted the role of power in mental institutions. Patients were aware that their need to smoke gave staff the power to control their behavior. Patient narratives on smoking were remarkably similar in the United States and other English-speaking countries, and control issues around cigarettes were apparent in all kinds of hospital settings, even in the Soviet Union, where political prisoners could be incarcerated in institutions masquerading as psychiatric hospitals.[56]

As patient experience and social-scientist observation both bear out, cigarettes were an important part of the culture in psychiatric hospitals through most of the twentieth century. And patients also understood that access to cigarettes reflected formal and informal relationships and power dynamics. Individuals who might not have encountered one another outside the artificial environment of the hospital structured their social interactions through cigarettes. Smoking provided a way for patients to connect with one another and sometimes with providers, including physicians and nurses. And smoking gave patients a concrete framework to understand the control that the hospital had over their lives.

In patient explanations, institutional limits on smoking were a gauge of control within mental hospitals. In the early part of the century, women's wards seemed to have more restrictions men's, based on staff assumptions about appropriate behavior. While the narratives by men before World War II discussed restrictions on smoking, the women's highlighted significantly fewer opportunities to smoke and fewer cigarettes allowed.[57] A woman hospitalized on the violent ward of a state mental hospital complained that the rules were explicitly different for women than for men. She pointed out that the men could smoke and would be given tobacco if they did not have money, "but the women—that is another matter! Even if they have their own money with which to buy their cigarettes, they cannot have them—it is 'immoral' for women to smoke. . . . If they become too nervous because of the sudden denial—they will be given drugs!"[58] Psychiatrists of the time admitted that they had a dilemma about whether to allow women to smoke as much as men as they strove to promote appropriate decorum for patients.[59]

While providers claimed that limitations around activities such as smoking were part of the treatment, patients pointed out that staff enforcement of regulations were subject to variation depending on the situation. A state hospital

patient, who wrote in the 1930s to educate the public about life inside the institution, explained that tobacco was very important to mental patients to help
them manage their time on the wards. In order to make sure that patients had an
adequate supply, he suggested that family and friends send in cigarettes, even
though it was likely that attendants would confiscate extras. He described various graft operations taking place in the hospital, primarily around goods such as
cigarettes and better food.[60] Patients understood that cigarette exchanges were
based on power and relationships. A nurse, star-struck when 1930s film actress
Frances Farmer was admitted as a patient on the ward, gave her cigarettes even
though she had not been given permission by the doctor.[61] Wealthy patients had
the power to bestow gifts. A morphine addict who was hospitalized in a federal
narcotics facility in 1947 purchased a carton of cigarettes from the commissary
and gave a couple of packs to a friendly orderly. He made a point of saying that
he gave him the cigarettes because he was nice, and not that the orderly became
nice because he received cigarettes.[62] Others writers matter-of-factly outlined
the casual bribery of attendants to get more smoking opportunities.

The reason that there was so much underhanded behavior by both patients
and staff around smoking was the high value placed on tobacco. Access to cigarettes symbolized a step up in a series of privileges toward discharge from the
hospital. The highest-status patients at hospitals were those who had gained
the right to carry their matches and cigarettes around with them for unlimited
access to smoking opportunities.[63] Cigarettes were also tied up with economic
issues. As one former patient explained in the 1930s, "Honestly, no one outside
can ever know how much tobacco means to men in a place like St. Charles. If
we had no money we were given a corncob pipe and a small supply of tobacco,
free—pretty bad tobacco, too. Of course we were glad to get any at all, for men
are men everywhere, and when there is little to do, time on one's hands, and
trouble to bear, tobacco is almost more welcome than food."[64] And patients
were willing to do all kinds of chores or work around the hospital in order to
get more tobacco.[65] Journalist Albert Deutsch complained in 1948 that men at
the Manhattan State Hospital were exploited for their labor and paid not in
money but in extra rations of tobacco.[66]

As Deutsch's concern suggests, one of the vulnerabilities of psychiatric
patients then (and now) was that they were often on the economic margins of
society and struggled to make ends meet. Individuals who spent time in public
mental hospitals often had unstable (or nonexistent) sources of funds. Early
in the century, patients measured true destitution by whether someone could
afford his or her cigarettes.[67] Although some institutions provided individuals
with (usually small) supplies of tobacco, patients agreed that the quality was

poor.[68] Cigarettes could make ideal prizes or rewards and were recognized as a commodity with significant value.[69] Visitors from benevolent societies supplied cigarettes and lighters.[70] Patients often needed to beg money from reluctant family members to pay for cigarettes during hospitalizations.[71] And cigarettes could be used as effective bribes for underpaid staff members.[72]

Tobacco supplies were particularly an issue for patients at state hospitals, and the mindset of institutional reformers at the time was that men and women in hospitals needed to have their basic needs attended to—including their need for cigarettes. A wife of a Pilgrim State Hospital psychiatrist published a novel in 1945 exposing the problematic aspects of the thinly fictionalized state hospital. Among the outrages she noted was that the institution was not good about providing tobacco supplies for patients. In the novel, patients resorted to smoking dried leaves crumpled in toilet paper. The psychiatrist main character in the novel displayed his heroism by giving money to purchase tobacco for the patients.[73] Patients with resources sometimes helped others in need by supplying money for cigarettes—or money for other treats if patients were only using their scarce resources on cigarettes.[74] And occasionally staff would help out by giving cigarettes to patients too poor to buy them.[75]

Smoking was critical to a subset of patients in the early part of the century who were hospitalized for their inability to control their use of alcohol or other drugs. While there were special hospitals for alcoholics in the early twentieth century, some individuals had such severe problems they were sent to full psychiatric hospitals.[76] The patients who were struggling with alcohol and drug difficulties were especially attuned to the issues around cigarette access. Writer William Seabrook went to a mental hospital in 1933 because he was unable to stay sober. In the first few days of his stay—when he was actively going through alcohol withdrawal—one attendant made him go to a lounge (where staff held matches) and smoke. Another, though, was more understanding and allowed Seabrook to have a cigarette in a place where smoking was technically not allowed. As he moved between wards, Seabrook judged the environment by the comfort of the smoking room.[77] Other writers in the grip of addiction to alcohol and other substances were particularly attached to cigarettes and smoking as they endeavored to stay sober. Several biographers of Bill Wilson and historians of Alcoholics Anonymous (AA) commented that AA grew out of a regular meeting of a small group of men who would drink coffee and smoke cigarettes in order to avoid going out to get drunk.[78] An alcoholic woman writing advice so that other women could recognize and get help for alcohol problems noted that it was terribly dangerous to drink and smoke at the same time. Her solution was to quit drinking—not quit smoking.[79]

While some found cigarettes to substitute for (in their view) more problematic substances, others used smoking opportunities to relate to one another or to staff. In their narratives of illness, patients repeatedly explained the ways in which cigarettes helped forge connections between patients. These relationships often started with an offer of a cigarette. A patient hospitalized in the 1940s described being intensely confused when he arrived on a psychiatric unit. He understood, though, that another patient was trying to be friendly when he offered him a cigarette. Later, he had a pleasant conversation with a recreational therapist who gave him free access to cigarettes whenever they talked about uncomfortable topics.[80] Patients found that they could talk to each other over cigarettes, even when they could not talk to their treatment providers.[81] In a novelized account of mental illness, a patient who wanted to reach out and thank another patient for a kind action decided to leave cigarettes under her pillow.[82] Patients gathered together in order to smoke, and often used each other's cigarettes to light their own (since attendants to light them were in short supply).[83] An anthropology doctoral student found that patients began to treat her as a peer when she dressed in casual clothes and smoked quietly in the lounge of a mental-health center.[84] One schizophrenic man put it very simply—"Smoking help [*sic*] us to share our life with other."[85]

Cigarette smoking helped to define the community of individuals struggling with emotional issues.[86] And many patients noted the unspoken agreements among mental-hospital inmates, which was observed by researchers who described life in the hospital, that usually those with cigarettes would share with those less fortunate. Patients had elaborate rituals of exchange involving puffs of cigarettes, portions of cigarettes, and lights from lit cigarettes (to avoid going to staff to get access to matches or a lighter).[87] Patients from long-term, chronic wards might exchange cigarettes or beg them from others, while some patients were too shut down to interact with anyone, even over cigarettes.[88]

The understanding among patients regarding cigarette exchange even allowed patients who spoke different languages a way to interact with one another. A Canadian man who was forcibly hospitalized against his will in Spain described giving a cigarette to a psychotic man who asked for it in the context of his delusional idea that they were co-conspirators: "Others must have seen me give him a cigarette, for the next second I was surrounded on all sides by nervous, wide-eyed inmates begging for a smoke. One full packet was gone before they would leave me alone."[89] Even patients who were profoundly impaired were able to ask for cigarettes. A woman described her encounter with a mute patient on an inpatient unit in the 1970s: "When she indicated that she wanted them, I would give her cigarettes. I had even become familiar enough with her language and gestures to know a little about what she meant. She came up to us and stood right in front of me, with her hand outstretched. I didn't have any cigarettes with me. 'Go over to Ellen,' I told her firmly. 'She'll give you a cigarette.'"[90] The exchange was so fluid that Mary Jane Ward's semi-autobiographical main character Virginia in *The Snake Pit* noted that she would give away cigarettes to fellow patients, only to have them get confused and offer her the same cigarettes in return.[91]

Patients explained that cigarette exchanges were not always friendly, though. One alcoholic who was hospitalized at Bellevue in New York at mid-century noted that there was a hierarchy of patients—the one at the top took cigarettes from others and passed them out to those he was disposed to view with favor.[92] A woman who recounted her (mostly unpleasant) interactions with psychiatric providers and hospitals in the 1970s relayed a story of a patient who provoked her fellow patients by getting a nurse to light her cigarette, then looked around for an open purse into which she would drop the lit cigarette.[93] Another patient complained that it was hard to sleep while in a mental hospital because patients would wake her up to demand cigarettes even though she did not smoke.[94]

Smoking was common among patients, and also among people around them. Cigarette smoking eased interactions between confused or frightened family members and hospital staff. Family members could smoke with mental-health providers, who would explain the psychiatric issues, and families interpreted these interactions as signs that providers understood the patient and were trying to be helpful.[95] An American couple in the 1970s, Janet and Paul Gotkin, narrated their grim experiences of the mental-health system as Janet was repeatedly hospitalized for mental disturbance and suicide attempts. But throughout their challenging experiences, there were moments of clarity and connection with providers. At one point, Paul waited for a doctor after one of Janet's attempts: "I tapped out a cigarette for myself and he held out his hand, gesturing for me to pass him one. 'I thought you'd finally stopped smoking,' I said. He shook his head. 'I stop and I start again.'"[96] The men smoked together, united temporarily over cigarettes and their concern about Janet's safety.

Patients also smoked with staff, especially hospital aides. Strategic rule breaking helped patients feel that aides understood their distress. A man who was in a VA psychiatric hospital for a year and a half described his confusion and desperation around the experience. A number of episodes of smoking with attendants helped him to calm down and learn the system of the hospital.[97] Patients gauged their relationships with staff by whether or not they could share the experience of smoking with them. New York writer Eric Hodgins described his irritation with many nurses who tried to save him by preaching about the evils of tobacco (evils of which he was well aware, since he became mentally ill after a stroke that he acknowledged was probably connected to his smoking). Hodgins was grateful and enthusiastic about a nurse who said she wanted to ask him something. He was initially worried, but, "thus did I traduce, on less than fifteen minutes' acquaintance, the lady who turned my life around and made it *go* again—in short, who saved it. Her full sentence turned out to be, 'I hope you smoke.' Delighted into incoherence, I assured her I smoked like a fish. Our rapport began then. It was so nice to meet a human being again, after so many plaster saints and a full fair share of Furies."[98] Patients recognized nurses and attendants who smoked as kindred spirits.

Clare Wallace, a British woman who was both a patient and a psychiatric nurse and went back and forth between the two roles, documented the ways in which staff bonded with one another over cigarettes. The nurses smoked together when it got busy on the ward, or when they were particularly upset about protocol issues. Wallace also described the ways in which her nurse friends smoked with her and attempted to comfort her as she slid into illness and had to be hospitalized herself.[99] A short-story writer who shared her experiences with mental illness illustrated the power of nurses who could be friendly and joke with patients during smoke time rather than just rigidly controlling cigarette supply.[100]

Patients also connected to their physicians through shared smoking experiences, and a physician's willingness to smoke with them illustrated his—or her—essential humanity. While doctors gave cigarettes to patients, they also occasionally borrowed. In one narrative, a man illustrated how his doctor helped him understand his internal conflict in a scene involving cigarettes. He described a moment in which the doctor (Lawsky) reached for the patient's cigarettes at the same time that he made a challenging interpretation. The patient responded, "'You torture me and you mooch my fags!' 'You exaggerate on both counts,' said Lawsky. 'I doubt if I have mooched half as many fags from you as you have from me. I even recall providing you with a complete pack when you complained one week of being short of funds.'" This conversation helped the patient explain the ways in which he was getting better. He could banter about cigarette supplies with the doctor, and even had the power to donate to the authority figure.[101]

Patients made efforts to analyze and understand their relationships with their physicians, and smoking helped give structure to the interactions. A British patient conveyed a story of her deep attachment to her psychiatrist in an extended narrative addressed to him. The breakthrough moment for the patient came when she and her doctor admitted to each other that they both smoked (and she still did while waiting outside his office). While she initially did not like the idea of his smoking forty cigarettes a day, the mutual confession was an important part of their evolving relationship: "I could not imagine you chain-smoking. The idea revolted me. Your whole personality would have taken on a different aspect. In return, I let you know that I smoked six cigarettes a day. I had never mentioned it before, and I had hidden my cigarettes in the bottom of my bag, or under the tins of soup and potatoes in my basket or old paper bag. You said it made no difference to what you felt towards me."[102] For this patient, the interaction between the power and authority of the physician with what the patient perceived as the shameful act of smoking helped the patient reach a new level of insight in her treatment.

While most of the physicians described in patient narratives were men, there were a few women, and their smoking patterns with their patients helped them appear less authoritative. A British actress tried out several psychiatrists as she struggled with worry and thoughts of death in the 1960s. She went to one psychiatrist who sat on a couch behind her and made her more anxious. She switched to a woman psychiatrist and knew right away that it would be better because the doctor gave her a cigarette as she showed her around her office area. She reflected on the contrast with the old doctor, "Sitting in a chair, often with a cigarette, this difficulty sorted itself out with Dr. Pemberton. It was a conversation; I could ask if something was worth mentioning and find a reaction that encouraged me and kept me going."[103] For this patient, the ability to sit and smoke face to face with her doctor provided reassurance that she was a human being who could relate to others. At the same time, though, the more intimate interaction with the doctor made her uncomfortable, and the patient went back to a male psychiatrist who was more traditional and made her lie down on a couch.

In Joanne Greenberg's semi-autobiographical novel *I Never Promised You a Rose Garden*, one of the first signs that the main character, Deborah, had found a sympathetic psychiatrist was that Dr. Fried seemed to listen and echo Deborah's feelings by her smoking. When Deborah recounted her terrible experience with childhood cancer, Dr. Fried was described as so upset on Deborah's behalf that she angrily stubbed out her cigarette while muttering about how bad it was to lie to children. Although Deborah was apparently not a smoker, the narrative noted in several places that Dr. Fried smoked intensely during therapy sessions in which Deborah discussed overwhelming emotional issues.[104] Interestingly enough, the Hollywood depiction of this relationship removed the doctor's smoking entirely (along with her Jewish identity) and made Deborah the smoker (but only in front of a bad psychiatrist).[105] The real-life Dr. Fried, influential analyst Frieda Fromm-Reichmann, used smoking and cigarettes to connect with patients.[106]

Patients did not always view their psychiatrists' smoking behaviors with approval. One woman recounted numerous disastrous encounters with psychiatrists, and her impression of the worst of them was tied up with his smoking: "The inner office was heavy with smoke. Through the fog I saw a man with a long, soft, yellow face and pale eyes and light straw-colored hair. There was weakness and pain in the face, but the deciding characteristic was pain. I noticed his tobacco-stained fingers, and his thin wiry neck. He looked something like a chicken, I thought. A depressed chicken."[107] Another woman observed her psychiatrist's smoking behavior and criticized the way he would smoke instead of engaging with her. She commented, "Psychiatrists always armed themselves with tobacco, it seemed, as though it were a signal they would say little or nothing."[108] A nonsmoking depressed patient noticed that her psychiatrist's office smelled like the cigarette he smoked before he saw her and wondered, "Did he need to try to compose himself before he could leap from the problems of the earlier appointment into an approach to my needs?"[109] And while cigarettes were everywhere in mental hospitals, not all patients appreciated their role. Psychologist Al Siebert candidly acknowledged that he had been psychiatrically hospitalized at a VA hospital in 1965, and since he did not smoke, was disgusted with the fact that an aide offered him a cigarette. When Siebert met the psychiatrist, Siebert was confident that the man knew nothing because the doctor was overweight, smelled of cigarette smoke, and with fingers stained from years of smoking lit up a cigarette during their interview. Siebert left against medical advice and never returned to another psychiatrist.[110]

Beyond patients' sometimes unfavorable impressions of smoking doctors, cigarette-based interactions could signal problems with the dynamic between doctors and patients. A woman in a New Zealand hospital engaged in manipulation of a physician to get cigarettes even while she was in seclusion for aggressive behavior.[111] A father of a psychotic young man reported that his son reached for a psychiatrist's cigarette in their shared ashtray during an interview. The patient became agitated when he was told that it was not his cigarette. He became so unable to control himself that he had to be hospitalized.[112] When patients were confrontational and angry about psychiatric authority, their narratives were more likely to frame psychiatrists' attempts to share cigarettes with them in negative terms. Actress Frances Farmer described her difficult psychiatric hospitalization and the conflicts with staff. She initially was very reluctant to talk to her doctor, but finally did. She noted, "He offered me a cigarette, probably some sort of reward for talking, then took one himself."[113] Other patients bitterly recounted times when providers—doctors and other mental-health workers—demanded cigarettes from patients under circumstances that created resentment and adversely affected their treatment.[114] Patients' ability to control their situation while in mental-health settings was limited at best, and cigarette access and exchanges reinforced their lack of power.

As both providers and patients attested, smoking was an entrenched feature of psychiatric hospital life through the 1970s. At a time when smoking was normal for many Americans and an accepted element within routine social interactions, smoking within psychiatric settings illustrated the complex dynamics within the institutions. Psychiatric hospitals had been designed to create an ideal environment, to structure life for mentally disturbed persons in order to help them on the road to recovery.[115]Although twentieth-century hospitals hardly lived up to the ideal, staff within the hospital were attuned to the environment and the need to manage it effectively to help keep patients safe and in a position to get better. The ecology of smoking shows that not everyone interpreted these elements in the same way. Staff set limits over patients' smoking behaviors to promote safety and to assert control, and patients understood the power dynamics that emerged around smoking negotiations.

By the 1960s and 1970s, most public attention outside psychiatric hospitals regarding smoking was focused on growing concerns about health effects. Within mental-health settings, the ubiquity of cigarettes was increasingly visible—but the issue was not health. Instead, smoking became a key symbol of both the potential and the problem of psychiatric institutions during those decades of social and cultural upheaval. And while smoking was an element of normal social behavior at the time, psychiatric patients often had a unique relationship to their cigarettes that was a direct result of their illness. Both of these aspects of smoking—the role it played in institutional power dynamics and the particular connection of mentally ill patients to their cigarettes—were critical to the changing response within mental-health circles to smoking in subsequent decades.

Chapter 2

Conflict and Smoking in Mental Hospitals in the 1960s and 1970s

In the 1960s and 1970s, psychiatrists faced growing public criticism for their treatment settings, their approaches to patients, and even their definitions of mental illness. Social-science theorists and researchers such as R. D. Laing and Erving Goffman, along with psychiatrist Thomas Szasz, publically castigated the profession for confining patients for no reason, treating them badly while confined, and making up categories of illness. Some of these critiques aligned with shifts within psychiatry itself, but others dovetailed with growing distrust for authority in these turbulent decades, and psychiatrists found themselves on the defensive about their care of patients, especially in hospitals.[1]

In that context, it makes sense that the issue of smoking would have appeared in a different light than in the contemporary battle between health advocates, who emphasized that smoking caused disease, and the tobacco industry, which claimed that buying and using cigarettes was a part of free consumer behavior. The contest over smoking within mental-health settings during the 1960s and 1970s revealed that patients had relationships with cigarettes that went beyond that of typical consumers. And mental-health professionals had many other issues other than physical health on which to focus within increasingly contested hospital settings. It is hard to understand the experiences of individuals with mental symptoms, but their interactions with cigarettes highlighted their financial instability, family issues, and some of the challenges in determining the boundaries between reality and delusion. And psychiatrists understood that cigarettes offered a kind of anchor for patients to try to help them move toward other forms of recovery. For critics outside psychiatry who attested to the coercive power of mental hospitals and denigrated psychiatric treatments, smoking represented yet another form of normal behavior that was controlled in total institutions. And smoking exchanges highlighted gender roles and conflicts. Smoking was not an incidental behavior; it was one with meaning for many patients and staff, and a symbol of freedom for critics.

Special Role of Cigarettes

Smoking played a special role for individuals with mental illness, one that had been recognized by psychiatric providers for decades. By the 1960s and 1970s, it was increasingly clear that mentally ill individuals, especially those who struggled with serious illnesses (variously diagnosed as psychosis, schizophrenia, depression, or manic depression) had a particular relationship to cigarettes. They smoked with great frequency and intensity, and usually without apology, and others did not demand that they quit. Family, friends, and providers expected that patients would smoke. Smoking was so widely accepted as part of the mental-illness experience that film representations of psychiatric patients before the late 1980s routinely illustrated patients smoking, usually as a way of signaling the emotional intensity of the environment.[2] And smoking also illustrated some of the unique challenges faced by mentally ill smokers.

Chronically mentally ill individuals often lacked the skills or the resources to take care of themselves and as a result suffered serious financial hardship.[3] This was particularly acute for the many patients who smoked. One sign of the desperation experienced by patients was that if they could not afford cigarettes (or had limited access), they frequently resorted to smoking fragments in order to get tobacco. Patients understood the value of parts of cigarettes—they were better than nothing. And perhaps as part of their illness, they treated fragments as important currency even when this made no sense to the people around them. For example, in the film *One Flew over the Cuckoo's Nest* (the 1975 portrayal of the 1962 Ken Kesey novel), the men were shown betting cigarettes and one of the patients bet a piece of a cigarette. The main character (McMurphy as played by Jack Nicholson) rejected the idea of cigarette pieces, saying they were useless. But patient narratives throughout the century suggested that patients did value even parts of cigarettes.[4]

And patients openly enjoyed smoking. As one woman observed in the hospital, women in her unit gathered around a nurse to get her to light their cigarettes, then did activities while "taking long, satisfying drags from their cigarettes."[5] Mindy Lewis, a New York writer, described the intensity with which the teenagers at the New York State Psychiatric Institute engaged with their cigarettes in the late 1960s:

> Smoking is our most serious ritual, more natural than breathing: the
> sharp sulfurous hiss giving way to a subaudible crackle, inhalations like
> gasps of surprise followed by grateful exhalation. I watch people smoke.
> Some take deep drags, "steaming" their cigarettes, so the tip grows red.
> Others, frozen, forget to smoke, and their cigarette turns to one long, gray
> ash. . . . Patients smoke different kinds to suit their moods: menthol in
> the morning to perk them up, regular for serious afternoon contempla-
> tion, nonfilters for an espresso-like kick. Packs are stowed in pockets;
> hospital bathrobes provide two, pajama tops one. Matches are always
> in demand; lighters, prized. People trim their wicks carefully, lovingly.[6]

Even after she got out of the hospital, Lewis commented on her ongoing relationship with cigarettes, and emphasized that they helped keep her going
through difficult times.

Patients invested meaning in their attachment to cigarettes. Some borrowed psychoanalytic jargon to explain it. A woman who was unable to quit
smoking, even while feeling guilty about it, explained, "Cigarettes became
phallic symbols. I kept lighting them and throwing them in the toilet."[7] Others discussed their delusions and the roles that cigarettes played within them.
In one account, a narrator explained that he had developed an idea that he
needed to destroy a man sitting on a bench near him in the hospital because
he thought the man was a threat to him. He explained that he thought that by
smoking really hard and swallowing all the smoke, he would generate enough
heat to disintegrate the man. He smoked all his cigarettes one right after another
(even though he had wanted to save them) and believed he saw the other man
shrinking before his eyes.[8] More distressed patients harmed themselves with
cigarettes by burning holes in their skin, sometimes in specific patterns. One
patient burned holes in his hands that he likened to the nail holes in Christ's
hands.[9]

Whether or not individuals agreed with professionals about being mentally
ill, they could often recognize, because of changes in their smoking patterns,
that there were times in their lives when they lost touch with reality (at least
with the benefit of hindsight). One well-educated British patient had an experience of hearing voices that commanded him to do things, including when and
how to smoke. He reflected later, "I was controlled and dominated by what I
thought to be a divine voice, without which I dared do nothing, even so much
as light a cigarette."[10] Another woman heard a voice that insisted that she had
to make a sacrifice to help humanity—and that sacrifice was to give up smoking. She was not happy about this: "With dismay I realized that I had been slyly

tricked. Though the sacrifice might be small, the last thing I wanted to do was to give up smoking. Yet there seemed to be no other way out. How else could I free myself and at the same time keep my integrity and good intentions intact? With a sigh of resignation I took the only course open to me and gave up smoking."[11] The patients measured their recovery by their ability to smoke without psychotic interference.

Patients struggling with mental disturbances engaged in unusual or bizarre behaviors with cigarettes or fragments of them. New Zealand writer Janet Frame wrote a thinly fictionalized account about real patients she encountered through her own experience in mental hospitals. In her novel *Faces in the Water,* Frame reported that a hospital patient "had an engaging personality and a facility for finding cigarette butts and transforming them into smokeable cigarettes." This was fine until an older, delusional woman snatched one of the butts and a fight ensued.[12] A Canadian man hospitalized in a Spanish mental institution (while on vacation) encountered an old man who gathered cigarette butts, took them apart, and collected piles of tobacco and paper—even though he had sufficient funds to buy intact cigarettes.[13]

A California man, who wrote under the pseudonym John Balt, killed his wife in the throes of a delusion and was eventually found not guilty by reason of insanity. Balt described his eccentric behavior while in jail awaiting the proceedings after the murder. He was too psychotic to be able to understand a form he needed to sign to authorize using his money to buy cigarettes—he thought he was being asked to sign his death warrant. He had to rely on the jail's free but poor-quality tobacco. Despite a severe cough from this tobacco, he smoked instead of eating, and kept missing when he tried to throw the butts into the toilet so the floor was covered with them. Later, Balt attempted to kill himself with cigarettes: "I remembered that nicotine was poisonous; so I started to eat cigarettes. They had no effect, not even nausea. The filters, too, were apparently completely digestible. All I could manage with cigarettes was to burn myself and I did so constantly. Much later I found another use for them, one which Madison Avenue has never thought of. I tried to use the smoke to destroy my brain cells."[14] When Balt went to see a physician, the doctor pulled toilet paper, cigarette butts, and matches out of Balt's ears.[15]

Cigarettes were often fully enmeshed in the mental-illness experience. Increased smoking could be a sign of worsening agitation or distress in individuals with reality problems or even those who struggled with addiction to alcohol or drugs.[16] And cigarettes appeared in delusional utterances. A psychiatrist in the 1970s recorded that one of his patients ranted: "I'm trembling also smoking a lot cause it hurts it hurts to know this but I MUST MUST MUST know this I don't want any more secrets."[17] Smoking behaviors were both a part of their lives and a way to understand acute illnesses for both individuals and their providers.

Family members of mentally ill individuals also wrote narratives that described their loved ones' behavior through episodes of illness, and smoking patterns often signaled problems.[18] One father with a seriously mentally ill son knew something was wrong when all his son did was smoke: "He spent much time off in his own world, lying in bed evenings, smoking one cigarette after another, chewing at himself, uncommunicative, formally polite."[19] Another woman explained that her son's smoking conveyed his feelings right before admission to a new hospital: "He said nothing, reaching for a cigarette, but by his short harried puffs that smoked the car like a defective flue, I know his anxiety was still high."[20] A Virginia woman knew that her three-pack-a-day son was becoming ill when he threw a packet of cigarettes across the room and talked about not being able to smoke.[21] For these family members, certain emotional states—suggested by intense smoking—were the problem.

And smoking also highlighted the precarious lives of individuals with mental illness. A man who described his wife's mental illness and eventual suicide relayed the many ways in which her smoking heightened his alarm about her condition. At one point when she was not in a good state, the husband tried to ask her if she needed to be in the hospital, but "Anna wouldn't answer, if she indeed heard the question. She smoked as though the world was about to end, hysterically, her eyes wild and fearful."[22] She eventually died from injuries sustained when she set herself on fire.

Patients were aware—certainly after the first surgeon general's report in 1964—that smoking was dangerous to their physical health, but they seldom framed any efforts to quit in terms of improving or maintaining health.[23] In the 1970s, a California man shared his experience of psychosis with a group that was conducting experiments on LSD since he thought it might be useful information for investigators (a not entirely farfetched idea at the time as some psychiatrists thought that LSD intoxication was a good model to understand psychosis).[24] He explained that during one episode of illness during which he wrote voluminously, had a mood of "indescribable joy," and gave away a lot of things, including a carton of cigarettes. He was very pleased that he was able to quit smoking during this episode. Yet, "after about three months abstinence, my psychosis faded, and like an ass I bought a pack and it seems I haven't been able to quit since. So it may just be that when these things are better understood and controlled that good may be realized out of what we know as insanity."[25]

So this man was able to accept that quitting smoking was good, but questioned whether psychosis was really a bad thing.

Did psychiatric patients believe they were self-medicating with smoking? It is hard to say, as there were so many ways in which patients articulated their attachments to cigarettes. Some patients believed that smoking helped reduce side effects from their psychiatric medications.[26] But self-medication could also be viewed broadly as a way of coping with the stresses and strains of life. An interesting perspective on this came from comic Lenny Bruce in the early 1960s who defended his drug of choice, marijuana, on the grounds that everyone self-medicates: "So I do not understand the moral condemnation of marijuana, not only because of its nontoxic, nonaddicting effects as contrasted with those of alcohol, but also because, in my opinion, caffeine in coffee, amphetamine, as well as tranquilizers—from Miltown to aspirin to nicotine in cigarettes—are crutches for people who can face life better with drugs than without."[27] Most patients assumed that they needed their cigarettes, however they expressed that need.

During this time period, the tobacco industry kept up their mantra that everyone had the right to buy and consume products—including cigarettes. But the evidence from narratives of mentally ill smokers suggested that this population had a somewhat different relationship with cigarettes and smoking behaviors. It is hard to know how much these individuals responded to marketing or how they incorporated public discussion about smoking into their behaviors. But was clear was that mental-health professionals recognized the relationship their patients had with smoking and saw no barriers to trying to harness that connection to improve patients' overall mental health.

Behavior Therapy

As we have seen, psychiatrists were aware of their patients' attachment to smoking, and during the 1960s and 1970s, at a time when the profession was under intense criticism, they used that attachment to attempt new forms of treatment. Psychiatrists insisted that they were doing something active to help patients and that hospitals could be important research sites. And mentally ill individuals' motivations for cigarettes and smoking opportunities were reframed as a key tool for investigators. In the 1950s, psychiatrists began to use state-hospital settings as ideal research locations because patients were contained for long periods of time, and there were few administrative barriers to putting patients into studies. By the 1960s and 1970s, with growing calls to get patients out of hospitals, energetic psychiatrists worked to make state hospitals more relevant to patients by increasing treatment options and to the profession by increasing research at the same time.

Several professionals noted that smoking was prevalent among alcoholics and used this to study alcohol problems further.[28] Harvard investigators in the late 1960s tried to standardize the lives of alcoholics on a research unit in order to understand the effects of alcohol. One of their interventions was to provide each subject with a daily pack of cigarettes.[29] Another group of researchers examined alcoholics and their behaviors at St. Elizabeth's Hospital in Washington, DC. In order to assess their patterns of use, the investigators provided the subjects with tokens so that they could purchase their own drinks. For the men who did not use all of their tokens on alcohol, they had the opportunity to purchase cigarettes with them.[30] The same investigators did a study of memory loss in alcoholics' blackouts to find out if the men really did not remember anything. They used cigarettes to reward positive answers and expected that this would help the validity of the test of recall: "Cigarettes were awarded for correct responses on the tests; these were the only cigarettes available to the subjects during the study. Since all were heavy smokers, the aim of using cigarette reinforcement was to maximize attention and motivation during the testing procedures."[31] The fact that the men did not seem to remember much during their blackout periods—despite the inducement of cigarettes—suggested to the investigators that the memory impairment was real.

Beyond these rudimentary efforts to examine behaviors, using cigarettes as rewards, investigators formally employed behavioral techniques to try to understand and change patients in psychiatric hospitals.[32] During this time, behavior theories and treatment interventions were important for a growing number of psychiatrists who were disenchanted with the prevalence of psychoanalytic theory in the profession. From the 1950s through the 1970s, researchers used cigarettes within sophisticated behavioral research programs designed to explore behavior of chronically mentally ill individuals in psychiatric hospitals. The researchers worked on behavioral understandings, drawing heavily on the work of Harvard psychologist B. F. Skinner.[33] In the process, they highlighted the limitations of psychoanalysis, especially through patients' relationship with cigarettes, and advocated for different types of treatment options in the hospital.

Within a behavioral framework, the basic idea was that any stimulus naturally induced a reaction, and a subject could be trained so that a second stimulus could induce the same reaction. In the classic behavior experiments conducted by Russian physiologist Ivan Pavlov, a dog's response of salivating at the sight of food was paired with a sound. After a period of time, the sound itself caused salivation.[34] Skinner elaborated on Pavlov's findings and conducted years of experiments with animals (especially rats) to understand how to condition subjects to respond to different stimuli.[35] The idea that behavior could be reduced to stimulus and response also galvanized professionals who wanted to have a more concrete understanding of humans. Psychologists who studied human subjects with behavioral interventions had no interest in the elaborate interpretations promulgated by Freudian psychoanalysts. Instead, they attempted to understand and shape behavior through concrete stimuli. And researchers in both psychology and psychiatry challenged traditional psychiatric authority even as they conducted research in traditional mental-hospital settings.[36]

Investigators who used behavioral methods liked cigarettes because they were concrete objects that could be tied to specific behaviors. In fact, a couple of researchers used cigarettes in an experiment to prove that behavioral conditioning was more valid than psychodynamic psychiatry. In 1965, two researchers published a widely cited study in which they conditioned a schizophrenic woman to carry around a broom by offering her cigarettes every time she did it. They then invited in two psychoanalysts to interpret the woman's behavior. The interpretations were, of course, ridiculous—one said the patient was expressing unconscious desire for a child, while the other blamed an unresolved Oedipus complex.[37] The investigators were satisfied that psychoanalysis would not stand up to scientific scrutiny, and that cigarettes could help change behavior.

While most behavioral researchers had originally worked with laboratory animals, a few argued that chronically mentally ill patients in hospitals could also be studied using behavioral methods. Harvard psychologist Ogden Lindsley published foundational work in 1956 when he developed a mechanism for applying Skinner's rat experiments to humans in a laboratory setting. Lindsley, with advice from Skinner and influential psychiatrist Harry C. Solomon, designed a room with a chair, an ashtray, and a modified cigarette vending machine. Lindsley invited schizophrenic patients to stay in the room for an hour a day, and let them know that they could pull the knob on the vending machine to get candy or cigarettes. The point of the experiments was to see how and under what circumstances seriously mentally ill patients were able to organize themselves to pull a lever to get a reward—in this case, cigarettes. Lindsley and subsequent researchers explored how long it would take for patients to learn to dispense cigarettes from the machine, how long they would continue to pull on the lever before the response was extinguished, and how far the behavior could be reinforced.[38]

Investigators from a hospital in Anna, Illinois, visited Lindsley's lab and followed up on his work. The Illinois team published a number of reports of their behavioral interventions with chronic schizophrenics. Two of the patients had not spoken for decades, and others were chronically ill without much prospect for improvement. While cigarettes were not used for every patient, in general the investigators chose patients for their studies who would respond to readily available inducements such as cigarettes or candy.[39] The patients were taken one at a time to the experimental room and left there for an hour. They were not locked in, but if they left before the hour was over, they were made to wait in a waiting room and were not given the cigarettes that were typically offered to subjects after they completed the daily experiment. The investigators' goal was to make sure that patients stayed in the room for all of the interventions in the study—this evidently worked.[40]

The next logical step in behavior therapy was to see if patients could be taught to engage in appropriate behaviors as a step toward discharge from the hospital. In 1968, the Illinois team published a book outlining a system of rewards for good behavior using tokens as a currency of exchange. This token economy was widely studied and copied in a number of institutions in the 1960s and 1970s. When patients engaged in behaviors considered desirable by hospital staff—including doing chores around the unit, bathing on a regular basis, and interacting with others—they would be given tokens that could be exchanged for goods or privileges.[41] And, as investigators pointed out, cigarettes were among the most common items redeemed for tokens in these economy systems.[42]

Many hospital psychiatrists around the country who replicated the Illinois program reported with satisfaction that their token-economy systems worked to help chronic patients for whom other interventions had failed.[43] A few researchers even tried token-economy programs in acute psychiatric hospitals.[44] Others adapted a home cigarette-rolling machine to provide a strongly reinforcing mechanism by which patients could be encouraged to interact with one another.[45] These interventions—including the use of cigarettes to induce desirable behaviors—came to be included in new models of hospital psychiatry, which emphasized a treatment environment over older custodial models.[46] Further, behavior therapy could be helpful for other challenging populations, including patients with alcoholism. One investigator who studied alcoholics in psychiatric institutions in the 1970s found that token economies worked wonders for patients who were able to substitute cigarettes, candy, and a nurturing environment for their need for alcohol as long as they were in the hospital. Unfortunately, those reinforcers were not enough to keep the alcoholics away from alcohol after they got out of the hospital.[47] Other outpatient providers of alcohol treatment programs believed that a sanctioned space for drinking coffee and smoking cigarettes helped patients avoid spaces where they might be tempted to use alcohol.[48] While smoking behaviors were sometimes the ones that needed changing according to hospital staff, for the most part psychiatrists were happy to use patients' baseline smoking desire as a wedge to develop other positive behaviors.[49]

Psychiatrists readily recognized the role of cigarettes in token economies, but they did not typically engage in much discussion of what it meant to be encouraging (directly or indirectly) smoking in patients. In fact, researchers in the 1970s accepted that basic ethics necessitated both allowing patients to smoke and setting limits around cigarette access. One investigator argued in 1975 that it was difficult to obtain informed consent for behavior programs with schizophrenics because, "when applied to operant procedures, it would seem as patently absurd to ask a patient if it were all right to withhold cigarettes until after he cleaned his room as it would be for an employer to ask his employees if it were all right to pay them only if they had worked."[50] While behavioral studies in institutions (especially hospitals and prisons) came under increasing criticism in the 1970s because of the coercive nature of the setting, the smoking or cigarette aspect of the studies was not seen as the problem at the time.[51]

While some therapists working with the general population had begun to use behavioral techniques to help individuals stop smoking, mental-health researchers were using chronically mentally ill patients' strong attachment to cigarettes to encourage healthy behaviors.[52] Providers saw smoking as a baseline need that could be harnessed for good, and until the late 1980s and early 1990s did not appear to be overly concerned about patient smoking. In fact, one Indiana psychologist tried to get support from a tobacco-industry research group for a project involving cigarettes within a token-economy system. The tobacco group was lukewarm about his proposal, though, and it was not funded.[53] By the 1980s, providers were more apologetic about using cigarettes to positively reinforce behavior, and by the 1990s they were blaming token-economy systems for the high rate of smoking among psychiatric patients.[54] But at the same time that they expressed concerns about using cigarettes, they continued to recognize that smoking was an important feature in their patients' lives and that behavioral expectations could be dramatically increased when tied to patients' cigarette supplies.[55]

Cigarettes and the Total Institution

While researchers felt confident in their use of cigarettes to induce positive behavioral change in patients, critics were horrified by psychiatrists' efforts to control patient behaviors—including smoking.[56] But the critics were not concerned about the fact that patients smoked in general; they were upset about the ways in which patients' behaviors were unduly constrained. By the 1960s, many institutions, including psychiatric hospitals, were under attack as illegitimate, and psychiatrists faced criticism from multiple political perspectives.[57] Social scientist Erving Goffman argued that mental institutions were like any authoritarian places, including prisons. British psychiatrist R. D. Laing deplored a culture of "treatment" that failed to acknowledge patients' essential humanity.[58] And other critics pointed out that patients had to play along with providers' expectations to be advanced in privileges. Within all of these complaints, smoking was a barometer of control in institutions as well as a marker of human interaction (or lack thereof). Patients' excessive smoking within hospital settings also highlighted the dearth of activity. And smoking was an area in which many patients defined a (gendered) clash between their needs as emotionally vulnerable individuals and providers' need to be in control.

In 1961, Erving Goffman published his three-year study of the interior dynamics of St. Elizabeth's Hospital, the large psychiatric hospital in Washington, DC. Goffman's conclusion after this exploration was that hospitals were harsh, restrictive, and untherapeutic. He used the term *total institution* for a setting in which individuals had every part of their lives controlled, which included prisons as well as mental hospitals.[59] Within his critique, Goffman explicitly commented on the control staff exerted over patient smoking. He pointed out, for example, that patients complained that they needed to make excessive pleas for things like cigarettes: "Attendants have been reported forcing a patient who wanted a cigarette to say 'pretty please' or jump for it. In all such cases the inmate is made to display a giving up of his will."[60] Goffman's sympathies were on the side of the patients, and he derived much of his data from his own observation and from talking with patients.

But provider-authored literature bears out Goffman's assertion that hospital staff used access to cigarettes as a way to force social niceties (and to manage their own irritation with patients). As Morris Schwartz reported in 1957 about an interaction at Chestnut Lodge in Maryland, nurses strongly expressed their opinion that a particularly difficult and demanding patient should learn to be polite as part of her treatment, and so they insisted that she say please before they would get her cigarettes. They alleged that the patient was the one insisting on the jumping. As one nurse complained, "Then she said that I'm supposed to jump and get her the cigarette when she asks. I told her I wasn't going to do it until she asked me in a more polite way." When the patient could not be polite, the staff took her cigarettes away entirely.[61] Both sides agreed that staff decisions about patient behavior governed their access to cigarettes, though they clearly differed in whether they thought this was appropriate.

Other critics echoed Goffman's concerns about power structures within psychiatric institutions. Purdue sociology professor Robert Perrucci did a year of fieldwork within a mental hospital and noted the extent to which the hospital environment controlled patient activities. As he explained, "Patients are told when to rise, when to sleep, what to wear, what to eat, how to talk, how to act, who to talk to, and even how to think. They are dependent upon the hospital for their food, clothing, cigarettes, and toiletries. Material possessions and goods that are taken for granted at almost every level of living outside the institution are transformed into scarce commodities. In most of these respects, the mental hospital closely resembles the prison."[62] Patient narratives also testified to the control exerted by staff over their every action. One New York writer, who was hospitalized at Payne Whitney for depression following a stroke, outlined the smoking privileges on the different levels of the hospital. He mused, "One need only be deprived of a small (and unhealthy) freedom for a little while to realize how precious all freedoms, small or large, are."[63] British nurse and sometimes mental patient Clare Wallace spent a lot of time going back and forth between patient and provider in the 1960s. At one hospital, she was startled by the casual attitude toward smoking since nurses could smoke wherever they wanted, and they could grant patients freedom in smoking without fear of management reprisal.[64]

Smoking was part of group dynamic behavior, not necessarily a concern regarding individual health, and providers' conceptions about what they could to do regarding smoking related more to the environment and the culture of rights for patients in the hospital. At Chestnut Lodge in Maryland in the 1950s, staff had noted that they had an excessively dirty ward because all the patients were dropping cigarette ash and butts on the floor. They reported, "With many misgivings, the order was put into effect that a patient who did not use an ash tray would be denied cigarettes for twenty-four hours. The effect was instantaneous and almost complete. Acceptance by the patients was immediate and cigarette butts were no longer found on the floor."[65] But while the use of wholesale restrictions on cigarettes to enforce rules was acceptable at mid-century, by the 1960s and 1970s mental-health providers seemed to have much less latitude to use smoking limitations to enforce desirable group behavior. During this time, psychiatrists and sociologists worried about the effect of institutional life on chronic mental patients, particularly that they were being infantilized because they had so little control over their everyday activities. Goffman pointed out in 1961 that allowing patients to sit and smoke a cigarette (after being brought in with a straightjacket) lulled them into a false sense that that they were in a place that would look after them, rather than a total institution that would control every part of their daily lives.[66] Psychiatric leader Jack Ewalt explained in

1964 that progressive mental-health measures meant making patients respon-sible for their own behaviors on inpatient units, and he advocated for letting patients have their own clothes and manage their own cigarettes and matches.[67] This tension between staff control and development of patient initiative and autonomy was reflected throughout the next several decades in psychiatric lit-erature that illustrated the ongoing contradictions in mental-hospital life.

In 1963, for example, one Seattle hospital group reported on a major con-flict among staff regarding cigarettes. The chief of the hospital had instituted strict rules on cigarettes, including rationing patients' supplies and allowing patients to smoke only with permission. When a new staff psychiatrist arrived on the maximum-security ward and tried to lift the restriction, however, staff did not perceive that she had sufficient authority to do so and conflict ensued. As the psychiatrists from the hospital explained, "Some staff members, par-ticularly those who identified closely with the patients, believed that the men-tally ill were entitled to nearly complete gratification of their oral demands and viewed rationing as unnecessary oral deprivation and cruelty." Aides also resented having their own smoking restricted (since they could not really smoke when the patients were forbidden). Patients became more unruly and harder to manage, and the staff interpreted this as acting out because of conflicts they witnessed among members of the team. The staff members were finally able to have a group meeting to work out the conflicts and settled on a program of rationing of cigarettes in order to get control over the environment.[68] In this case, smoking represented a policy issue, a source of splitting among staff, and a rich example of the challenges in relating the necessary constraints of a men-tal hospital to social norms and patients' needs.[69]

Smoking was also caught up in the increased questioning of psychiatric authority over patient's lives. In the 1970s, patients' rights groups challenged psychiatrists' power to hold patients in hospitals for long periods of time. Activists endeavored to set limits around circumstances in which psychiatrists could keep patients against their will in hospitals or restrict their rights within hospitals.[70] The legal standard set by the United States Supreme Court in 1975 (*O'Connor v. Donaldson*) was that patients had to be a danger to themselves in order to be involuntarily committed. But how to define danger? As one New York writer pointed out, this involved decisions about social context: "Can a woman with peculiar smoking habits in which she occasionally burns her bed and clothing be locked in a hospital for years against her will because she might accidentally kill herself?"[71] Although the author left the discussion open, it was clear that she favored limitations on psychiatrists' power to take charge of patients' everyday lives, including smoking.

Critics were concerned with what happened when power became entrenched in institutions, and this was particularly evident in the ways that smoking was managed. In filmmaker Frederick Wiseman's controversial documentary *Titicut Follies* about the Bridgewater Correctional Mental Institution in 1967, smoking was part of an institutional culture of power and privilege. As revealed in the film, which consisted of footage of patients and their interactions with staff (without explanatory frame or narration), physicians and other staff smoked at will while patients were limited in their opportunities. Staff members appeared to be the only autonomous adults, while the patients were dependent and powerless as illustrated in multiple ways. According to *Titicut Follies,* patients had their clothes taken away if staff had concerns about their behavior. Smoking was only possible in the outdoor settings or on higher functioning wards. At the same time, staff seemed more attached to their cigarettes than the patients. The film had a memorable scene in which a psychiatrist inserted a feeding tube in a patient who had been refusing to eat. The area was not particularly sterile, and the psychiatrist had ash dangling from the cigarette in his mouth as he poured food into the feeding funnel.[72]

Critics of psychiatric hospital practices by the 1970s expressed concern about the role of cigarettes in getting patients to cooperate with unit routines. In 1976, Douglas Biklen from the Center on Human Policy at Syracuse University looked at a token-economy program at a local state hospital. He described the way that the program was introduced to the patients—including the head psychiatrist's distribution of cigarettes to help reinforce the idea that the token program would be good for the patients. Biklen pointed out, though, that the whole program functioned as a way to control patients: while greater mobility around the unit and cigarettes were "often considered privileges in the mental hospital context, and therefore qualif[ied] as rewards from the behaviorists' perspective, their use in this program put the experimenters in a position of intensifying control over patients' lives." He also commented that it was "dehumanizing" to use basic freedoms—taken for granted by individuals outside institutions—as positive rewards.[73] Thus the problem was not that the token economy encouraged smoking—the problem was that it restricted patients' basic rights to smoke.

Although the patient narratives I located did not explicitly describe the token economies extolled by providers in the 1960s and 1970s, patients were aware that providers used cigarette access to shape behavior. As Canadian activist Carla McKague complained, "Cigarettes and money are used routinely as 'behaviour modification' tools—doled out as rewards for appropriate conforming behaviour and withheld as punishment for anger or rebellion."[74] New York writer Mindy Lewis, who was hospitalized at the New York State Psychiatric Institute in the 1960s as a teenager, reported that at one point the unit doctor got upset with how messy the unit had become with cigarette butts and threatened to take away smoking in the main area and restrict it to certain spaces. She explained the reaction to the threat: "Jaws drop, ashes fall. Impossible, and unfair. If we can't smoke in Center, how will we pass the time? How will we stay calm? What will happen? Gidro-Frank is unyielding, 'You can smoke in the living rooms.' He knows as well as we do that patients on observation can't go into a living room by themselves. That either means no smoking (unthinkable) or we'll have to go smoke in groups. And that means the end of what little semblance of privacy the living rooms provide. At least temporarily, because suddenly everyone becomes incredibly neat."[75] This episode highlighted the precarious position that patients felt themselves in with regard to their control over their smoking environment.

While patients in the early part of the century accepted—with a lot of grumbling—that hospitals had rules that would include restrictions on smoking, patient narratives by the 1960s were much more critical of the control with which staff managed cigarette access. Patients were acutely aware of ranks of privilege within the hospital. Advancement to a higher status meant that they had access to facilities where they could buy cigarettes and could also smoke with fewer restrictions.[76] They were also conscious that earning smoking privileges involved pleasing staff members. And as Erving Goffman pointed out, privileges were a way of coercing cooperation from patients.[77] As one Oklahoma alcoholic explained about her hospitalization in 1968, "if you got on the 'good behavior' list and could smoke—one of the privileges won by acting 'normal,' that is docile behavior and unrelenting anxious eager subservient smile—you could politely ask a nurse to light your cigarette with the lighter she carried tucked away in her pocket."[78] Another woman complained that hospital staff would not let her go off by herself because they wanted her to socialize: "So they took away my cigarettes. I'm a real addict and after half-a-day I broke down and said I'd sit at the table with the other ladies if they'd let me smoke again."[79] Patients, therefore, could theoretically gain some control over their smoking—but only by giving over control to the hospital staff in defining normal behavior.[80]

Smoking restrictions and privileges were a major area of disagreement between patients and providers and seemed to emphasize that mental patients were not treated with respect that should have been due to suffering human beings. Patients and critics were often outraged by restrictions on smoking and complained that they were likely to affect patients' ability to recover. California physician and medical writer Walter Alvarez compiled a volume of mental-patient narratives and commented on patients' experiences. He particularly noted difficult circumstances, such as one case in which "the superintendent was needlessly cruel in that he did not permit the patients to have books or magazines. As a result, they had to sit silently all day, looking into space. They were deprived, also, of tobacco, which would have given great comfort to all of the smokers and chewers. They way people were treated in this hospital was likely to deprive a sane man of his reason."[81] According to Alvarez, it was cruel to not offer patients everyday opportunities to take care of their needs, including smoking.

But while patients usually wanted chances to smoke, they recognized that staff used smoking to calm them down—and thus control their behavior. In one narrative, a patient became repeatedly agitated as he tried to fight through his delusions and make plans for discharge from the hospital. The social worker who was trying to help him kept offering him cigarettes when he got upset. The patient got even more upset and demanded to talk to a supervisor, and the pattern continued: "As an afterthought, he took a package of cigarettes from his pocket and offered to me. 'Have a cigarette, won't you?' I took one, wearily recognizing the pacification routine."[82] In this context, smoking was not a way for humans to connect to one another, but rather the symbol of condescension of staff toward a powerless patient.

Though critics pointed to limitations in smoking opportunities as evidence of total institutions, others suggested that the atmosphere of mental hospitals was problematic in that it encouraged smoking as part of a maladaptive culture. By the 1960s and 1970s, critics were increasingly pointing to the absence of any activities on many inpatient psychiatric units. Patients noted this, too, and complained that the only thing they could do was to smoke.[83] University of Georgia sociologist John Belcher observed that there were in effect two cultures within a psychiatric hospital that could be in conflict—one created by staff and the other constructed by patients. After doing an observation in a southern mental hospital, he noted that many of the women patients were smokers, though more had not been smokers when they entered the hospital and had said that it was wrong to smoke. When talking to the women, he found that they said that doctors told them to smoke to help with their nerves, and other staff suggested that smoking would help them get along with others better. Cigarettes were passed out at parties, and the nonsmokers took that cue and thought they might as well start smoking. Belcher pointed out that the boredom of hospital as well as the cultural pressure within the hospital, led more women to smoke than would have if they had been on the outside.[84]

The habit of using cigarettes as a way to frame behavior for mentally ill patients was so entrenched that a psychiatrist during an early 1970s commitment hearing used the fact that a patient quit smoking (because the cigarette package said that smoking was harmful) as evidence that the patient was paranoid. The doctor explained, "That means that he is confusing the danger of cigarette smoking, which is enjoyed by many people, even prisoners, with his unreal fear that he might be killed. . . . The point I am making is the inappropriateness of his making so much of the little notice on the cigarette package, smoking may be harmful, which he would obey."[85] The doctor presented this patient as psychotic solely because he believed the package warning on cigarettes. Attorney Bruce Ennis, who was active in the move to reform commitment laws in the 1960s, provided this testimony to illustrate the absurdity of psychiatric assessment.[86] And while this psychiatrist did seem to be stretching it to see psychosis in this patient, it was a reality for providers in mental-health settings that patients seldom expressed a desire to quit smoking, and the warning on the packages seemed entirely irrelevant to this population.

Because smoking was such a normal behavior within mental hospitals, it was also a medium through which power relationships could be structured. This was particularly apparent in the dynamics described by both patients and staff in cigarette exchanges. Providers could count on patients' need to smoke, and freely used—or exploited—that need to manage patients. While this continued through most of the twentieth century, critics of psychiatry noted more and more the problematic power dynamics inherent in psychiatry by the 1960s and 1970s, especially around issues of gender.

Gender and Smoking

In 1972, psychologist and feminist critic Phyllis Chesler extended the critique of power in mental health to analyze the gender implications of psychiatric diagnosis and treatment for women patients in both inpatient and outpatient settings in the United States. She argued that the social and cultural role of women was to be dependent and needy, and these were the qualities diagnosed as mental illness (and despised) by a male-dominated psychiatric profession.[87] And as women patients' experiences bear out, their expressed need for cigarettes played into this dynamic.

Janet Gotkin, who had numerous encounters with psychiatrists in the 1960s and 1970s, had a conflict over smoking that illustrated the gender and power issues. She was in treatment with a Freudian psychiatrist who wanted her to lie on a couch facing away from him. When she was on the couch and reached for a cigarette he reacted strongly:

"I prefer that you do not smoke during the session," Dr. Berman said. And I realized, again, that he was watching me carefully.

"I have to smoke," I said.

"I am sure you can survive for an hour without a cigarette," he retorted, his cool voice crackling with impatience.

"I have to smoke," I repeated. "I can't lie here without smoking."

"My patients do not smoke during their analytic sessions," Dr. Berman said.

"I'm the boss around here," he was saying, "and you're just a puny sniffling subject."[88]

Gotkin understood that in forbidding her to smoke, the doctor both dismissed her needs and tried to control her behavior.

Women who were unafraid to assert their right to smoke faced challenges with psychiatric power. A woman who shared her experiences with mental hospitals in the 1960s contrasted the "bad hospital" that took away all her things (including cigarettes) with a good hospital where she got better (and she kept her personal possessions).[89] Feminist writer Kate Millet described an incident in which she tried to stall for time before the police took her to a psychiatric hospital: "The last gesture of freedom, the need of calm—I find a cigarette." Another time when she was facing a psychiatrist at an intake interview for the hospital, she explained her resistance: "I still sit in the chair by the door, my purse in my lap—my last possessions: money, cigarettes. He would have me sit nearer, across from his desk. The procedure. To hell with your procedure; it is simply this that I refuse to partake of." She later caused problems with staff when she decided that she needed to have an adequate supply of cigarettes. As she thought to herself, "Begin first though with cigarettes: if you have cigarettes you can outlast a siege; if not, you're in trouble." And, "The day you run out of cigarettes is the day your passivity ends."[90] At the same time that women tried to define what they needed for their recovery, they also asserted an adult identity that included the right to smoke without staff taking away their belongings and their smoking opportunities.

While women patients' assertiveness could result in turmoil within hospitals, another problem was manifested through the figure of the psychiatric nurse who limited access of patients to smoking. This power dynamic appeared particularly wrong to critics when female nurses were exerting control over male patients. Novelist Ken Kesey used access to cigarettes as a marker for the troubling Nurse Ratched in *One Flew over the Cuckoo's Nest*. In the 1962 novel, the narrator (the Chief) noted that for a while the patients would not play cards with the antisocial McMurphy because he won all their money, "and they can't play for cigarettes because the nurse has started making the men keep their cartons on the desk in the Nurses' Station, where she doles them out one pack a day, says it's for their health, but everybody knows it's to keep McMurphy from winning them all at cards."[91] In Kesey's novel, nurses who controlled others were unfeminine and violated social and cultural norms. It is not an accident that Kesey chose a nurse to symbolize all that was wrong with psychiatric institutions, nor that one of her ways of enforcing her power was to deny access to cigarettes.[92] And in the film version of *One Flew over the Cuckoo's Nest,* Nurse Ratched's stranglehold on the cigarette supply provoked more than one patient rebellion. Her unreasonable efforts to control carried much of the blame for the tragedy at the end of the story.

As smoking became more common among women after the middle of the twentieth century, the power dynamics between mental-health providers and patients over cigarettes were shaped by gender. Women's demands for smoking opportunities were interpreted as part of their mental illness, while women providers' efforts to control male patients appeared as emblematic of psychiatry's inauthentic use of power. These expectations around gender, power, and smoking did not just exist within mental institutions—they were visible in film portrayals of mental illness as well. And the potential dangerousness of a mad woman—symbolized by her aggressive smoking behavior—represented the fearsome spectacle of women empowered to assert too much freedom, a caricature of tobacco industry marketing to women.[93]

Within discussions about smoking among providers, patients, and critics in the 1960s and 1970s, there were striking absences. First, smoking cessation was generally not an issue. Patients smoked a lot, usually without apology. And few providers appeared concerned about their smoking habits. The other significant absence was mention of particular brands of cigarettes. Although tobacco leaders justified their advertising budget with claims that they were merely promoting their own brands, psychiatric patients appeared oblivious to brand-based marketing.[94] They smoked for many reasons, but never mentioned self-image, sophistication, rebellion, or any of the other reasons promoted by the tobacco companies, and almost never articulated awareness of advertising campaigns.[95]

For more than a century, the tobacco industry represented smoking as a conscious consumer behavior taken on rationally by adults (or youth aspiring to be adults). Public-health activists countered that it was due to addiction. But many mentally ill smokers failed to fit into the cigarette company profile of classic consumers, nor were they simply addicted to cigarettes. For years, psychiatric patients' ability to make choices about how they spent their time was curtailed by their location within mental hospitals. Further, seriously ill patients faced economic hardships that affected their capacity to function as consumers. And many had relationships with their cigarettes that reflected their mental illness. The testimony of mentally ill individuals and their caregivers illustrated that cigarettes and smoking were a complicated aspect of the mental-illness experience, and that physical-health concerns were less important than other considerations for this group.

From the perspective of both providers and patients, smoking was an integral feature of mental-health-care settings through most of the twentieth century. Providers recognized the role of smoking in the lives of their patients and tried to use it to foster communication and to control behavior. Patients engaged with their cigarettes in much more elaborate and complex ways within their mental illness, against limitations set by hospitals, and in relationships with one another. But though it was common knowledge that mentally ill individuals often had a strong attachment to cigarettes, this was not widely studied or addressed until the 1980s and 1990s, well after the first major efforts of what would become the tobacco-control movement. Within and around mental-health settings, cigarettes were signs, symbols, and tools, and the issue was how to manage them.

Psychiatric hospitals during the 1960s and 1970s were a world apart from the experts who emphasized the physical hazards of cigarettes. The other obvious world where health consequences of smoking did not appear was within the tobacco industry. As many scholars have pointed out, cigarette companies actively obscured the physical risks of their products. But they also, like mental-health providers and patients, attended to the emotional aspects of smoking and created an industry-based research enterprise that eventually dovetailed with concerns of academic mental-health investigators. Tobacco companies explored what psychiatrists already knew—that smoking involved emotions and behavior.

Chapter 3

Smoker Psychology and the Tobacco Industry through the Early 1980s

In 1964, the United States surgeon general released a report confirming what many had suspected for a decade—that smoking caused cancer and significantly contributed to other major health problems.[1] The report galvanized action in the public-health community, and advocacy groups such as the American Cancer Society worked to educate the public about the health hazards of smoking.[2] The surgeon general's report acknowledged in a small section, though, that some individuals might have psychological reasons to smoke, despite the health risks. The authors commented that humans had a long history of using pharmaceutical substances for psychological purposes, and it was likely that they would continue to do so. The report did not condone this rationale for smoking and suggested that the emotional benefits would likely not outweigh the risks.[3] But while psychological connections to cigarettes were only occasionally addressed by health experts, this was one area in which the tobacco industry had a keen interest.

Cigarette companies faced a serious problem with the growing number of medical findings on the health consequences of smoking, especially when they were publicized through the surgeon general's report. One way that tobacco combated the threat to the industry was through support of research that questioned the connection between smoking and serious health problems, often through methods designed to protect themselves from legal liability.[4] But in the process, they also explored other factors—especially psychological ones—that were associated with smoking. Tobacco-industry researchers and executives asked the question not usually broached by public-health efforts to combat smoking: what did people get out of smoking? And why might they continue to smoke in the face of evidence that it was bad for them? In the aftermath of the surgeon general's report, some within the industry quietly conceded that not everyone was going to continue to smoke. And if their customer base was going to shrink, they needed a better way to understand their remaining consumers. Like other businesses faced with an existential threat, the tobacco companies had to innovate to survive. And like other industries, they used psychological insights to change their practices.[5]

The tobacco industry investigated the same phenomenon observed by psychiatric providers and their patients—the strong emotional relationship between some individuals and their cigarettes. And they made strategic decisions about what psychological factors to investigate in smoking and how to look at them. Tobacco companies, like other business organizations, employed a calculus to determine how much research to pursue within their own walls and how much to develop in partnerships with investigators in academia. Academic researchers in turn used the big budgets of large corporations to explore their interests. Over the decades, the tobacco-funded research of smokers and their psychological attachment to cigarettes evolved into a series of programs to understand the neurobiology of nicotine. By looking at the emergence of tobacco-industry-sponsored work in this area, we can see how and where tobacco interests were well entrenched by the time that questions about the biological relationship between mentally ill individuals and nicotine were explored in the 1990s.

From our perspective now, it is easy to focus on the nefarious uses to which the tobacco industry put their sponsored research, particularly their legal defense. But for decades, cigarette companies were viewed by many investigators as important sources of research funding. And tobacco industry leaders were skilled at engaging researchers' personal ambitions and professional aspirations. Tobacco-industry funding—through ostensibly neutral research organizations—supported serious investigators in several robust scientific fields of the time, including the field of psychosomatics, which used psychiatric insights to understand the physical manifestations of disease.[6] Individual companies also conducted internal research programs to understand differences between smokers and nonsmokers, with the help of psychological tools and insights. Through their explorations of their customers' feelings and behaviors, the tobacco companies became important experts in the psychology of smoking.

Psychosomatic Research

In the 1950s and 1960s, tobacco companies responded to potential threats posed by research on the health problems of smoking by doing their own investigations. In both the United States and Europe, they collaborated to create research organizations to provide grants to researchers that would support per-spectives strategically useful to the industry.[7] Although the intent of their sup-port was undoubtedly defensive, tobacco companies, like other businesses in the decades after World War II, also invested in research in order to improve their products and their place in the market.[8] The United States' tobacco research group was the Tobacco Institute Research Committee (TIRC), later named the Council for Tobacco Research (CTR). The British tobacco industry organized its own research group, originally called the Tobacco Manufacturers Standing Committee (TMSC), later renamed the Tobacco Research Committee (TRC). Both the TIRC/CTR and the TMSC/TRC funded investigators in coun-tries around the world, and carefully monitored the latest scientific investiga-tions. In addition, individual tobacco companies, especially Philip Morris (PM) and R. J. Reynolds (RJR), created internal research projects and contracted with external researchers. Some of the investigators who consulted with one tobacco group also worked with others, and research organizations sometimes collabo-rated and periodically compared notes on their research findings.

In their strategy to support the tobacco-industry position that cigarettes were not harmful, tobacco industry leaders looked to academic investigators who had a compatible point of view and needed help (that could be provided by the industry in exchange for public defense of cigarettes). In their perusal of scientific trends, tobacco personnel noted areas with professional conflict or new avenues of inquiry where grant support might be particularly valued. One of these was the field of psychosomatic medicine in which both psychiatrists and psychologists argued for the relevance of mental phenomenon to the rest of medicine. Within a psychosomatic framework, chronic illnesses such as peptic ulcers, heart disease, and even cancer appeared to be the result of emotional stress played out through physical symptoms.[9] For cigarette companies, the psychosomatic emphasis on emotions (especially stress) helped to deempha-size environmental elements such as smoking. For investigators struggling for professional recognition for their field, grants offered by the tobacco industry represented both financial support and validation. Initially, tobacco research organizations narrowly focused on funding investigators who could directly support their argument that smoking did not cause disease. But as they devel-oped relationships with researchers over time, the tobacco companies became involved with a broader field of psychological and psychiatric investigation.

When they first explored the implications of psychosomatic theories on illness, the tobacco industry looked for researchers who were experts in their field (and who could enhance the companies' reputations with collaboration).[10] Geoffrey Todd, head of the British TMSC, toured the United States in 1956 to see how Americans were dealing with the lung-cancer issue and met with psychosomatic researchers, including the dean of psychosomatic medicine, Franz Alexander in Chicago.[11] While Alexander did not become a tobacco industry collaborator, some of Todd's other contacts had been or would become connected to the industry.[12] Many investigators in this struggling field were eager to be consulted and to take advantage of the tobacco industry's deep pockets.[13]

In the late 1950s and early 1960s, the TMSC funded British physician David Kissen, a pioneer in psychosomatic medicine.[14] Kissen argued not only that emotional factors were key in causing physical illness, but also that personality makeup was the most important factor in lung cancer. With TMSC encouragement, Kissen developed research projects at a Glasgow hospital and created a network of psychosomatic researchers to promote further research in this area. In 1960, Kissen began a collaboration with British psychologist Hans Eysenck.[15] As Kissen explained to the TMSC, they were working on a theory, "based on clinical observation, that lung cancer patients have a poor outlet for emotional discharge."[16] They argued that lung-cancer patients could be separated from other smokers based on their personality types, and that other kinds of psychological profiling could predict who would be likely to display psychosomatic symptoms. Eysenck and Kissen classified respiratory symptoms (including asthma, bronchitis, and cough), heart conditions, and nervous diseases among those likely to be caused by psychosomatic mechanisms.[17] The British sponsorship of these investigators seemed so promising for the tobacco industry that in the late 1960s the American CTR took up support of Eysenck and further explored the relationship between personality and smoking behaviors.[18]

Hans Eysenck's relationship with the tobacco industry illustrated the evolving interest of cigarette companies in psychological insights. His prominent position at the influential Institute of Psychiatry in London was obviously valuable. And tobacco industry support helped promote Eysenck's efforts to advocate for psychology—and for himself. Before he began to collaborate with the tobacco industry, he had developed a personality-assessment tool that eventually became the Eysenck Personality Inventory (also known as the Maudsley Personality Inventory). He mobilized this tool to evaluate medically sick patients in his work with Kissen, and he later helped other psychologists—including some within tobacco companies—to use the Eysenck Personality Inventory to help understand smokers and their behavior. The fact that Eysenck was colorful and engaged in multiple academic and political controversies (that earned him the distinction of being one of the most-cited psychologists of his era) made him a particularly attractive partner to his tobacco sponsors.[19]

Eysenck had a long and fruitful collaboration with the CTR that lasted through the 1960s and into the 1970s. Throughout his research, he never wavered in his fundamental assertion that it was personality, not cigarettes themselves, that led individuals to succumb to cancer and heart disease. In the early 1970s, Eysenck was invited to collaborate with internal research teams at both PM and RJR and partnered with their lead psychologists to further explore the relationships among stress, smoking, and physical disease.[20] By the early 1980s, his insights about individual psychological makeup and response to stress permeated the research programs within the tobacco industry and helped investigators connect to the broader literature on personality outside the industry.

Psychosomatic researchers, especially Eysenck, eagerly looked to tobacco support to help them explore human factors in health and disease. Although Eysenck was criticized at the time (and even more since his death) for his extensive research funding by the tobacco industry, his involvement with the issues he raised about smoking and personality go well beyond the sometimes-voiced opinion that he was paid to be a spokesman for the industry. Instead, Eysenck (who himself quit smoking in the 1950s) found in the tobacco industry a partner and facilitator for his grand agenda of promoting his own view of science.[21] The result of tobacco industry funding into psychosomatic illness was that researchers became convinced that the individual was a key factor in both smoking and the propensity to disease.

And as a result of their explorations of the types of people who smoked and collaborations with investigators such as Eysenck, tobacco researchers recognized that their best customers had a relationship to cigarettes that was different than the ways that most Americans used corporate products. Through tobacco-industry-sponsored research in psychosomatics and personality, several investigators commented that the mentally ill seemed to be a population of people who proved the assertion that individual differences (possibly even genetic ones) drove both behavior and propensity to disease. Tobacco leaders were intrigued by the observations by several psychiatrists that schizophrenics appeared to have a low incidence of lung cancer.[22] Montreal researcher David Horrobin submitted a research proposal in 1977 to the TRC to investigate his assertion that schizophrenics had a lower risk of lung cancer, even though they were heavy smokers. While British epidemiologist Richard Doll agreed with Horrobin about the lower incidence of lung cancer in schizophrenics, the TRC turned down Horrobin's proposal on the grounds that his hypothesis about cancer causation was too complicated to be verified by his research.[23]

The tobacco industry continued to track both the incidence of cancer in schizophrenics and their propensity to smoke. Eysenck discussed the possible connection between the two in his 1980 book, *The Causes and Effects of Smoking:* "There does, however, seem to be no doubt that there is a (negative) relationship between cancer and schizophrenia, and probably psychosis as a whole. This again suggests that genetic factors play a part in determining who shall be at risk to cancer."[24] If individual differences—manifested by genetic factors and displayed through personality—were the primary determinants in cancer causation, then maybe cigarettes were not to be blamed after all. In the meantime, the work of Eysenck and others on personality variables made it abundantly clear that not every user of cigarettes was a dedicated smoker. Companies continued to be concerned about how to best understand their customers' psychological makeup. And internal psychology research further reinforced the importance of individual differences, including responses to stress, in smoking.

Philip Morris and Project 1600

It is well known that tobacco companies benefitted from psychological insights in their marketing and advertising campaigns from the 1920s on.[25] But the tobacco industry more broadly employed psychologists to help manage employees and understand their customers.[26] In the context of growing market segmentation and a push toward individualism in the broader culture, cigarette companies explored their customers' thoughts and feelings.[27] Research and development divisions within tobacco companies began psychological studies of their customers, especially after the 1964 surgeon general's report. Litigators and others have pointed out that partly as a result of this research, tobacco company leaders knew that smoking was addictive.[28] But the point of tobacco-company psychological research in the 1960s and 1970s was to ask what smoking did for people. In this time period, the company with the most active psychology program was Philip Morris.

In 1961, PM hired psychologist William L. Dunn Jr. to consult with them regarding personnel decisions, but he quickly moved beyond employee relations. His dissertation had been on schizophrenia, and he worked for several years in mental hospitals before making the move to PM.[29] He had a keen understanding of the range of human emotions and psychopathology. Over the decades of his tenure with PM, Dunn built a program of psychological research involving human behavior, animal research, and collaborations with academic psychologists.[30] His major work was identified within the company as Project 1600, a vigorous behavioral psychology program to understand PM's consumers.

While Dunn is remembered by attorneys and historians as someone who admitted that cigarettes were essentially delivery vehicles for nicotine, Project 1600 was more broadly conceived.[31] Dunn's original mission was to add psychological insight to the existing structure at the Philip Morris Research Center. Dunn helped to develop consumer panels—large groups of individuals (often housewives or college students) who could be asked to evaluate products and provide feedback.[32] He also weighed in on concept development for cigarette designs before they went to the marketing division. As he explained in 1963, "The overall objective for this project is to develop more sensitive testing procedures for the evaluation of subjective differences in cigarettes and to develop more adequate devices for eliciting judgmental or preference statements about cigarettes from smokers."[33] Dunn not only helped to evaluate cigarette preferences, he also expanded panels to include evaluation of other kinds of products (including shaving equipment).

After the first surgeon general's report, Dunn and his group began to look at smoker behavior in light of health concerns. In February of 1964, Dunn's staff conducted an attitude survey among their panelists regarding response to the report—they found that 5 percent of the panelists quit smoking, 20 percent cut down, and 75 percent continued smoking at the same rate (numbers similar to a national poll outside the company).[34] Through the rest of the decade, Dunn was able to expand his research group, hire more psychologists, and broaden the mission of Project 1600 to include the "psychodynamics of smoking."[35] By 1968, Project 1600 psychologist Frank Ryan reported that their group was planning to study physiological events reflecting the need or motive to smoke, changes during the act of smoking, and changes in the body ("baseline tension") after smoking. Ryan emphasized that this group was engaged in cutting-edge scientific research with innovative projects and techniques.[36]

As research director Helmut Wakeham explained to the PM board of directors in 1969, the point of Project 1600 was to try to understand why people smoked despite health warnings, including the question of "what benefits do smokers wittingly or unwittingly find in smoking that outweigh the real or imaginary risks that the same smokers feel?"[37] The spirit of inquiry within Project 1600 seemed to be one of genuine curiosity—why did people smoke even when they had heard over and over that it was bad for them? Dunn was convinced that the answer was to be found through psychological research, and he worked on a variety of projects to uncover the motivations for ongoing smoking behavior. His group organized numerous experiments, often involving college student subjects from nearby Virginia Commonwealth University. In addition,

Dunn expanded his network of professional contacts and increasingly collaborated with academics who were interested in similar questions.

In 1970, Dunn conceived of the idea of an international conference that would bring together "nationally recognized authorities to discuss short term (beneficial) consequences of smoking."[38] Dunn postulated that smoking might reduce anxiety and stress and that quitting smoking might result in increased aggression. Very early on in the planning process, he and his colleagues decided to have this conference in a place that would draw participants—the Caribbean during winter.[39] And while Dunn originally framed the question of the conference in terms of the benefits of smoking, he eventually broadened it to address motivations for smoking. Dunn secured industry-wide support for the conference, and well-respected researchers and academicians from around the world accepted his invitation to speak and discuss the role of smoking in modern life.[40]

One assumption that ran through much of the work within Project 1600 was that stress was a major factor in smoking. Dunn was able to get renowned stress researcher Hans Selye to deliver the opening address for the Motivation in Smoking conference that took place in January 1972 in St. Martin. Selye's book, *The Stress of Life,* had been published in 1956, and the McGill investigator was widely regarded as the international authority on the subject of stress.[41] PM (and the CTR) had been working with Selye for several years before the conference, as Selye believed that humans necessarily engaged in risky behaviors in order to relieve stress.[42] In his address, Selye commented, "Few investigators have made a point of the possible benefits of smoking; yet, as I have said in my testimony before the Canadian Senate, there would be no need to create a committee on smoking if nobody found cigarettes advantageous or desirable. Certainly smoking is one of the diversional activities which, to many people, has proved to be so much more useful than complete rest after exposure to severe stress."[43] Selye provided a brief but elegant explanation of the physiology of stress and explained that all people needed some way to distract themselves. Cigarette smoking was one option, and like almost every activity in modern life, carried its own risks.[44]

Not all of the participants at the 1972 conference agreed with Selye's supposition that smoking provided a respite from stress, but they did all accept that on some level smoking had a function in individuals' lives. Columbia University psychologist Stanley Schachter pointed out the apparent paradox that smoking reliably increased heart rate and blood pressure but smokers reported that it helped calm them down. Johns Hopkins epidemiologist Caroline Bedell Thomas explained that smokers appeared to experience elevated levels of anger and nervous tension, which led to increasing use of cigarettes. And anthropologist Albert Damon, who studied smoking in preliterate societies, found that the habit was important for personal gratification, not for social status.[45]

A few of the conference participants focused specifically on the role of nicotine. University of Michigan pharmacologist Edward Domino explored the neuropsychopharmacology (effects in the brain and on behavior) of nicotine in animals and humans, while Murray Jarvik (who was at the Albert Einstein College of Medicine at that time) explained that nicotine was the reinforcing agent in smoking. In addition, Walter Essman, of the Queens College of the University of New York, explored the neurochemistry of nicotine and suggested ways in which the chemical might function in the brain.[46] From our perspective now, it may seem startling that these researchers presented evidence suggestive of the power of nicotine—including its addictive potential—at a conference sponsored by the tobacco industry. The findings from this conference were certainly not hidden. Dunn published the papers of the participants in an edited volume, and his CTR sponsors hoped that the book would influence academic research. Further, the industry did not try to hide from the work of researchers in nicotine. Domino, Jarvik, and Essman all had grants from the tobacco industry to support their work before and after the conference.[47]

While some of the researchers who presented their projects during the St. Martin conference looked at smokers in general, others investigated nicotine in animals or speculated about the role of smoking in certain subsets of the population. For example, researcher Ronald Hutchinson, who collaborated with Dunn and other PM research staff before and after the conference, emphasized the role of nicotine in aggression in stressed animals. Hutchinson suggested that nicotine's function was similar to that of the major tranquilizer, chlorpromazine, which was being used in psychiatric hospitals to treat agitation and psychosis.[48] University of South Dakota investigator Norman Heimstra explored the role of smoking in mood and hypothesized that smoking might help reduce negative affect (emotion) and help performance for some individuals.[49]

After the conference, Dunn and his colleagues at PM continued to investigate the idea that smoking served some role in alleviating anxiety and stress. Project 1600 personnel began to differentiate types of smokers and identified factors such as socioeconomic level and status-inconsistent behaviors that might be stressful and result in smoking.[50] PM researchers also recognized that there were individuals who seemed to be particularly attracted to smoking and tracked research that suggested that individuals with strong psychological reasons to smoke might be harmed if they quit smoking.[51] Although they were not able to follow through on their ideas, PM Project 1600 psychologists designed studies to collaborate with the Virginia mental-hospital system and some local schools in order to follow psychiatric patients and hyperkinetic children; they assumed both populations would be more likely to smoke in the present or in the future.[52]

While PM appeared to have been the first of the tobacco companies to devote substantial resources to smoker psychology, their work was emulated throughout the industry in subsequent decades. In 1977, an international group with representatives from both European and American tobacco companies gathered for a follow-up conference on work done since the St. Martin meeting.[53] In 1978, the tobacco facilitators of the 1977 conference published another volume of papers on smoking behavior, including contributions by some who had also given papers at the 1972 conference.[54] Many of the 1978 papers focused on individual differences, particularly the role that smoking might play in arousal or in stress relief. While the conference participants did not necessarily reach consensus on the motivations for smoking, conferees repeatedly suggested that individuals had their own reasons to smoke and that important factors included stress, levels of arousal, and extent of addiction. And tobacco companies were eager to keep exploring these elements.

Biobehavioral Research at R. J. Reynolds

In the late 1970s, research-and-development personnel at RJR anxiously reported that they were falling behind PM in the area of consumer psychology and encouraged leaders within the company to take action through the creation of a behavioral-psychology research program. The argument was that RJR needed to understand more about how consumers chose brands and what element of smoking made it so enjoyable. A research manager proposed that RJR hire a behavioral scientist to help bring RJR up to speed on topics that had been under investigation at PM for many years. The new scientist would be responsible for exploring consumer relationships with cigarettes, monitoring the professional psychological literature, and acting as the primary contact for the company's outside consultants.[55]

RJR management agreed with this assessment, and in 1980 the company hired psychologist David G. Gilbert. Gilbert was made part of a new Biobehavioral Division, which helped take psychological research about smoking to the next scientific level. He and a group of researchers within the division immediately went to work getting advice from external researchers, including Hans Eysenck and University of South Florida psychologist Charles Spielberger. Spielberger was already a well-known investigator by the time he began to collaborate with RJR. He had spent time as a research fellow with the National

Institute of Mental Health (NIMH) and was also active in the American Psychological Association (he became president of the organization in 1991). He acted
as a consultant to RJR from 1979 to 1985 and worked on projects funded by the
company through the 1990s.[56] Much of the focus of the RJR internal and external research was on new methods of measuring stress, including techniques to
assess both physiological and emotional variables.

By this time period, the concept of stress had become increasingly
important within medicine and in popular understandings of health and disease. Many accepted the idea that certain intense behavior patterns—type A
behavior—directly contributed to cardiovascular disease. And the widespread
perception about stress in American life was both evidence of and cause for the
rise of blockbusting medications for anxiety.[57] Though smoking was increasingly problematic from a physical-health perspective, it remained a widely recognized mechanism for stress relief. Spielberger, who worked on stress, type
A behavior, and heart disease, did not directly defend smoking per se. But he
understood the potential connections between smoking and stress. For example, his 1979 self-help volume *Understanding Stress and Anxiety* had a picture
of a visibly distressed woman smoking a cigarette on the cover, and he mentioned the fact that millions of people in America smoked to relieve stress.[58]

Stress researchers flourished with tobacco company sponsorship. In 1983,
RJR funded a conference organized by Spielberger, Eysenck, and Robert Ader,
a psychologist from the University of Rochester and former president of the
American Psychosomatic Society. The conference, which brought together a
large number of investigators—many of whom had collaborated on tobacco
projects in the past—aimed to "clarify what is known about the role of stress
and psychosocial factors in the etiology of coronary heart disease (CHD) and
cancer." Further, the conference coordinators agreed to provide RJR with a
position statement on future research directions regarding the relationship of
type A behavior patterns and heart disease. The organizers of the conference
held their meetings at a law firm that represented RJR (Jacob, Medinger, and
Finnegan in New York), and yet these researchers seemed primarily intent on
emphasizing the importance of psychological factors in research.[59]

Industry attorneys were watching their work, however. Internal correspondence indicated that Spielberger was considered valuable as a potential wit-
ness on behalf of the industry during the increasing number of congressional
inquiries and the tobacco litigation of the 1980s.[60] Investigators sympathetic to
the tobacco industry testified during a round of congressional hearings in 1982
on cigarette advertising. Spielberger, who could not attend the hearings in person, submitted a statement to Congress explaining that his research supported

the idea that young adults smoked because of family issues and peer pressure—not media influences. Further, his research demonstrated that constitutional and genetic factors determined an individual's ongoing smoking behavior (as well as their propensity to become physically ill).[61] While Spielberger did not speak to the public-health concerns that prompted the hearings, he was willing to defend the idea that individual personalities were too different for public-health interventions to make sense, and he criticized a use of government power to limit individual choices. In this area (and so many others), the tobacco industry—along with other businesses—used academic connections to support their efforts to avoid government regulation.[62]

Within RJR, David Gilbert used what he learned from external academics to initiate innovative new programs and interventions.[63] Gilbert obtained permission from his company to construct a panel of consumers in Winston-Salem who could be called upon to participate in a variety of research studies about the effects of smoking.[64] He and his colleagues initially focused on how smokers in different stages of smoking (and deprivation) completed tasks. They quickly moved, though, toward more of a focus on nicotine and cognitive performance. In 1985, Gilbert presented a paper on the effects of nicotine on brainwaves (using an electroencephalogram, or EEG) at the Society of Behavioral Medicine and also participated in a symposium on the role of smoking in affect regulation.[65] The researchers in this symposium, including prominent tobacco investigators John Hughes and Ovide Pomerleau, concluded that there was evidence that nicotine had some stress-reducing properties and appeared to enhance cognitive performance.[66]

Throughout his tenure with RJR, Gilbert made lasting connections with researchers in the area of personality assessment. He collaborated with Eysenck and Spielberger, as well as a number of others. He also developed his research skills and made himself known at national conferences. Gilbert was successful enough at his position in RJR to step directly from there into an academic research appointment. In the fall of 1985, he left RJR to become assistant professor of psychology at Southern Illinois University, though he retained a close relationship with RJR and worked with researchers there on a number of papers. He also continued to act as a consultant for his old division.[67]

After Gilbert's departure, the company hired University of Texas psychologist Walter S. Pritchard for the Biobehavioral Division, and the group as a whole made a turn toward more molecular pharmacological approaches to the issue of nicotine and its effect on smokers. While Pritchard and the others in the division continued to rely some on the personality types utilized by Eysenck, they also began to focus on nicotine as a chemical that had significant effects in the brain.[68] So fruitful was this line of research that by 1987, the Biobehavioral Division had formed a separate research entity to explore nicotine receptor pharmacology.

As is clear from the extent of tobacco company research on the psychology (and eventually the brain differences) of smokers, tobacco companies were not merely marketing and selling cigarettes. They asked important questions about differences among individuals and with their consultants and collaborators created important new knowledge about psychological factors and smoking. Although they only occasionally directly addressed the population of mentally ill, tobacco investigators were aware that mental and emotional stress had a direct relationship to smoking. And their research networks significantly contributed to emerging questions about how nicotine, the key ingredient in cigarettes, affected the brain.

By the 1980s, the tobacco industry had an increasingly nuanced understanding that individual psychological makeup, mental and emotional processes, and external stress all played a role in smoking behaviors. Tobacco companies obviously attempted to use their knowledge to support their products. But their awareness of the complex issues for smokers far outpaced that of psychiatrists of the time, even though mental-health professionals had been immersed in a smoking culture for decades. While the tobacco industry had a commercial interest in gathering information about the multiple factors that led their customers to smoke, psychiatrists had professional motives for expanding their expertise to include smoking behaviors as broader health concerns finally caught up them. In subsequent decades, mental-health professionals struggled with conceptual models to deal with smoking, first in the general population and then among the chronically mentally ill.

Chapter 4

Psychiatry Engages Smoking

From the pages of the flagship journal of the American Psychiatric Association in the 1960s and 1970s it would be impossible to tell that the surgeon general had published an important report in 1964 or that smoking caused illness. The *American Journal of Psychiatry* had only five articles that even mentioned smoking between 1960 and 1970, and none of them addressed health issues.[1] A few psychiatrists mentioned smoking in the context of other concerns in the 1970s, but in general there was a deafening silence about smoking in mental-health circles, despite robust public attention to smoking and active tobacco-industry response outside of psychiatry. This was perhaps not surprising given the consuming struggles within the profession to define its scope in relation to the rest of medicine and to other talking professions such as psychology and social work. In that context, smoking was not even on the professional radar.

As psychiatrists dealt with divisions within their own ranks about how best to treat patients (psychoanalysis, pills, or attention to social context) and encountered criticism outside the field, smoking appeared initially within the profession's efforts to define the field. In the 1970s, a small group of psychiatrists attempted to capture mental illness within a system of categories in a new *Diagnostic and Statistical Manual* (what would become *DSM-III*). But though a smoking disorder appeared within *DSM-III* and continued to evolve in successive editions of the *DSM*, psychiatric engagement on cessation of smoking in both the general population and among the seriously mentally ill revealed more about professional psychiatric issues than clinical truths about smoking or nicotine. As we might expect given the long-term presence of a cigarette culture in psychiatric settings and the relationship between mentally ill individuals and their smoking habits, psychiatrists' approach to how, whether, or when to help, tell, or ask people to stop smoking was complicated.

Smoking as an Illness

Although it may seem logical for psychiatrists to be experts on the topic of addictive drugs, both psychiatric engagement with addiction and the concept of addiction itself have changed over time. For decades, psychiatrists were only sporadically interested in drugs of abuse, which until the 1970s seemed to be mostly morphine/heroin and cocaine, with the addition of marijuana during the political upheavals of the 1970s.[2] Until that decade, drug abuse was primarily contained within legal and policy domains. During the Nixon administration's war on drugs (which involved both domestic and foreign policy), physicians—especially psychiatrists—began to articulate the need to treat substance abuse as a medical condition rather than just a legal issue.[3] And research leaders within the biological faction of psychiatry, as exemplified by the American College of Neuropsychopharmacology, claimed investigation of all mind-altering substances, whether legal or illegal, as part of their professional purview.[4]

When psychiatrists began to look at smoking among other substances of abuse, it was not necessarily with the foregone conclusion that smoking had the same negative consequences.[5] A few psychiatric interpretations of smoking in the 1960s, in fact, stressed challenges in smoking cessation rather than the problems with cigarettes. For example, a few psychiatrists used their expertise on the dynamics of relationships to explain difficulties for men at a Veterans Administration (VA) hospital attempting to give up heavy smoking. While the men had physical symptoms, "others referred to the loss in more personal terms. 'A cigarette is like a companion,' said one; another described his state of abstinence as 'like not being able to call on a friend.'"[6] The investigators appreciated that smoking was about a relationship to cigarettes. John Tamerin, a Connecticut psychiatrist who did research on substance abuse and smoking, conducted a study on psychodynamic factors in a group of women who were attempting to quit. He found that grief was a real issue in giving up cigarettes: "The depression was so pervasive in each group that, on the day the subjects were to stop smoking, they all looked as if they were attending a funeral."[7] The particular expertise of psychiatrists in this case was that they were able to understand the complex emotions attendant on giving up such a beloved practice.

The psychoanalytic training of many practitioners of the time led them to ask about the meanings of interventions, including the process of having patients quit smoking.[8] In 1971, Tamerin presented a paper with Charles Neumann at the APA annual meeting in which they outlined the psychological hazards of smoking cessation. They were critical of excessive public pressures to make people quit and cautioned that this could result in guilt and shame that would translate into serious symptoms, especially because cigarette smoking was unlike alcohol or other drugs.[9] A member of the audience commented that he thought that too much of the emerging work on smoking cessation was being done by people without adequate psychological background. A trained professional, he insisted, was necessary to understand the ramifications of such a drastic behavior change. (Not surprisingly, a representative from a tobacco-industry public-relations firm was at the meeting. He tried approaching Tamerin about his criticism of the smoking-cessation movement, but Tamerin told him that he thought that smoking was harmful and did not understand why tobacco companies could not take the dangerous elements out of cigarettes.)[10]

Tamerin followed up on this topic to observe that psychiatrists were less likely than other kinds of physicians to tell their patients to quit smoking. While one issue was that a lot of psychiatrists smoked, Tamerin also thought that psychiatrists recognized that quitting smoking might actually harm emotionally unstable patients: "In general, they are more hesitant than internists to encourage patients to stop smoking because they feel that the consequences of cessation may upset the patient's homeostatic equilibrium."[11] And while it might not be a good idea to upset a mentally ill patient by asking him or her to quit smoking, it seemed incomprehensible to try to ask individuals coping with other substance-abuse issues to quit cigarettes, too. For most who contributed to medical literature in this time period, tobacco was in a completely different category from other drugs.

Instead, cigarettes represented a stable object that patients could grasp while they were undergoing treatment for other things. Narcotic-treatment expert and methadone-maintenance pioneer Marie Nyswander shared cigarettes with her patients. Although she told them about her (mostly unsuccessful) efforts to quit smoking as a way of trying to understand their struggles to stay away from drugs, it was clear that she did not expect them to stop smoking, too.[12] As one physician pointed out in 1970, patients who were in treatment for drug abuse sometimes shifted their addiction of choice from substances such as heroin to others such as caffeine or nicotine. But at the same time that these behaviors were related, he advised against trying to get patients to quit smoking, also—he said the results were not good.[13] In the grand scheme of things with regard to drug addiction, tobacco seemed the least of anyone's problems. While some physicians who specialized in addiction argued that tobacco was similar to other drugs of abuse, treatment involved a matter of priorities. Those who observed the drug culture in the 1960s and 1970s argued that tobacco and caffeine use were nothing like illegal drugs such as heroin for which users faced legal prosecution. As one social scientist pointed out in 1971 after spending time observing the illicit drug culture, legal drugs were used to cope with stress, while illegal drugs were used for the high.[14]

In the mid-1970s, New York psychiatrist Jerome Jaffe—who had been Nixon's drug czar in the early part of the decade—began to try to break down that dichotomy. He presented a paper at an international psychiatry meeting in which he argued that excessive smoking was equivalent to the hard-core use of heroin, a substance about which he had a great deal of professional expertise.[15] After the test run of the idea of smoking as addiction at the conference, he worked to expand it to influence psychiatrists' thinking on smoking.[16] From his position at the New York State Psychiatric Institute (NYSPI), he was able to effectively suggest to his faculty colleague Robert Spitzer, the architect of the upcoming third edition of the *Diagnostic and Statistical Manual* (*DSM-III*), that there should be a diagnosis about smoking. Tobacco industry leaders became aware of the possibility of the diagnosis, and lobbied professionals at academic institutions to block it. Despite strenuous objections from several influential psychiatrists, Spitzer and his task force included tobacco dependence within the 1980 *DSM-III*.[17]

The diagnosis of tobacco dependence was pretty vague and could theoretically be applied to patients with symptoms such as smoking for at least a month, unsuccessful attempts to quit, experiencing significant withdrawal while trying to quit, or continuing to smoke even with a serious tobacco-related disease such as lung cancer. But though the diagnosis was there, it had almost no clinical significance. The description of tobacco dependence mentioned that it affected a "large proportion" of adult men and a significant number of adult women in America. But, "since nicotine use rarely causes any identifiable state of intoxication as does alcohol, there is no impairment in social or occupational functioning as an immediate and direct consequence of tobacco use."[18] The diagnosis was broadened somewhat and reincarnated as nicotine dependence in the 1987 revision of the *DSM* in which nicotine was lumped with all the other drugs of abuse, including cocaine and heroin. At the same time, though, the statement about the lack of clinical impairment remained which suggested that smoking really was different.[19]

The inclusion of tobacco (and later nicotine) dependence within the pages of the APA's diagnostic manual revealed more about the politics of diagnosis and the profession's efforts to define itself than it did any particular science around smoking or nicotine. As critics of the time noted, psychiatrists had voted to exclude homosexuality from *DSM-II* in 1973 because it was too common—too normal—to be considered a disease. And yet the next edition of *DSM* less than a decade later included a disease that represented the behavior of close to half the adult population of the United States. Influential New York psychiatrist Alfred Freedman, who was the president of the APA when homosexuality was eliminated, was particularly vocal in his opposition to what he regarded as a naked professional turf grab on behalf of psychiatry. (And not surprisingly, the tobacco companies were quick to support Freedman in his opposition. They funded a conference in which Freedman and colleagues criticized American psychiatry for its diagnostic overreach.)[20]

But while on paper psychiatrists claimed that smoking represented a disease—a dependence or addiction to tobacco or nicotine—in practice they were much more ambivalent about what this meant for patients who had mental-health issues besides smoking. Whether or not patients were addicted to their cigarettes, psychiatrists and other mental-health providers had to decide what to do about the behavior during the 1970s and 1980s when it became increasingly problematic to turn a blind eye to smoking behaviors in health-care institutions.

Problems Emerge in Smoking among Psychiatric Patients

When mental-health professionals began slowly to address the issue of smoking among psychiatric patients by the late 1970s and 1980s, health concerns were barely mentioned. Instead, psychiatrists and others worried about the meanings of smoking behaviors, the economic issues for poor mentally ill individuals who could not afford cigarettes, and eventually the role of cigarettes in limiting active treatment in psychiatric hospitals. Mental-health policy during this time period was focused more on the movement of patients from mental hospitals toward community care, not on what seemed to be private behaviors such as smoking.[21] While some became more concerned about the presence of smoking in mental-health settings, there was by no means professional consensus that this was a problem worth tackling at this time.

In the early part of the century, the only patients for whom treatment teams regularly recommended significant restrictions on smoking were adolescents. At the same time that smoking was widespread among adults in American society, mental-health providers consistently commented that smoking for young people was a sign of juvenile delinquency.[22] In later decades, psychiatrists recognized that smoking had a meaning for younger patients and that it would not be sufficient to simply ban smoking or cigarettes. As Joseph Noshpitz, a Maryland psychiatrist, explained in 1962, smoking was a highly symbolic activity for young men that involved growth toward adulthood and defiance of authority. He pointed out that at a treatment unit at the National Institute of Mental Health, staff were split about whether to allow smoking for teenage boys who had major behavior problems. While permitting smoking resulted in more acting out behaviors by the patients, it also accomplished more communication among patients and staff: "During smoking time, a great deal of easy-flowing conversation ensued, sometimes of rather dramatic character and often with an openness only rarely to be achieved under other circumstances."[23] Noshpitz concluded that smoking was a contentious issue that depended on understanding where patients were coming from and the meanings smoking had for the patients.

And because smoking was an important activity for psychiatric patients, it was logical for many psychiatrists in the 1970s and 1980s to advocate for their patients by trying to ensure a supply of tobacco to those with limited resources. By the 1980s, increasingly deinstitutionalized patients faced major financial problems, which affected their ability to get cigarettes. Even patients in the Canadian system complained about the economic disadvantage of mentally ill individuals and the problem of a lack of money for cigarettes.[24] Anthropologist Sue Estroff pointed out in 1981 that the patients she interacted with at a mental-health center admitted that almost all of them had at one point approached a stranger to ask for money or cigarettes.[25] Limited funds was a pressing problem even before tobacco control measures resulted in increased prices.

As the economic conditions of mentally ill smokers continued to worsen by the 1980s, some chose to reach out to the tobacco companies for help. Psychiatrist and patient advocate E. Fuller Torrey wrote to R. J. Reynolds in 1980 from his position as medical director at St. Elizabeth's Hospital after federal legislation made it illegal for the government hospital to supply cigarettes. He asked the company to assist the patients who could not afford cigarettes, because of their attachment to smoking. (He was turned down because the company wanted Torrey to lobby to change the legislation.)[26] But the most poignant requests to the companies came from patients themselves. A man wrote to RJR in 1987 from a California mental hospital, "We mentally ill, or allegedly mentally ill, smoke a lot. Most patients here are smokers and we buy *a lot* of your cigarettes. Many of us like or are addicted to cigarettes—we are often too poor to buy them—then we have to share them and suffer. Do you think your company could send us free samples? . . . Any brand would do?"[27] Some mental-health providers also saw tobacco companies as logical partners in the broader goal of taking care of mentally ill patients because of individuals' strong attachment to cigarettes.[28]

By the 1980s, psychiatric providers increasingly articulated the reality of life for mentally ill patients—they smoked in large numbers even as the rest of society began to move away from cigarettes for health reasons.[29] And though psychiatric hospitals became less central to mental-health services and more and more education suggested the value of smoking cessation, the tradition of smoking in psychiatric settings remained pretty well entrenched and was noted by investigators. Some blamed hospital staff for the high rate of smoking among psychiatric patients by either situation or example. A psychoanalyst argued, "By stocking cartons and packages of cigarettes on the wards, by 'pushing' cigarettes to patients, and by providing a constant example of casual, routine, or occasionally frenetic smoking, staff have led patients to observe and closely imitate the use of cigarettes by hospital ward personnel." He criticized nurses for being waitresses to their patients' smoking needs rather than care providers and said that common courtesy should dictate that providers not smoke in front of patients.[30] Other observers of hospital smoking behaviors noted that smoking nurses perceived their job to be more stressful than nurses who did not smoke, with the highest percentage of smokers occurring among psychiatric nurses (and the lowest among pediatric nurses).[31]

Although many psychiatric units continued to tolerate—and even encourage—smoking, by the 1980s more members of treatment teams expressed unease about its prevalence. One psychiatrist commented on conditions he found at a VA hospital in Massachusetts: "Twenty-five patients chainsmoked in the dayroom and hallways. When their cigarettes were consumed, stolen, taken or given away, they smoked 'snipes' (rubbed out butts) scavenged from floors, rubbish barrels, or ashtrays. . . . Their incessant search for snipes was usually the only goal-directed activity apparent. Interactions between patients themselves, and between patients and nursing aides, centered on requests and demands for, or arguments and fights over, cigarettes and matches." He further commented that aides used cigarettes for behavior management. While the observations the psychiatrist noted could have been from any time over the previous decades, he was much more harsh in his conclusion: "In short, the milieu was utterly dominated by the procurement and consumption of cigarettes." The solution at this hospital was to set strict limits on smoking locations, supplies, and circumstances in which patients could smoke.[32] This perception of the status quo was not only much more critical than those of previous decades, it was also more judgmental than the perspectives from other countries. For example, a visitor from the Soviet Union to a United States mental hospital was favorably impressed with the ventilation areas in the smoking rooms and electric lighters on the walls.[33]

Smoking also highlighted the inadequacies of treatment and interactions with staff on inpatient units. As a psychiatry resident recalled during his inpatient rotations, staff used cigarette distribution every forty-five minutes as a substitute for talking with patients. He noted that staff would hand out cigarettes with a condescending smile and a demeanor that suggested the patients had little else going for them: "It was also a subtle way of rejecting the patient by in effect saying, 'All you're going to get out of me is a cigarette. Don't expect anything else, and don't bother me for the next 45 minutes.'" While nurses would help patients smoke even in times of stress (such as when restrained on a bed because of psychosis), staff use of cigarettes as a substitute for therapy appeared increasingly problematic.[34]

Provider-authored literature by the mid- to late 1980s suggested that smoking could become a contentious issue, but there was no consensus on how to handle it. E. Fuller Torrey did not mention smoking in the first edition of his family guide for schizophrenia in 1983 but in 1988 modeled acceptance of smoking behaviors, observing the power of patients' (especially schizophrenics') attraction to cigarettes: "In my own experience among inpatients with schizophrenia, I have been impressed by the strength of nicotine addiction among many of them; cigarettes are a frequent cause of fights and women in psychiatric hospitals occasionally turn to prostitution in order to acquire them."[35] While he did not hesitate to identify the patients' addiction, he suggested that family members of patients avoid fighting about cigarettes because they would not be able to win.

But while Torrey was tolerant of patients' smoking, other providers became more insistent that the culture needed to change. In 1983, a psychoanalyst contributor to a special issue in the *New York State Journal of Medicine* argued that hospital psychiatrists were neglecting their patients' physical health in order to continue using cigarettes to reward behavior.[36] Though smoking in general-medical hospitals was still fairly common through the mid-1980s, psychiatric facilities lagged behind in addressing the issue because of staff assumptions that mentally ill patients needed the opportunity to smoke and because of staff members' own use of cigarettes.[37] As general hospitals began to be more consistent in limiting smoking, it became increasingly obvious that smoking played a special role for mentally ill patients, including those with substance-abuse problems.[38] The question became whether these settings should continue to allow smoking on the assumption that psychiatric patients had particular needs, or ban smoking because mentally ill patients should be treated like everyone else. There were no obvious answers.

By the late 1980s, a few psychiatric hospitals had begun cautiously to explore what it might take to ban smoking entirely. One unit at Western Psychiatric Institute at the University of Pittsburgh surveyed patients after a temporary smoking ban because of an environmental problem. The results were mixed, and the administrators reflected, "While giving up smoking may be too stressful for many people, and the right to smoke remains a personal choice, the psychiatric clinic, like other health care facilities, should consider whether it is appropriate to permit and therefore promote patients' smoking."[39] While they recognized that patients—and possibly staff members—might object, psychiatric administrators began to articulate the idea that allowing patients to smoke was in effect condoning their behavior. Further, hospitalization might provide a setting in which to try to get patients to quit.[40]

Some psychiatric hospital administrators, particularly on the west coast, could not tolerate the idea of appearing to sanction tobacco use in the era of increased awareness of the health consequences of smoking. Still, a deliberate outright ban on smoking on a psychiatric unit was notable enough that it warranted a published report in the literature. Psychiatric providers at the Oregon Health Sciences University (OHSU) surveyed the state to find out about attitudes toward smoking among psychiatric hospital administrators. Despite determining that staff at most of the facilities in the state were pessimistic about whether it was possible to reduce or eliminate smoking, OHSU proceeded in the late 1980s.[41] Staff noted that prior to the ban most of the nurses thought that smoking should still be permitted, but they were won over by the end. The advocates of the ban pointed out that it did not seem to make patients worse and also helped the smoking nurses to quit. They urged psychiatric facilities to follow general trends to improve physical health by banning smoking in psychiatric care settings, despite a culture of entrenched patient smoking.[42] Other hospitals in Oregon followed suit, and OHSU investigators proudly advocated facility peer pressure to make changes on behalf of patient and staff health.[43]

Yet hospitals in other states did not immediately model the Oregon program. Most facilities tried to deal with smoking by instituting more specific policies around when and how patients could smoke.[44] While earlier administrative manuals for institutions for the mentally ill did not mention smoking as an issue to be addressed, later procedural guides outlined the balance between safety and patient freedoms.[45] But though psychiatric administrators were increasingly aware of the issue, there was not a smooth progression toward reduction or elimination of smoking on psychiatric units. The use of the hospital to push a particular health behavior highlighted conflicts between paternalistic doctors and patient choices. A couple of London editorials in the *Journal of Medical Ethics* complained that the aggressive promotion of patient health sometimes came into conflict with patient autonomy and that the push toward health behaviors (including avoiding smoking) was being engineered by zealots who ignored individual responsibility.[46] For some, smoking remained a symbol of individual rights. Psychologists noted that older behavior-modification programs using cigarettes were no longer possible because patients' rights advocates had insisted that it was not permissible to limit patient smoking to just times of reward for behaviors desired by staff.[47]

The issue of smoking became touchy by the late 1980s among psychiatric providers. On the September 1987 cover of *Hospital and Community Psychiatry*, the editors placed a reproduction of a 1935 painting—in which an individual smoking a cigarette was visible—to highlight an article about the Oregon psychiatric unit that went smoke free. A number of psychiatrists wrote to the journal to complain that this illustration was in effect supporting smoking among patients. Further, one New York psychiatrist accused the journal of doing the work of the tobacco industry by advertising smoking on the cover. As editor John Talbott reflected, "We have also portrayed violence, overeating, psychosis, and depression in our cover art when papers in an issue dealt with one of those subjects. But I think it was clear that we were not endorsing or promoting violence or mental illness; I think it was less clear in the case of smoking."[48] Fewer psychiatrists seemed willing to defend the existing mental-hospital culture of permissive smoking, though there was no professional consensus on the role of psychiatrists with regard to their patients' smoking patterns.

Two issues that a number of investigators raised in the late 1980s and early 1990s were whether patients could tolerate a smoking ban in a hospital and whether it would make any difference in their smoking behaviors once they left. These were loaded questions for psychiatric hospitals. As west coast hospital administrators explained, "For a smoker with a psychiatric illness, cigarettes may take on a unique, sometimes magical and ritualistic significance. If one further considers that psychiatric patients use relatively more tobacco compared with the population at large, it is easy to see how the restriction of psychiatric patients' smoking could raise numerous concerns, both real and fantasized, among members of the psychiatric treatment team."[49] As these administrators and a number of other investigators reported, psychiatric units were able to go smoke free without major problems, even though staff had worried that patients would become aggressive or violent when they were not permitted to smoke. But there was no guarantee that a period of abstinence from smoking while in the hospital would have any effect on patients' long-term smoking behaviors.[50] Further, providers who restricted smoking in a community mental-health setting were able to see that patients simply smoked more outside (rather than in the center).[51]

Psychiatric debates about smoking in mental hospitals by the 1990s became quite intense. A growing number of activists from public-health and voluntary organizations coalesced around the broad program of reducing smoking in the United States. Advocates for more controls on tobacco pushed for smoking bans in more and more public spaces. Meanwhile, concerned providers within mental health became increasingly worried about the physical effects of smoking on psychiatric patients. But at the same time, patients' rights leaders insisted that patients had a right to choose and that their mental illness did not make them incompetent to make informed decisions. Finally, policy analysts became involved, as well as the accreditation agency in charge of hospital standards.

JCAHO and Smoking

In the 1980s, voluntary health organizations that had organized around the problem of tobacco began to actively take on what seemed to be a particularly pressing problem—the fact that patients and staff at many hospitals were exposed to cigarette smoke. General hospitals were slower to take action against cigarettes than might be expected given the clear risks elucidated in the surgeon general's report. Some hospitals put up signs to discourage smoking, though many were reluctant to limit smoking for fear that stressed patients would have a hard time with their recovery.[52] And discussions of smoking bans in hospitals involved other considerations beyond long-term health consequences for patients, as sales of cigarettes in hospital gift shops had an economic impact on the hospitals.[53] But in the 1980s, hospitals began to take seriously the potential conflict between their role as health-promoting institutions and the fact that patients could buy cigarettes and smoke at their sites. Across the United States and Great Britain, general hospitals began to set limits on smoking for visitors and patients and suggested that hospital personnel refrain as a good example to their patients.[54] Yet there were no national standards to force institutions to enact this health promotion step.[55]

Critics put increasing pressure on regulatory bodies to take action. In 1989, for example, Joe Tye, David Altman, and Andrew McGuire (academics and advocates from an organization to push reductions in teen smoking) published an article in *Hospital and Health Services Administration* to exhort hospitals to do their duty by halting the spread of tobacco-related problems.[56] At the same time that they pointed fingers at the tobacco industry for obstructing public health, they also chastised the American Hospital Association (AHA) and the American Medical Association (AMA) for failing to take action. They were particularly critical of the ways in which hospitals took advantage of the deep pockets of the tobacco industry for endowments and donations while turning a blind eye to the evils of their products—a critique that had also been made about the AMA's approach toward tobacco funding for its activities.[57] Tye, Altman, and McGuire advocated for new guidelines from the Joint Commission on Accreditation of Healthcare Organizations (JCAHO) that would address this problem.

JCAHO (at the present called the Joint Commission) had been founded in 1952 through a merger of the accrediting programs of the American Council of Surgeons (ACS) and the AMA. From its inception, the Joint Commission consisted of representatives from the ACS, AHA, AMA, and the American Council of Physicians. By the time that federal funds were being used for health care in the 1960s (through Medicare), the Joint Commission had become a nationally recognized organization whose accreditation standards were necessary to allow hospitals and other health-care organizations to receive reimbursement for services.[58] And by the 1980s, JCAHO standards were a powerful means by which to motivate widespread changes in hospitals.

With pressure from tobacco control-activists, who also leaned on the AHA and the AMA, the Joint Commission announced in 1991 that for the following year, hospitals needed to prohibit smoking to receive accreditation.[59] The intent of the new standard was to promote positive health for patients and to limit their exposure to second-hand smoke, a growing concern in public-health circles. The standard was not designed to address individual patients' smoking habits, but rather to provide a clean environment when patients were in the hospital.[60] And while the policy directors at the Joint Commission were not specifically thinking about the implications for mental-health institutions, the new smoking policy became applicable at the same time that the Joint Commission combined their accreditation standards for general hospitals and behavioral-health programs (including substance-abuse and psychiatric hospitals—both short and long term).[61]

The Joint Commission's publication of the new expectation regarding smoke-free hospital facilities resulted in a wave of protests from the mentally ill and their advocates. Activist groups on behalf of the mentally ill had already been fighting smoking bans on a local level for several years. In Indianapolis in 1989, an editorial in the local newspaper criticized the local state hospital for taking the "needlessly harsh" measure of limiting freedoms for mentally ill smokers. Further, a legal-services organization filed suit on behalf of the involuntarily committed psychiatric patients at the hospital who alleged that their rights were being violated by a smoking ban.[62] Advocates noted that these patients were locked up against their will and that the state did not have the right to take away their opportunities to exercise freedoms enjoyed by everyone else in society.

Before the Joint Commission standards, those who opposed smoking bans or restrictions for the mentally ill made the argument that individual treatment settings had capriciously acted ahead of state and federal laws. Further, as argued by Tim Coleman, an attorney for the Oregon Advocacy Center who explored legal action against the Oregon Health Sciences Center that forbade smoking in the late 1980s, a smoking ban was in essence forced medical treatment for patients committed to the hospital against their will.[63] Michael Lavin, a philosophy professor from the University of Tennessee, argued in 1989 that psychiatric patients had the right to choose whether to be treated for their dependence on nicotine. He insisted that just because they were dependent did not make them incapable of making that decision.[64] Lavin did not suggest that patients had a right to smoke but did insist that physicians did not have a right to make them stop against their will.[65]

Arguments about smoking and the mentally ill were not just academic squabbles contained within the professional literature. The national media covered the dispute about the potential problems with smoking bans in psychiatric hospitals.[66] As a *New York Times* author pointed out in 1990, mentally ill smokers had a much harder time in the new climate of aggressive tobacco-control measures since they could not just step outside of locked psychiatric units in order to smoke. As he explained, "For psychiatric patients, cigarettes have traditionally been a special fix: an escape, a reward, a defense against boredom and drowsiness induced by antipsychotic drugs."[67] Against the long-standing tradition of smoking in mental hospitals, the new standards seemed particularly cruel to psychiatric patients.

Although the logical argument for tobacco-control enthusiasts regarding smoking in hospitals was based on long-term health risks, this issue was somewhat more contentious in the case of the mentally ill. First, advocates for the freedom to smoke in this population argued that mental-health (rather than physical-health) issues were more immediate and primary. But also the long-term health issues for chronically mentally ill patients were more complicated than for those without mental illness. As a Swedish researcher pointed out in 1989, patients with schizophrenia had long been noted to have shorter life expectancies than those without serious mental illness. Further, the rate of death in the mentally ill was higher even as the causes of death changed over the decades (especially from tuberculosis to cardiovascular disease).[68] While the observation about the higher mortality rate among the mentally ill later became a reason to focus on smoking cessation, in the 1990s observers used this to suggest that the calculus regarding smoking bans should be different for patients with mental illness. For example, Tulane investigator James Wright pointed out in 1990 that the usual health promotion advice made little sense among individuals who had overwhelming socioeconomic issues, little control over their environment, and living situations that made it absurd to thinking about long-term health issues.[69]

Though the Joint Commission rules intended to put mental-health hospitals on the same regulatory level as other hospitals, administrators involved in psychiatric care were acutely aware that there were special problems. New Jersey investigators pointed out, "In designing policies for smoke-free psychiatric settings, emphasis needs to be placed not only on the patient's risk of pulmonary disease, cancer, and stroke from smoking but also on the effect that smoking has on overall psychiatric treatment. Smoke-free policies can have significant effects on unit ecology, effectiveness of pharmacotherapy once drug-nicotine interactions are eliminated, treatment compliance, patient-staff relationships, and outcome of hospitalization."[70] Others pointed out that behavioral disturbances were often the product of problems of cigarette supply within locked psychiatric units.[71] Many feared that elimination of smoking within these settings would lead to massive behavioral disturbances.

But early reports about smoke-free psychiatric units presented a fairly rosy picture of the results, especially in contrast to fears of riots or other catastrophic consequences. Some wondered whether the real story was being told. Minneapolis social workers Michael Greeman and Thomas McClellan argued in 1991 that adverse events after smoking bans had probably been underreported. They contrasted the situation in a VA hospital that had a relatively permissive policy before a 1988 ban with the situation after the ban. A number of patients left the hospital to get cigarettes without permission, vulnerable patients were victimized because of an aggressive underground barter system, and 20 percent of the patients had major behavior problems because of the ban. Greeman and McClellan gave examples of assaultive behavior, agitation, prolonged hospital course, as well as episodes of illicit smoking and contention among staff members. They concluded, "An attitude of casual indifference or undue optimism about instituting a smoking ban may result in serious problems."[72] Further, as Massachusetts General psychiatrists pointed out, symptoms of nicotine abstinence (which looked a lot like other psychiatric symptoms) could distort providers' understandings of what was going on with patients. They advocated caution about abrupt discontinuation of smoking for psychiatric patients in need of hospitalization.[73]

While the 1992 Joint Commission standard about smoking bans created widespread anxieties among psychiatric providers, most hospitals complied. Further, the rules did allow a few exceptions for smoking such as for terminally ill patients and others for whom physicians could write a specific order. A Joint Commission spokesman suggested that an example might be a patient who was being treated for alcohol or drug dependence: "the physician may desire to treat only one addiction at a time and not potentially complicate the primary addiction treatment with treatment for nicotine withdrawal."[74] In the initial iteration of the Joint Commission rule, psychiatric patients as a class were not given permission to smoke but individual patients with psychiatric problems could be given a prescription to allow them to smoke while in the hospital.[75]

Yet a physician prescription was a problematic mechanism for psychiatric patients to evade the ban. As a journalist pointed out in *Washington Post* coverage of the smoking ban in 1992, physicians found it ethically and legally troublesome to write a specific prescription. While the standards were intended to put pressure on patients and staff to prohibit smoking (rather than just discourage it, as the old standards purportedly had done), Joint Commission staff acknowledged that they were primarily focused on physical health rather than the specific issues around mental health that were raised in the wake of the ban announcement.[76]

As many reported at the time, one major issue for psychiatric patients was that the new smoking policy flew in the face of decades of cigarette-related culture inside psychiatric institutions, at least some of which had been the direct result of mental-health professionals' efforts to shape patients' behavior. In the same vein, critics pointed out that the system of VA hospitals, which had began a slow process toward becoming smoke-free in the late 1980s, was trying to turn back a long history that had begun with the government dispensing cigarettes to soldiers in wartime.[77] Further, as a New York University School of Medicine faculty member explained, the VA was substituting individual patients' ideas about their health priorities with a new social standard of increased longevity. As a result, "health promotion to attain the goal of personal longevity is . . . the popular personal ethic of today that is largely replacing older ethics, such as living life for the betterment of society or the attainment of an afterlife. To act contrary to the ethic of life extension and/or personal health is to receive the approbation of society and to be considered morally blameworthy for one's disease."[78] Psychiatric patients were also forcibly put into the framework of maximizing personal health when put into psychiatric hospitals.

Although some complained about the smoking bans in general hospitals, especially in areas of the country with strong relationships to the tobacco industry, the culture within most nonpsychiatric hospitals rapidly shifted.[79] As a Boston investigator noted, administrators found that the Joint Commission regulations had helped change how they were viewed: "They were no longer antismoking zealots out to persecute the smoking minority, but concerned managers ensuring continued operation of the hospital."[80] Yet the same kind of change in culture did not happen as rapidly for psychiatric hospitals. Some refused to go along with the Joint Commission standards, arguing that it would be too hard on psychiatric patients if they were told they could no longer smoke.[81] Veterans groups were particularly incensed and staged protests outside VA hospitals across the country.[82]

As a result of pressure by psychiatric patients and their advocates, the Joint Commission decided late in 1992 to grant an exemption to psychiatric and substance-abuse patients regarding smoking options.[83] One of the senior vice presidents of the Joint Commission noted that this issue raised the most comment from the public than any regulatory decision previously rendered by the organization.[84] While the Joint Commission did not require hospitals to allow a smoking area nor demand that patients be given the opportunity to smoke, the regulatory body did agree that mentally ill patients and individuals in long-term care units could be allowed to smoke as a class without specific physician prescription.[85] Many state hospitals responded to this with a compromise that allowed smoking in outdoor areas while maintaining a smoking ban inside. Observers of this change in state-hospital culture insisted that the inside ban helped with patient behavior and patient-staff interactions.[86]

The Joint Commission's slightly more relaxed stance on its standards regarding mental-health-care settings did not eliminate the controversy around smoking in psychiatric or substance-abuse units, however. In New York City in 1994, an activist mayor and city council pushed through comprehensive public-space smoking bans that included psychiatric hospitals. This measure was opposed by mentally ill patients and their advocates who argued that their episodes of hospitalization were for mental illness, not smoking detoxification.[87] A grassroots campaign was generated by advocacy organizations, including the Alliance for the Mentally Ill (AMI) and the Friends and Advocates for the Mentally Ill (FAMI). Helen Konopka of FAMI, whose chain-smoking schizophrenic sister had refused hospitalization multiple times because of the smoking ban, distributed literature, encouraged a letter-writing campaign, and testified before the New York legislature in an effort to protect the rights of the mentally ill to smoke.[88]

In a pamphlet published and distributed by FAMI to (presumed) non-mentally-ill voters, readers were asked to put themselves in the position of a person with a mental illness in the midst of a crisis: "Imagine, the Police have just taken you in handcuffs to the Psychiatric Emergency Room of the local City Hospital. The doctor is trying to explain something to you but everything is confusing. She tells you that you will be held against your will until you are stabilized. You are given medication for your psychosis. You are nervous and scared. You ask for a cigarette. The nurse sarcastically tells you that you won't be able to smoke, the hospital is smoke free and there are no discrete smoking areas."[89] In this nightmare scenario, the physician was not the authoritarian figure (and was actually a woman psychiatrist), but the nurse became a mocking dictator who was using her position of power to control patients through the smoking ban.

While some of the advocacy material asked readers imagine the position of an individual deprived of consolation and freedom at a time of serious emotional crisis, other publications from the campaign stressed the ways in which the mentally ill were uniquely vulnerable. In another publication, the reader was asked, "What has happened to individual freedom and our respect for the human dignity of New York City's most vulnerable citizens—the seriously and chronically mentally ill?"[90] In this context, the smoking ban became an example of social injustice perpetrated on those without a voice to defend themselves. (It might be logical to conclude that the tobacco industry was behind this. But while Helen Konopka reached out to Philip Morris to tell them about the campaign, there is no evidence that the tobacco industry did anything more than track their activities.)

In an effort to bring justice for the mentally ill, a number of advocates filed lawsuits on behalf of patients who alleged that their civil rights had been violated by the new smoking restrictions. While lawsuits had been an important way for patients' rights groups to win reforms in civil commitment laws in the 1970s and 1980s, by the 1990s there was so much concern about the harmful effects of smoking that advocates were unable to convince courts that mentally ill patients had a right to smoke. In 1993, for example, the Ohio Court of Appeals upheld a smoking ban at a psychiatric facility despite patient allegations that the ban violated their rights to equal protection. The court said that the facility had the authority and that a ban on smoking in order to promote health was reasonable.[91]

In Connecticut, a group representing patients in public mental-health facilities brought suit to demand a change in a plan for implementing a smoking ban. The group initially approached the commissioner of mental health in the state, but he was politely incredulous that the group could ask for an exception to the smoking ban given the well-documented health risks of smoking for both smokers and those around them.[92] But as the representative from the Connecticut Legal Rights Project explained to a state representative after the ban was announced, "We were immediately flooded with distraught calls from patients who were overwhelmed with having to give up the one thing that allowed them some control within their lives. Many of them claimed that they had almost nothing to do all day and smoking was essential to keep them from exploding in frustration and boredom."[93] While the attorney expressed his awareness of the stickiness of the situation, he emphasized the pain and suffering of the patients he was representing. The suit was not successful, however; the case was dismissed by a Connecticut Superior Court ruling ten months later.[94]

While few of the lawsuits had any effect on smoking options for the mentally ill, the Alliance for the Mentally Ill published a position statement in 1995 asserting the rights of psychiatric patients to smoke. The AMI statement argued that these individuals were locked up in mental hospitals against their will and did not have opportunities to exercise the freedoms available to others. It also noted that because patients with serious mental illnesses such as schizophrenia and depression had higher rates of nicotine addiction than many others, "it is inhumane to rob patients of their autonomy and dignity by infringing on one of the few remaining freedoms historically allowed patients." The AMI advocated for special smoking areas, as well as smoking-cessation programs specifically designed for the mentally ill.[95]

One issue raised by the AMI statement was that mentally ill individuals seemed to have a special relationship to smoking and nicotine, and advocates argued for more research on this issue rather than just outright bans on smoking behaviors. Many popular and academic commentators made note of this unique relationship and suggested that there might be important biochemical reasons for the high prevalence of smoking in the mentally ill population. Columbia University psychiatrist Alexander Glassman explored psychiatric symptoms among patients undergoing smoking cessation and found a strong association between depression and smoking. He also suggested that smoking was doing something specific for patients with schizophrenia. He postulated that it might be important to learn about this connection for mentally ill patients: "I believe that not only is cigarette smoking relevant to clinical psychiatry but its association with particular psychiatric illnesses offers an opportunity to increase our understanding both of normal brain function and of psychopathology."[96] Glassman and others suggested that smoke-free units might raise issues for some psychiatric patients. At the least, providers should be attentive to the critical issues of nicotine withdrawal in this population.[97]

The conflict around smoking bans in mental hospitals highlighted professional issues for psychiatrists in this time period. The diagnosis of tobacco (later nicotine) dependence suggested that the profession was ready and willing to claim smoking as a mental-health issue. At the same time, though, psychiatrists were more focused on other issues, especially the gradual movement toward biological psychiatry and the increasing use of medications for broader segments of the population. For those who continued to treat seriously mentally ill patients, smoking could become a point of conflict between psychiatric patients' desire to assume more autonomy in their treatment decisions and medical authority that dictated what was right to patients. Some in the profession took an uncomplicated view of the issue—smoking caused physical problems (and could affect blood levels of medication) and therefore psychiatric patients needed to stop smoking whenever possible. Others were more uncomfortable with the conflict between their goals for treatment and patients' expectations about their lives.

But through the 1990s, as more and more psychiatric hospitals and other public settings in the United States became smoke free, the emphasis around smoking among the mentally ill shifted. Instead of accepting smoking patterns of mentally ill populations and framing the issues in terms of behavior, many mental-health-care professionals moved toward a focus on nicotine. In this area, they joined with researchers in multiple existing networks involving academic centers as well as the tobacco and pharmaceutical industries that had developed knowledge about the role of nicotine over the decades. For industry-sponsored investigators, there were lucrative potential markets to develop based on both the need for smoking cessation and the recognition that nicotine might have some function in the brain. And for psychiatrists, the reminders that the brain was the seat of psychiatric illness helped to shore up their status as a medical specialty. A shift in the focus toward nicotine helped mental-health professionals and business, even the increasingly embattled tobacco industry.

Chapter 5

The Many Faces of Nicotine

In May of 1988, a new surgeon general's report, *Nicotine Addiction,* synthesized research from a variety of fields to support the conclusion that people continued to smoke despite the health consequences because nicotine was addictive.[1] Many perceived this report as a direct assault on the tobacco industry's claims that smoking represented personal choice. But the publication of *Nicotine Addiction* also signaled the beginning of tobacco research, policy, and practices directed toward the brain rather than the rest of the body and highlighted the potential significance of nicotine itself.

The stance that nicotine was addicting was a step up from that of the 1964 surgeon general's report that had identified smoking as a habit. In his preface to the 1988 report, Surgeon General C. Everett Koop argued that Americans should be as outraged by nicotine addiction outcomes (which he defined as mortality from smoking-related diseases) as they were by the epidemic of illegal drug use, which the federal government was combating with its ongoing war on drugs.[2] But on some level it was hard to compare nicotine addiction to dependence on other drugs since nicotine dependence did not have legal consequences. Instead, the report focused on withdrawal symptoms, tolerance, and the inability of a user to quit despite the health risks.[3] The first section of the report explored the pharmacology of nicotine and its availability in the brain through different smoking patterns. Another section addressed the reasons why many became addicted to nicotine, including its effects on weight, cognition, and perceived effects on stress. And the volume concluded with a discussion about treatment of dependence, including the availability of nicotine-replacement medications.[4]

But though the emphasis on nicotine might have suggested a straightforward application of principles of addiction to cigarettes and smokers, in fact the growing awareness of the role of nicotine in the brain complicated conversations about addiction. It also raised the possibility that business enterprises could make use of the chemical for profit outside of cigarettes. As early as 1978, a National Institute of Drug Abuse (NIDA) conference featured researchers who speculated about whether there were brain receptors that could be blocked by medication to help people quit smoking.[5] Pharmaceutical companies were actively looking for sites in the brain to target drug development.[6] And New York psychiatrist Jerome Jaffe (who had proposed the diagnosis of tobacco use disorder) and UCLA researcher Murray Jarvik were involved in the development of nicotine medications with pharmaceutical companies.[7] Further, one of the investigators at the 1978 NIDA symposium, who discussed the most promising approach toward nicotine, was directly supported by the tobacco industry—and freely disclosed this in the conference publication. University of Rochester biochemist Leo Abood presented the neuroscience of nicotine infusion experiments he had conducted with rats, and demonstrated new methodology for detecting neurotransmitter binding with nicotine and other substances.[8] The focus on nicotine over the decades made it clear that there was more to the chemical than just keeping smokers hooked. Nicotine exposed the challenges in psychiatry's approach to addiction. And both the tobacco and pharmaceutical industries became increasingly engaged in the area of nicotine neuroscience as they continued to innovate with new products and approaches to problems.[9] Tobacco-company researchers and academic investigators collaborated to explore the effects of nicotine on the brain and the potential of the nicotinic receptor as a site for pharmaceutical drug development. This basic science research shifted the ground for medical attention to smoking. Instead of exclusively focusing on the physical harm of cigarettes (and the damage to innocent bystanders), investigators and clinicians began to look at brain chemistry. The tobacco industry did not just fight off conceptualizations of nicotine addiction, it joined in studying the neuroscience of nicotine.[10] And in conversations about the brain effects of nicotine, researchers included another corporate partner: the pharmaceutical industry.

Meanings of Addiction

Although it may seem self-evident now that cigarettes are addictive, it was not a foregone conclusion that medical and research opinion would coalesce into labeling nicotine as an addictive drug. It was not until the 1970s and 1980s that smoking was identified as a form of substance abuse. And as in other kinds of addiction, there has been a tension between understanding users as victims of a disease or viewing them as social deviants.[11] As I discuss in the next chapter, psychiatrists slowly eased into a model of diagnosis and treatment for nicotine dependence in clinical settings. But the conversations about addiction also centered around how to understand smokers and their relationship to the world of drug abuse. For much of the last century, substance abuse involved legal, financial, and social issues for users.[12] A declaration that nicotine was similar to other drugs of abuse raised the question of what to do with users of cigarettes. Was a cigarette smoker really like a drug addict? And what social consequences could follow from someone who was a regular (albeit addicted) user of a legal substance?

The tobacco industry fought policies based on the 1988 surgeon general's report. But tobacco defenders also battled the conceptualization of smokers as users of hard drugs. The 1988 report explicitly stated, "The pharmacologic and behavioral processes that determine tobacco addiction are similar to those that determine addiction to drugs such as heroin and cocaine."[13] Not surprisingly, tobacco industry spokesmen seized on the analogy between heroin users and smokers in order to ridicule it. They insisted instead that the more appropriate analogy was between smokers and coffee drinkers, a comparison intended to deescalate the rhetoric around smoking addiction and to highlight the normality of nicotine consumption.[14] In the wake of the surgeon general's report, tobacco-funded psychologist David Warburton from Reading University in the United Kingdom organized a workshop to address the problems of categorizing smoking (and nicotine) with other serious drugs of abuse and helped to form an organization dedicated to allowing people to enjoy pleasures such as coffee, chocolate, and smoking.[15] Warburton also edited a volume entitled *Addiction Controversies* that was published in 1992 with articles by a number of well-respected investigators (many, if not all, of whom had received tobacco industry funding at some point), who argued that it made no sense to define all substance abuse with one set of criteria.[16]

Those who wished to defend the differences between smoking/nicotine and other drugs of abuse engaged in multiple public and professional venues. In 1992, tobacco researchers debated advocates of the concept of nicotine addiction within the journal *Psychopharmacology*. R. J. Reynolds scientists John Robinson and Walter Pritchard argued that people used smoking as a coping tool and for nicotine's mild psychoactive properties. They cautioned about the slippery slope of viewing everyday substances as drugs: "If we lose this common-sense perspective of the role of nicotine in tobacco use, those of us who enjoy the 'lift' we receive from that first cup of coffee in the morning or that cola drink in the late afternoon may find that a few years from now a small group of researchers have equated our coffee/cola-drinking behavior to that of a hard-core crack or heroin addict."[17] Psychologist Robert West from St. George's Hospital in London countered that it was necessary to view nicotine as an addictive drug in order to get people the help they needed with smoking cessation and to shape public policy.[18]

In return, Robinson and Pritchard argued that West seemed to have diluted the meaning of "addiction" and that, "labeling smoking as an addiction 'just like heroin or cocaine' not only minimizes the tragedy of hard-core addictions, but may also provide people with a convenient excuse not to quit, and may even provide young people with an inaccurate perspective that could actually encourage experimentation with hard-core drugs."[19] Vermont psychiatrist John Hughes emphasized in 1993 in the same journal, though, that Robinson and Pritchard were misusing the analogies of use and stressed that dependence did not need to be identical for all drugs.[20]

For much of the 1990s, the tobacco industry combated efforts to label smoking as a form of drug abuse by highlighting what it would mean for smokers to be classified as drug addicts. In 1994, the British American Tobacco Company (BAT) produced a TV commercial in which respected scientists (who not surprisingly had ties to the tobacco industry) said that it would trivialize real drug addiction by classifying smokers as hard-core drug users. Further, the concept of addiction had become stretched to include "addiction" to chocolate or exercise, and individuals with those kinds of addictions would not "group themselves with heroin, cocaine or 'crack' users."[21] The tobacco industry was somewhat successful in holding back the tide of tobacco-control measures as long as they could emphasize how ridiculous it was to connect smoking, something that normal people would do, to illicit drug use.

But this argument did not last long, and not just because tobacco-control advocates were successful in beating back tobacco-industry influence. Instead, neuroscience researchers began to argue that evolving science was the best way forward. When the issue of how to understand nicotine's addictiveness was revisited in a 1995 issue of *Psychopharmacology,* Robinson and Pritchard were outnumbered, and their arguments were drowned out by other investigators. As UCLA researcher Murray Jarvik observed, terminology and assumptions had changed since the 1964 surgeon general's report that described tobacco as "habituating" rather than addictive. Jarvik pointed out that the author who wrote that section of the report had himself been a smoker, and as such was "not likely to stigmatize himself with the pejorative title of 'addict.'"[22] Not only had the terrain changed, but also new tools and techniques would help in the future. NIDA researchers Jack Henningfield and Stephen Heishman stressed the potential for nontobacco nicotine medications.[23] And psychologist Saul Shiffman said that it was time to be done with the issue of addictiveness and focus on the science.[24]

Although there were (and continue to be) tobacco-industry defenders who carped on failures in the analogy between smoking and other drugs, the dispute about what it meant to be hooked on smoking was only part of the tobacco-industry strategy. Instead, the emerging research on the neuroscience of nicotine was embraced by a number of tobacco research organizations. Both individual companies and tobacco research groups supported basic research on nicotine mechanisms. They funded some who supported the idea that nicotine was addictive,[25] but mostly they pursued the premise that nicotine had brain effects, and that their companies were—and should be—the experts in this area.

Industry-Academic Collaborations and the Therapeutic Value of Nicotine

With the evolution of new techniques to study the brain, investigators inside the tobacco industry and those sponsored by it began to look at what nicotine could do, including its potential in noncigarette applications. Tobacco-industry interest in therapeutic indications for nicotine appeared to have been part of a broader strategy to create new products and approaches in the wake of increasing concerns about health. The tobacco companies found research partners who had interests and skills in molecular neuroscience techniques. For example, tobacco research organizations had a long and productive collaboration with University of Rochester scientist Leo Abood, who had worked on developing new pharmaceutical agents for mental illness with Abbott Laboratories in the late 1950s and early 1960s.[26] In his tobacco industry relationships, including reviews of applications for Council for Tobacco Research and funding and consultations with Philip Morris, Abood brought his expertise in brain chemistry and his habit of thinking about neurochemicals from a therapeutic point of view. As the CTR connection with Abood suggests, as early as the 1960s tobacco research groups were on the lookout for academic researchers with expertise in the emerging field of psychopharmacology for grant reviews and sponsored symposia.[27]

Nicotine had been recognized by the early twentieth century as an important chemical that affected internal organs, muscles, and the brain.[28] It was also an agent that helped to differentiate types of receptors for acetylcholine, a neurotransmitter that is present in both the brain and the spinal cord. Acetylcholine's receptors include two types: muscarinic (which bind the chemical muscarine), and nicotinic (which bind nicotine). By the 1980s, researchers were exploring how neurotransmitters—including acetylcholine—were involved in normal brain function, as well as their role in brain diseases. Many investigators were beginning to target neurotransmitter systems to develop therapeutics. Tobacco-sponsored researchers were on the cutting edge of new discoveries involving nicotine and its action in the brain.

The tobacco industry invested in molecular biology through several mechanisms. The CTR granted funds to researchers through this time period and approved projects with molecular methods.[29] And they helped to promote scientific exchange through sponsorship of meetings. In 1985, for example, Rockefeller University scientist Bruce McEwen, an international expert in neurotransmitter structure and function, chaired a scientific meeting, "The Role of Receptors in Biology," at the CTR headquarters. The meeting included luminaries from a variety of academic institutions, as well as the National Institutes of Health, who discussed the knowledge to date about receptors and their functions.[30] While the CTR fostered industry-wide investigation, some of the cigarette companies also funded direct research programs and supported extramural researchers. BAT had a robust relationship with a number of investigators in Europe and funded projects on molecular mechanisms, while PM continued to closely monitor and periodically fund researchers.[31] And the Smokeless Tobacco Research Council (STRC) appeared in the 1980s, a group that funded research in an effort to distance the noncigarette portion of the tobacco industry from the health threats of cigarettes.[32]

A number of themes emerged from the tobacco-industry-funded view of nicotine. One was that nicotine was a powerful chemical that had far-reaching effects on multiple neurotransmitter systems. Another was that certain populations seemed to experience different effects of the chemical in the brain. Researchers in psychopharmacology—the study of chemical interactions in the brain and their emotional and behavioral consequences—were particularly interested in how nicotine might be implicated in serious mental illnesses, including schizophrenia and depression. Others explored the effects of nicotine on memory and movement in neurological diseases. Some of the basic science questions were driven by clinical observations—such as the fact that so many individuals with schizophrenia smoked. Others came about because of research, some of which had taken place in tobacco industry laboratories, that suggested that smoking helped with thinking and memory.

One area that captured tobacco industry researchers' attention (and funding) was the problem of Alzheimer's disease. Alzheimer's research was wide open to novel therapeutics. The inexorable course of the illness seemed to afflict more and more Americans, and it gained attention in the popular media in the 1980s. The tragedy of memory loss and withdrawal from society was even more poignant by the early 1990s when Ronald Reagan announced that he had been diagnosed.[33] In this context, tobacco companies pursued the idea that nicotine might be helpful in halting the progression of the illness or even treating it. They were explicit that they were looking for new business opportunities and that nicotine had the potential to address many of the physical problems that afflicted aging individuals.[34]

The classical appearance of brain pathology in Alzheimer's disease, microscopic plaques and tangles within neurons visible at autopsy after death, did not answer the question of why or how the brain defects emerged.[35] Researchers began to use new methods involving neurotransmitter function, and suggested possible therapeutic options. Investigators found that cholinergic receptors (those that bound acetylcholine) seemed to be affected in Alzheimer's patients. Therapy initially was based on muscarinic acetylcholine receptors. But some found that nicotinic acetylcholine receptors also seemed to be abnormally low in number in patients with both Alzheimer's disease and Parkinson's disease (a progressive movement disorder).[36] As investigators suggested, perhaps stimulation of the nicotinic receptors—with a substance such as nicotine—might help slow or halt the progression of these diseases.

Some Alzheimer's researchers made the observation that smoking status might have some relevance for individuals' propensity to develop the disease. In 1987, scientists at RJR commented that a British investigator found Alzheimer's disease to be less frequent among smokers. The investigator recognized that this news would make the tobacco industry happy, and the RJR staff agreed. As they commented, "A beneficial effect of nicotine on this disease could be of major benefit to Alpha [a project to develop Premier, a smokeless cigarette]."[37] Tobacco consumers also observed a potentially therapeutic role for nicotine. One woman wrote to the research group at RJR in 1989 to explain that her father had Alzheimer's and that he seemed to do better when he smoked his old cigars. She had done some reading about acetylcholine and wondered whether nicotine might have some important effects in the brain.[38]

This view of nicotine aligned the tobacco industry more with the pharmaceutical industry and its priorities in developing chemicals for treatment of disease.[39] In 1988, Professor Jeffrey Gray, who took over the chair in psychology at the Institute of Psychiatry in London from Hans Eysenck when he retired, wrote to a research director at BAT proposing a project entitled "A Behavioural, Neuropharmacological and Neurochemical Study of the Effects of Nicotine on Memory and Attention in the Rat."[40] Gray explained that this project would build on existing research that demonstrated that nicotine helped with cognitive performance. He pointed out that existing treatments for Alzheimer's already targeted acetylcholine receptors but they did not work. Instead, this project would help develop nicotine-like treatments for cognitive deficits.[41] BAT research executives were interested in Gray's research as they understood the financial implications of developing a treatment for a disease as prevalent as Alzheimer's.[42] Gray's investigations were so promising for the industry that he maintained cordial relationships with many of the funding streams available to tobacco-sponsored researchers.[43]

The suggestion that nicotine might have potential positive effects on the brain was not an industry secret nurtured only within research laboratories. Instead, investigators promoted the potential for nicotine (or even smoking) for some diseases, and the popular press was quick to pick up on this. In October of 1988 (several months after the surgeon general's report), the *New York Monthly* ran a story on the benefits of smoking, including prevention or amelioration of illness, based on basic science research.[44] And in turn, tobacco companies paid close attention to trends in research and popular opinion that might affect their bottom line or future business opportunities. For example, the research manager for BAT was alerted when the European Parliament in 1992 recommended investment in brain research—including Alzheimer's disease.[45]

Nicotine offered challenges in research and development that suggested the value of wide collaboration. One issue, as University of Bath investigator Susan Wonnacott pointed out in 1990, was that nicotine receptors did not behave in a typical way. She explained in an article in *Trends in Pharmacological Sciences* that the accepted dogma of receptors was that chronic exposure to an agonist (something that stimulates the receptor to respond in a positive way) would decrease the number of receptors, while exposure to an antagonist (something that shuts down receptors) would increase the number of receptors. For nicotine, however, the pattern was not nearly as clear. Wonnacott, who had consulted for BAT, linked the atypical receptor pattern to the usual practice of smokers adjusting their dose of nicotine: "It is perhaps apposite, in this context, to recall the common observation that cigarette smokers puff lightly for the stimulatory effects of nicotine (arousal), while inhaling deeply for more calming or depressant effects."[46] In order to understand the role of nicotine in the brain, it was helpful to know more about smokers' behavior. In this area, the obvious experts were the tobacco companies.

In December of 1990, a number of scientists from around the world participated in a roundtable discussion with researchers from RJR on the topic of nicotine. The conference was highly technical, with complicated conversations about dose-response curves for smokers and nicotine delivery. The scientists noted that this was a complex issue, involving steroids, receptor interactions, genetic differences, as well as smoker behavior. The roundtable participants also acknowledged that conferees brought different information—and priorities—to the meeting. Company researchers, for example, had a different agenda than their academic collaborators. Within this discussion, RJR investigator John Reynolds expressed regret that the company's Premier cigarette, a non-burning product, was not more commercially successful because it would have offered benefits with less harm. And psychologist Jeffrey Gray made suggestions to the company about possible development of new products. Within this discussion, researchers brainstormed about possible directions for research and gave each other feedback on project ideas.[47] In the roundtable, as with a conference on EEG sponsored by RJR the next year, the tobacco-company researchers had specific expertise that was of value to academic investigators.[48] And the deep pockets of the industry offered opportunities for research funding and collaborations.

Conferences such as the one in 1990 became increasingly common throughout the decade. At the same time that parts of the tobacco industry were geared up to fight accusations that cigarettes were addictive, other elements within the companies were looking for new business opportunities with nicotine. In a meeting on smoking issues at BAT, outside consultants were brought in who described research on potential benefits of nicotine, including treatment for Alzheimer's and Parkinson's disease. Although the research consultants were asked to leave before the company talked about internal strategy to respond to business threats, their presentations were explicitly tied to the issue of how to innovate in the wake of public-health concerns.[49] Some within the industry began to argue that research on the molecular effects of nicotine could allow the companies to act as good corporate citizens.[50] Obviously, the history of tobacco-industry behavior indicates that cigarette companies were hardly good citizens. And some in the media perceived the tobacco sponsorship of nicotine research to be highly suspect.[51] Still, tobacco-company organizations funded respected scientists on neuroscience projects not directly intended to disprove or muddy the criticisms of cigarette smoking.[52]

By the 1990s, many neuroscience investigators—including those with tobacco-industry support—focused on nicotine primarily as a neurobiological agent with no mention of its origins in tobacco. For some who interpreted these results, the benefits of nicotine were a happy consequence amidst the otherwise dismal news for smokers.[53] For the tobacco companies, new therapeutic suggestions for nicotine to treat diseases gave them alternatives to their defensive posturing regarding smoking and physical health.[54] And the potential benefit of nicotine for people with serious and otherwise hopeless diseases could only be positive for the companies.

Duke researcher Edward Levin, whose Nicotine Research Program was funded in part by generous donations from the tobacco industry, explained some of the possible commercial implications of his research on nicotine.[55] While nicotine itself might be problematic because of the possibility of addiction, "nicotinic drugs hold considerable promise as a new class of treatments for cognitive dysfunction, such as Alzheimer's disease, schizophrenia, and ADHD. Alternative forms of delivery, such as the nicotine skin patch, reduce some of the health risks and abuse liability. Development of more specific nicotinic sister drugs may separate the cognitive enhancing effects of nicotine from its cardiovascular, developmental, and reinforcing effects, so that adverse side effects can be further reduced."[56] Nicotine fit into a model for drug development in which chemicals were designed with a particular biological goal in mind, instead of trial and error with a series of compounds. In this type of process, collaboration between industry and academic science seemed to be particularly fruitful and provided mutual benefits.[57] RJR pushed this type of scientific interaction to the next level in developing novel pharmaceutical agents based on the company's traditional research interests.

Crossing the Line into Pharmaceuticals at RJR

As I discussed in chapter 3, the Biobehavioral Division within RJR originally looked at individual differences between tobacco consumers using personality assessments such as the Eysenck Personality Inventory. But researchers within the division had moved fairly quickly by the mid-1980s toward a more neurobiological approach on nicotine and its actions in the brain. RJR's first psychologist for the division, David Gilbert, was involved in a developing field of psychology known as psychophysiology, or the effort to measure behavior through physiological data, particularly brain activity. Gilbert found like-minded researchers when he attended annual meetings of the Society for Psychophysiological Research and talked to them about his work on psychophysiology and smoking.[58] When Gilbert left RJR to join the faculty at Southern Illinois University in 1986, his replacement, Walter Pritchard, also employed psychophysiological approaches and continued connections between the tobacco industry and academic investigators.

The tools available with psychophysiological research, including brainwave measurements with electroencephalography, tracking of eye movements, and correlation of stimuli with brain activity, all allowed investigators at RJR to take their inquiry about the brain effects of smoking beyond subjective reports.[59] In addition, they used the opportunity afforded by these research methods to look specifically at the brain effects of nicotine. Further, researchers within the growing Biobehavioral Division at RJR began to reach out to another set of researchers in pharmacology to more specifically explore the actions of nicotine.[60]

In 1986, the Biobehavioral Division announced several initiatives intended to push them to a new level of scientific achievement—and that would also help the company. First, leaders of the division reported that they were starting a project on nicotine-receptor pharmacology. They consulted with faculty at the University of North Carolina and Bowman Gray University and developed new techniques for binding and cell-culture methodology.[61] Second, they extended their relationships with key investigators on nicotine actions in the brain and expanded their expertise on the molecular mechanisms of this key chemical. As a result of this work, the division began to look less like a part of the tobacco industry and more like a pharmaceutical company.

Some may have seen this as a way of rescuing the tobacco industry from the impossible position that it found itself by the late 1980s as it faced the rising tide of opposition to smoking. During a 1986 nicotine conference, one of the company scientists explained, "The development of new products is vital to the future of the company, and we believe that success depends on developing a much better understanding of the pharmacology of nicotine." Further, it was important to be able to coordinate efforts between in-house researchers and experts in universities around the country.[62]

In 1987, the action plan of the Biobehavioral Division included pharmacokinetic studies of nicotine in human subjects, measurement of the rate at which nicotine appeared in smokers' systems, how fast it was metabolized, and the effects of smoking behaviors on nicotine levels. They also had outside research contracts to explore other issues, including genetics and nicotine exposure in rats with Allan Collins from the University of Colorado, antibodies to nicotinic receptors with Susan Wonnacott and George Lunt from the University of Bath, and the effects of nicotine on rodent behavior with Samuel Deadwyler at Bowman Gray University.[63] Though these areas of collaboration were well outside the tobacco industry's business of making and selling cigarettes, the mission of the biobehavioral group was to support product development—which suggested that RJR was looking at a different kinds of products.

In 1988, the division began to have preliminary conversations with pharmaceutical companies around partnerships in nicotine-receptor pharmacology.[64] They explored a possible relationship with Hoechst-Roussel (a German pharmaceutical company that later became Aventis). As an RJR document outlining the pros and cons of such an alliance explained, an advantage would be to "promote public welfare and social good, as well as potentially enhance our corporate image, by assisting in the development of treatment, cure or avoidance of ailments which could potentially affect millions of individuals," including Alzheimer's and Parkinson's diseases, as well as anxiety, depression, and schizophrenia. On the other hand, RJR executives recognized that the pharmaceutical company might have different corporate priorities—including the desire to "overdisclose" potential side effects of new products developed in order to avoid future litigation: "Hoechst does not have to be concerned about product liability and regulatory issues vis-à-vis cigarettes."[65] But in general, the reputation of the pharmaceutical industry was positive enough that tobacco researchers thought the association with them would be beneficial. Scientists at RJR focused on the scientific promise of research on the possible role of nicotine in schizophrenia as well as the business opportunities in devising a scan for Alzheimer's disease based on nicotinic receptor behavior. Each company would get something from the collaboration—the pharmaceutical company would get access to RJR's nicotine-testing information and compounds, while RJR would get positive public relations from their relationship with the pharmaceutical firm.[66] RJR executives suggested that this work would allow them to not only "promote social welfare" but also get financial reward.[67]

By the mid-1990s, the Biobehavioral Division was more explicitly moving toward pharmaceutical approaches based on their hypothesis that smoking conferred some benefits on selective populations.[68] If these benefits could be harnessed through selective pharmacology, the company would profit. Members of the division generated patents for new compounds and developed a computer-modeling system to help them screen possible drugs.[69] They also contracted with researchers who had experience with drug development and who had worked with pharmaceutical companies. They cited this as important expertise in their relationship with outside investigators.[70] RJR researchers endeavored to establish themselves as experts in nicotine and constructed arguments for the usefulness of the drug in terms of brain receptors. RJR's Carr Smith coordinated with other staff and outside consultants on a global statement about all the properties of nicotine and correlated behavioral change with nicotine administration. He was careful to cite areas of potential therapeutic potential, including Parkinsonism, Alzheimer's disease, Tourette's syndrome, schizophrenia, and depression.[71]

By 1994, the Biobehavioral Division formally became the Nicotine Pharmacology and Neurodegenerative Disease Team. The members of the team looked into new compounds to be tested for pharmacological activity and committed to working with other companies to develop pharmaceutical agents. The team envisioned that they would help find agents related to nicotine that would be of use in Alzheimer's disease and schizophrenia, as well as the relief of anxiety.[72] Although the division had no visible connection to the production of cigarettes, its role in the company was strategic. One outline of the work of the division explained their goal: "Execute, fund, and publish scientific studies on the positive aspects of smoking to: provide sound evidence in response to 'anti' claims of absolutely no redeeming value for tobacco products. Fight to maintain scientific credentials for scientists accepting tobacco funding (some currently under attack) and to establish scientific credentials for industry scientists, earning the right to be heard. Differentiate nicotine and caffeine from addicting drugs."[73] By stressing potential therapeutic value of nicotine, the company's research division attempted to redefine the chemical from an addictive drug to a tool in the noble goal of improving health. And RJR scientists in the nicotine pharmacology division emphasized that they had the best of both worlds—the cigarette company's long experience with smoking consumers' habits, as well as the neurobiology innovation needed to develop new therapeutic compounds.

In 1997, the nicotine pharmacology division split from RJR and became a subsidiary, Targacept.[74] The mission of the new company was to "discover, develop and commercialize pharmaceutical applications of RJR's basic research pertaining to the biology and pharmacology of the nicotinic acetylcholine receptor (nAChR) system."[75] In particular, the researchers' goal was to develop candidate drugs to treat schizophrenia, and they projected that the United States market for therapeutic agents for this disease was $1 billion. Among their assets, the new company listed several candidate drugs for which they had received patents, as well as a computer-modeling system to aid in drug screening. One of their drugs, RJR-2403, had already completed phase I trials by the time Targacept was created.[76] When RJR scientists announced the formation of Targacept at a pharmaceutical conference that year, they were congratulated on their rapid acquisition of the knowledge and skills of drug development.[77]

In 1999, Targacept announced a partnership with pharmaceutical company Rhone-Poulenc Rorer to collaborate in the areas of research, development, and commercialization. As the president of Targacept explained, "This collaboration marries Targacept's expertise in nicotinic chemistry and pharmacology with Rhone-Poulenc Rorer's strengths in developing and commercializing therapeutics for the central nervous system. . . . We are very excited about the potential to help alleviate some of the suffering experienced by millions of individuals with Alzheimer's disease and Parkinson's disease, and their families."[78] Targacept officially separated from RJR a year later, though RJR continued to hold majority interest in Targacept for at least the next decade.[79] The business plan of Targacept, born in the research and development laboratory of RJR, highlighted the interest and enthusiasm of members of the company to innovate and push into new markets. While the program at RJR is the most obvious, other tobacco companies also pursued a diversification of interests by following the molecular path of nicotine.

By the 1990s, nicotine was both evil, by enslaving those who used cigarettes, and good, as an exciting element of evolving neuroscience research and therapeutics. These aspects of nicotine were related. And tobacco scientists used their expertise with the chemical to ally with pharmaceutical companies, some of which were looking at nicotine's actions and receptors to design treatments for smoking cessation. Both the tobacco industry and the pharmaceutical industry had business reasons for exploring the role of nicotine in the brain. Both industries cast their research nets widely to capture the largest potential markets to treat widespread problems. As public-health leader Kenneth Warner and his coauthors argued in a 1997 paper, nicotine (as formulated in new non-cigarette entities) was a product for which both the tobacco and pharmaceutical industries could claim interest.[80]

By the late 1990s, even as tobacco-industry executives continued to battle litigation based on nicotine's addictive qualities, research and development groups in cigarette companies had moved beyond the issue of cigarettes to focus on business opportunities around nicotine. And, probably not coincidentally, stories about the benefits made it into the media. A *Charlotte Observer* writer reported in 1998 that there was "finally, some good news about nicotine. The long-vilified chemical, and designer molecules that mimic it, can improve memory, prevent brain cells from dying and—as smokers have long known—markedly reduce stress." Nicotine-based drugs were being developed for use in a number of serious conditions, including Alzheimer's disease, Parkinson's disease, schizophrenia, and anxiety disorders. The *Charlotte Observer* article cited Duke researcher Edward Levine, as well as RJR scientists who were studying nicotine "as an adjunct to cigarette development." According to the article, the RJR investigators were working with pharmaceutical companies to develop nicotine-like drugs.[81]

In 2000, reporters around the country picked up a story about presentations from that year's meeting of the American Association for the Advancement of Science at which researchers identified a potential value in nicotine for a number of illnesses. But while some of the investigators—including Paul Sanberg and Paul Newhouse—had been supported in their forays into nicotine neuroscience by the tobacco industry, the companies that were highlighted for this media coverage were pharmaceutical firms.[82] The newspaper articles contrasted nicotine's "evil image" with its potential, though one investigator was quoted as saying that companies wanted to make analogs—at least partly because nicotine could not be patented.[83]

An article the same year in the *Economist* highlighted the financial issues involved. The author noted that while cigarette companies did not advertise the health benefits of their products anymore, "it has been suspected for some time" that cigarettes protected individuals from Parkinson's disease. Further, the author pointed out, "Psychiatrists have observed for many years that ciga-rette smoking is almost ubiquitous among people with schizophrenia, leading to suggestions that this activity is a form of self-medication." The *Economist* author pointed out that the problem with nicotine was not the drug itself, but rather the delivery vehicle, and cited several drug companies that were work-ing on patentable compounds.[84]

But even while nicotine—and chemical entities that looked and func-tioned like it—enjoyed increasing status within neuroscience fields, advanc-ing tobacco-control measures were reducing the appeal and spread of cigarette smoking. And although policies to reduce smoking (restrictions on sales to minors, public-smoking bans) were not nearly as draconian as measures directed toward drugs such as heroin or cocaine, users of cigarettes increasingly seemed to be on the margins of society. Not coincidentally, tobacco-control activists and psychiatrists began to notice that the largest numbers of remaining smokers in the United States were among the mentally ill.

Researchers, policy analysts, and providers began to address the issue of smoking in the mentally ill by the 1990s: some focused on neuroscience impli-cations while others emphasized physical effects. Much of the difference in approaches toward mentally ill smokers depended on experts' perception of the different industries with an interest in the issue. Researchers and clinicians (often with connections to pharmaceutical companies) suggested that it would be less harmful for smokers to switch to nicotine replacement or use other medication. And they advocated for neuroscience research to design therapies for diseases centered around the nicotine receptor in the brain. At the same time, the increasingly negative reputation of the tobacco industry led many in the tobacco-control movement toward a vociferous condemnation of anything connected with tobacco past or present, including nicotine. But regardless of the approach, in the context of new possibilities for nicotine and the decline of cigarettes, it did not seem acceptable to tolerate smoking in anyone, even the mentally ill. Now it became something to treat.

Chapter 6

From Tolerance to Treatment

In 1992, the same year that the Joint Commission published its rule that all hospitals should go smoke free, New York State Psychiatric Institute psychiatrists Gregory Dalack and Alexander Glassman reviewed the challenges faced by mentally ill smokers, especially those on psychiatric units. Dalack and Glassman noted that many providers were unwilling to address the issue of smoking cessation among the mentally ill, sometimes out of an idea that patients needed to smoke for stress relief. The authors encouraged mental-health practitioners to take up the smoking issue with their patients. Dalack and Glassman pointed out, though, that enforced abstinence from smoking was not the same as actual cessation: "In some cases the decision has been made that because a patient is in a smoke-free environment he or she should quit smoking. However, this reasoning proves to be misguided, and obviously ignores the role of the individual's motivation in cessation."[1] The authors recommended waiting for patients' symptoms to go into remission before addressing the issue of smoking cessation.

While Dalack and Glassman had encouraged practitioners to talk about the issue but put it in context with patients' concerns, less than two decades later the tone of the literature had changed. In 2009, University of Kansas researchers insisted that there was no reason not to assess tobacco use and strongly encourage treatment in all hospitalized patients—including psychiatric ones. They further suggested that the Joint Commission could assist with this by mandating that smoking status be addressed in all patients regardless of their reason for admission, as it already was for smoking-associated illnesses such as cardiovascular disease.[2] These investigators assumed that the only limiting factor in smoking cessation among psychiatric patients was a lack of will on the part of their providers. If physicians and other health professionals pushed more with interventions, their patients would quit.

Some of the very rapid change in professionals' approach toward mentally ill smokers over the decades evolved out of better awareness of the harms of smoking, as well as effective policies to limit smoking opportunities. But this shift also happened because of major changes in psychiatry and its emerging reputation as a science-based specialty organized around brain diseases and medication treatments. Psychiatric investigators who explored smoking reframed it as a biological issue, which encouraged mental-health providers (and pharmaceutical companies) to claim it as a problem to be treated. Psychiatrists' use of power regarding their smoking patients also changed—from a dynamic in which smoking privileges were granted or withheld to a situation in which more of the patients' behaviors were framed as illnesses to be treated.

There was nothing inevitable about this way of looking at smoking or the mentally ill, though. A medical model of smoking was the result of deliberate choices on the part of a group of smoking-cessation researchers, followed by psychiatric professionals' interest in the brain effects of nicotine. Although psychiatrists increasingly discussed smoking as a manifestation of a brain disease, their framework depended on their own professional issues. As I discuss in the next chapter, public-health activists conceptualized smoking in this population a different way, through the lens of the plummeting reputation of the tobacco industry, and they emphasized controls on cigarette supplies. Psychiatrists were less focused on tobacco itself and instead incorporated nicotine use into their existing paradigms of treating brain chemistry disruptions with pharmaceutical products.

Pharmaceuticals and the Medical Model of Smoking

From the beginning of psychiatrist interest in the issue of smoking, there were ties to pharmaceutical solutions.[3] In 1978, Jerome Jaffe published an article with UCLA researcher Murray Jarvik to describe the problem of dependence on tobacco. Although the substance of the article was similar to Jaffe's other writings of the time that advocated for a psychiatric diagnosis of tobacco dependence, this one was published in a large volume under the auspices of the American College of Neuropsychopharmacology (ACNP). The ACNP had been founded in 1961 as an elite research organization to bring together investigators from around the world to support biological concepts of mental illness and pharmaceutical therapies.[4] The membership of the ACNP represented the vanguard of biological psychiatrists seeking to wrest the profession away from its attachment to psychoanalysis.[5] And the ACNP supported and promoted academic interactions with pharmaceutical companies for mutual benefit.[6]

Like the other articles in the 1978 ACNP volume, the one by Jaffe and Jarvik stressed brain chemistry and discussed tobacco as a drug with psychoactive effects. The authors acknowledged that there had been debate about how to conceptualize a mental disorder around smoking. But they insisted that, "both the medical profession and society in general have accepted the view that those individuals who use such substances to the point where they are producing obvious damage to themselves (socially or medically), or those who appear to have lost control of their capacity to refrain from use, may have a behavioral or mental disorder of some sort." People who were unable to stop smoking, therefore, had a mental illness.[7]

Critics of the time complained that psychiatrists were overreaching their professional bounds by claiming that normal behaviors (including smoking) were mental illnesses. How could something that common be a mental illness?[8] One of the ways that mental-health researchers managed this critique was through collaborating with pharmaceutical companies to design therapies. Investigators initially assisted in development and testing of forms of nicotine. The pharmaceutical market expanded over subsequent decades to over-the-counter nicotine products and other pharmaceutical agents. With the possibility for pharmacological interventions, smokers could be seen as patients with a disease that required treatment.

Not surprisingly, relationships with pharmaceutical options (and companies) affected psychiatric approaches toward smoking. Some researchers worked in collaboration with pharmaceutical companies to help with smoking cessation in the form of nicotine replacement. Initially, there was no consensus about whether it made sense to use nicotine in individuals who were trying to quit. As researcher Nina Schneider and her group (including her mentor Murray Jarvik) pointed out in 1977 in their study of nicotine gum, "The question of whether smokers seek nicotine in addition to the psychological reinforcements associated with smoking has not been answered. It has been claimed that smoking is clearly an addiction, with evidence of physical dependence, i.e., withdrawal effects; others claim that smoking is a psychologically determined habit rather than a true addiction."[9] But Schneider and her co-authors answered this debate by illustrating cases in which nicotine gum relieved the symptoms of withdrawal from smoking. Years later, Jarvik openly discussed the fact that this research was funded by a pharmaceutical company that was interested in marketing nicotine replacement.[10]

Although there was a diagnosis of tobacco dependence in the 1980 *DSM-III*, it initially had little significance in the world of existing psychiatric treatment. What it offered, though, was an opportunity for pharmaceutical companies to advertise remedies and for psychiatrists to expand their practice. These companies were careful to link their smoking-related offerings with an appropriate indication.[11] In 1984, for example, Merrell Dow Pharmaceuticals placed an advertisement in the *Journal of the American Medical Association* (*JAMA*) that identified connections (visually displayed as links of a chain) among "psychological dependence," "nicotine dependence," and "social factors" composing the difficulty many people had with quitting smoking. The advertisement explicitly cited the *DSM-III* diagnosis and emphasized that dependence was the problem to be overcome. They explained, "A possible answer to this question is currently under intensive investigation at Merrell Dow Pharmaceuticals, as part of our commitment to advancing respiratory and cardiovascular therapy."[12] The company was able to formally market its product, Nicorette Gum, when it was approved by the FDA later that year.

By the late 1980s, more within the profession were becoming vocal about the need for psychiatrists to take notice of the problems of smoking because of the physical-health consequences in the population. *DSM* architect Robert Spitzer promised to strengthen the criteria for a smoking disorder for the next edition of the diagnostic manual.[13] But the focus increasingly shifted to nicotine rather than smoking per se. Investigators emphasized that smoking behaviors were driven by dependence on a chemical that could be replaced with a medication.[14] Further, they argued that the process by which individuals became hooked on nicotine was analogous to that of other drugs, and so it was not necessary to get into philosophical questions about when and how smoking was or was not acceptable.[15] The pharmaceutical focus on nicotine was further reinforced when the 1987 revision of the psychiatric nomenclature (*DSM-IIIR*) changed tobacco dependence to nicotine dependence, with a separate section to identify the clinical symptoms of nicotine withdrawal.[16]

But though a diagnosis might help identify an indication for a pharmaceutical agent or an area of professional intervention, investigators faced further challenges with how to design and measure therapies. The *DSM* diagnostic symptoms were supposed to help create a common language for intervention among all practitioners, and originated in criteria used by researchers to make sure that interventions were tested with the same subject populations.[17] The successive diagnoses of tobacco and nicotine dependence, though, were very broad and not especially connected to therapies. As investigators looked at treatments such as nicotine gum, they attempted to quantify the extent of subjects' attachment to cigarettes through different kinds of measures to be able to judge the efficacy of medication.

In order to differentiate smokers who might be more dependent—and theoretically more in need of treatment—many investigators turned to a scale developed by Swedish researcher Karl-Olov Fagerström.[18] Fagerström first published what he called the Fagerström Tolerance Questionnaire (FTQ) in 1978, and it was widely used around the world to gauge the relationship between smoking and nicotine dependence.[19] The Fagerström scale allowed researchers to assess patients' attachment to their cigarettes and the extent to which it would be difficult for them to give them up through questions such as how long after waking an individual lit up a cigarette. The use of the FTQ was explicitly tied to medication research. When Fagerström and his collaborators found that the FTQ did not predict treatment success with nicotine replacement, they revised the scale.[20] In 1991, the newly published Fagerström Test for Nicotine Dependence (FTND) was promoted as a way of measuring the effects of new products that could assist practitioners in helping their patients quit smoking. Fagerström's focus on tests to guide pharmaceutical interventions was intentional. He was a researcher with drug manufacturers (Pharmica and Upjohn), and later became the executive of his own company that developed smoking cessation products.[21]

As treatment options for nicotine dependence continued to evolve, psychiatrists increasingly formulated a diagnosis of nicotine dependence in line with the other drugs of abuse for which the profession claimed expertise. Though Robert Spitzer had initially commented in *DSM-III* that a diagnosis of tobacco dependence was of unknown significance, nicotine dependence within the later revisions of *DSM-IIIR* (1987) and *DSM-IV* (1994) was placed with all the other drugs (including heroin and cocaine) with standard language around abuse and dependence. Further, changing conditions for smokers such as smoking bans in public places now made their behaviors appear the result of a disease: "Giving up important social, occupational, or recreational activities can occur when an individual forgoes an activity because it occurs in smoking restricted areas."[22] So while smokers were not seen to have social or occupational impairment in the 1980 criteria, the declining acceptance of smoking created impairment— even for those who smoked in 1980 and continued to 1994.

Psychiatrists' disease model of smoking moved into mainstream professional and popular literature by the time that *DSM-IV* was published. Part of this no doubt came from increasing social and cultural acceptance of psychiatric disorders and pharmaceutical treatments. Although there were still critics of the wide reach of psychiatric diagnosis, many within the population enthusiastically bought into the idea that their problems could be given a name and treated with medication. The introduction of blockbuster medications such as Prozac for outpatient treatments helped make psychiatric diagnosis a regular occurrence rather than a drastic action connected with inevitable hospitalization.[23]

The American Psychiatric Association made formal recommendations for smoking cessation in a set of treatment guidelines outlined by a Task Force on Nicotine Dependence in 1995. (And even though *DSM-IV* had made a point of stressing the common features of substance dependence—including nicotine— the APA guidelines for alcohol, cocaine, and opiates were significantly different and published separately.)[24] The statement by the task force emphasized not only the very high prevalence of nicotine dependence (20 percent of the United States population at some point in their lives) but also the expertise of mental-health professionals in treating it. As the task force explained, "Nicotine dependence can be treated by using pharmacological, behavioral, or psychosocial treatments or a combination. Treatment of nicotine dependence can reduce the health consequences of smoking. Psychiatric knowledge and skills in psychotherapy and pharmacological therapy are relevant to treatment of nicotine dependence."[25] The next year, the APA followed this up with a booklet of practice guidelines to assist practitioners in identifying and treating nicotine dependence in their patients.[26]

While the APA presented information about treatment for nicotine dependence in health terms, not all psychiatric interest in this issue was purely altruistic. In their practice guidelines, the APA task force emphasized not only the enormous prevalence of nicotine dependence but also psychiatrists' specialized knowledge in treatment. In both the practice guidelines and in the APA position statement from the year before, it was stressed that psychiatrists should take an active role in making sure that insurance companies understood the problems—and were willing to reimburse psychiatrists for treatment of smoking cessation. The guidelines included recommendations for both therapy and medication to help with smoking cessation, though the focus was primarily on nicotine replacement.[27]

Mental-health providers' increasing awareness and discussion of nicotine dependence helped promote smoking-cessation medications. Psychiatrists— many of whom had relationships with the makers of the nicotine products— emphasized the utility of nicotine available in patch or gum form. And in the mid-1990s pharmaceutical giant GlaxoSmithKline with its academic collaborators pushed for approval of a formulation of the antidepressant buproprion (which had been marketed under the name Wellbutrin) for smoking cessation (under the trade name Zyban). It was not approved at the time of the APA practice guidelines, but the Task Force on Nicotine Dependence chair, John Hughes, published a column in 1997 suggesting that the data on buproprion from the Food and Drug Administration (FDA) hearings looked promising.[28] Hughes had developed significant expertise in a variety of medicinal remedies for nicotine dependence in his capacity as consultant to numerous pharmaceutical companies over his career.[29]

By the time of the approval of buproprion for smoking cessation, published reports about smoking emphasized the evils of cigarettes and the benefits of medicinal remedies to help patients quit smoking. And these were often authored by psychiatrists with ties to the pharmaceutical industry. For example, Jack Henningfield, a researcher at Johns Hopkins University (and former head of the National Institute on Drug Abuse), was the senior author on a 1997 article highlighting all the terrible things that could happen to patients addicted to nicotine. Henningfield and his co-authors emphasized that smokers were trapped in a cycle of use because of the strongly addictive nature of the product. But they made a distinction between the nicotine in cigarettes and the nicotine available in drug form and advocated for easier passage of medicine through the FDA for treatment of smoking cessation. They further suggested study of longer-term use of nicotine replacement and advocated for policy changes to make medicinal nicotine cheaper and easier for patients to obtain. While the passion displayed by Henningfield and his coauthors was obvious in this article, Henningfield's objectivity about the use of pharmaceutical products might have been affected by his roles as a consultant to pharmaceutical giant GlaxoSmithKline and as vice president for Pinney Associates, a consulting firm for the pharmaceutical industry.[30]

With the shift of many nicotine products (gum, patch, lozenge) to over-the-counter status in 1996, medicinal remedies for the disease of nicotine dependence became even more widespread.[31] Further, pharmaceutical companies continued to create new forms of nicotine (including an inhaler that is still available only by prescription) and the smoking cessation medication varenicline (trade name Chantix).[32] Most of the research on nicotine dependence, though, was done within a general population of individuals whose only mental disorder involved their use of cigarettes. It was not until fairly recently that psychiatrists began to turn back to their traditional populations of mentally ill patients to address the issue of smoking.

Smoking Cessation and the Mentally Ill

Though (with pharmaceutical company help) psychiatrists had expanded their definitions of mental disorders to include smoking, seriously mentally ill patients got a pass until the late 1990s. Even within the 1996 APA tobacco practice guidelines, patients with active psychiatric symptoms were exempted. The reason that it seemed to take so long before smoking appeared to be a problem among mentally ill individuals was partly because of the difference in health ideals for the general population and psychiatrically ill groups, who were generally stigmatized. But the issue really took off among psychiatric researchers when they were able to understand smoking as a neuroscience puzzle in the brains of mentally ill individuals, especially those with schizophrenia.[33]

At the time when the general focus on smoking turned to nicotine, psychiatric investigators were in the midst of exploring different neurotransmitters in the brain through a study of the mechanisms of psychiatric medications. Researchers had found, for example, that by reasoning backwards from the apparent effectiveness of medications such as haloperidol (Haldol), one major problem in schizophrenia seemed to be that the neurotransmitter dopamine was at abnormal levels. But medications to adjust dopamine levels were only partly effective for patients with schizophrenia and so researchers continued to explore other brain-chemistry options.[34]

To search for biological markers for the illness, a team at the University of Colorado (led by Robert Freedman) refined a measure to assess attention and information processing, both of which appeared to be abnormal in schizophrenic patients.[35] In a test called the P50, repeated sounds were used to measure how subjects' brains responded. Normal subjects who were exposed to a rapid series of two sounds had less of a brain response (picked up by an EEG) for the second sound, which investigators connected to their ability to screen out extraneous stimuli. Schizophrenic subjects, however, responded equally to repeated stimuli, which appeared to be part of their difficulty in processing their environments. Biological investigators were excited by a specific psychophysiological marker that seemed to be associated with schizophrenia. Researchers found not only that these measures were abnormal in schizophrenic patients, but also that normal relatives of schizophrenics had this abnormality—which reinforced the idea that schizophrenia was definitely biological and probably genetic.[36]

What was also interesting for Freedman and other investigators—who noted the attachment of mentally ill patients (especially schizophrenics) to their cigarettes—was that nicotine fixed the P50 abnormality for a short time. Researchers knew that nicotine bound at the acetylcholine receptor in the brain, and some speculated that nicotine might actually be doing something possibly connected to the brain systems that either produced schizophrenic symptoms or alleviated them. Schizophrenic patients who smoked might have been correcting a deficit, or they could have had a specific genetic defect at the nicotinic receptor or were perhaps trying to mitigate the side effects of medication. This further suggested that there could be a biological link between smoking and mental illness that would help illuminate the biology of psychiatric disorders in general.[37]

From this perspective, investigators in psychiatry and neuroscience approached the connection between smoking and mental illness to ask what mentally ill patients might get out of smoking. And did smoking do something different for patients with different psychiatric diagnoses that might suggest specific brain chemistry abnormalities?[38] Further, what was happening to the brains of seriously mentally ill smokers who were hospitalized on inpatient units that were increasingly smoke free? As researchers and clinicians became more aware of smoking in their patient populations, they began to note that smoking changed the blood levels of psychiatric medications, with implications for patient care both inside and outside the hospital.[39]

Even with increased awareness of the potential biological linkages between smoking and mental illness, providers did not necessarily come to the conclusion that smoking cessation in this population was the answer. At the same time that tobacco-control measures and a cultural shift away from smoking decreased social acceptance of the behavior, many within mental health suggested that the biology of mental illness made smoking a unique issue among psychiatric patients. While most did not openly endorse the idea that mentally ill individuals should smoke at will, providers thought that an exploration of the connection might be useful, and might even help uncover the genetic basis for schizophrenia.[40]

As researchers continued to evaluate the biochemical connections between smoking and serious mental illness, companies (both tobacco and pharmaceutical) took notice. Tobacco company scientists felt vindicated when a potential genetic link between smoking and schizophrenia was uncovered, as industry spokesmen had been arguing for years that genetic connections explained the connection between smoking and physical illness.[41] But as researchers continued to investigate the biological implications of mentally ill patients' smoking patterns, it seemed likely that the pharmaceutical industry would be the real beneficiary of this knowledge. Duke researchers in 1996 pointed out that smoking seemed to help schizophrenics overcome cognitive deficits that accompanied administration of the antipsychotic drug haloperidol. They suggested that nicotine replacement was important for this population: "It is an intriguing possibility that nicotine administered via the skin patch or other nicotinic agonists may be useful as adjuncts in the treatment of schizophrenia."[42] Although this approach left open a role for nicotine, mental-health researchers understood this to mean a pharmaceutical, rather than a tobacco, product.

And for the pharmaceutical industry and the researchers who partnered with them, smoking-cessation options among mentally ill individuals provided different kinds of brain investigations and new markets. Several research groups began to try to enroll patients with serious mental illness in clinical trials (with medication) to help them quit smoking. Most of the trials were small and had fairly high dropout rates and low rates of long-term smoking cessation.[43] Still, investigators emphasized that any progress in getting patients to quit smoking was going to make a difference. And they stated that the solution to the problem lay in the particular brain chemistry of individuals with mental illnesses.

Since mental-health researchers had differentiated psychiatric diagnoses based on response to medications, it made sense to see whether specific psychiatric populations needed different treatments for smoking cessation.[44] Investigators speculated that schizophrenics' failure to quit smoking in substantial numbers might be due to the benefits (real or perceived) they received from cigarettes.[45] While schizophrenics might be using nicotine in cigarettes for a specific purpose, patients with depression seemed to be unable to tolerate the dysphoria that came with nicotine withdrawal. Some patients even smoked more when experiencing depressive symptoms.[46] Psychiatric symptoms might even affect how those without a formal diagnosis approached smoking cessation. Louisiana State University psychologists found that smokers' baseline higher depression scores predicted greater difficulty with smoking withdrawal, even for those not already in treatment for depression.[47] Researchers from the Center for Disease Control suggested that there might be interaction between smoking and depression such that smokers should be given antidepressants in order to quit (an approach already in use with buproprion).[48]

Though medication interventions for smoking continued to gain in popularity among psychiatrists and other mental-health providers, the specific aim of finding medications to treat the unique role of smoking within each diagnosis did not work out. Investigators did not find much generalizable information about other types of disorders such as problems with alcohol or other drugs, anxiety disorders, or post-traumatic stress disorder other than to note that patients with these problems smoked at higher rates than the general population.[49] The studies based on clinical samples might have been limited because of patient selection, while epidemiological investigations might have been confounded by socioeconomic variables.[50] It is perhaps not surprising that this research failed to yield much concrete information, since mental-disorder diagnoses were (and continue to be) fuzzy and vague.[51] Investigators who attempted to understand the relationship between smoking and anxiety states, for example, recommended lumping all anxiety disorders together since there were no patterns to differentiate them.[52]

But though specific chemical answers to the problem of smoking in different psychiatric diagnoses did not work out, researchers continued to look
at what nicotine might be doing in the brain. A number of investigator groups
focused on the action of nicotine at the nicotinic acetylcholine receptor. Some
tried to imitate the effects of nicotine with analogs, chemicals that have similar
properties to nicotine. Others found ways to block the nicotinic receptor. Basic
science researchers began to look at the complex cascade of chemicals in the
brain triggered by the nicotinic receptor to see if there was any connection
to abnormalities in schizophrenia.[53] On a more immediate and practical level,
pharmaceutical (and tobacco) companies began to devise treatments based on
this research. And the newest pharmacological agent on the market for smoking
cessation—varenicline (trade name Chantix)—is a drug that acts at the nicotinic receptor in the brain.[54]

The biochemical framework to understand smoking among the mentally ill
generated important research. But it also promoted an enthusiasm for medications in a population that could be at higher risk for adverse events. This was
particularly an issue for the pharmaceuticals promoted for smoking cessation.
The two main agents on the market now (apart from nicotine replacement)—
buproprion and varenicline—have had a number of problems associated with
them, including serious psychiatric consequences such as increased suicidal
thinking or aggressive behaviors.[55] Further, traditional clinical wisdom would
suggest that it is not a good idea to give an antidepressant (to which class
buproprion belongs) if a patient has a history of bipolar disorder (manic depression). Smoking-cessation enthusiasts have argued, however, that it is okay as
long as there is monitoring.[56] There were enough reports of serious psychiatric
symptoms in non-mentally-ill individuals who used varenicline that the FDA
mandated a black-box warning regarding its use. But promoters of the drug
have insisted not only that it is safe for psychiatric patients, but also that it
may help depression.[57] (In a line of reasoning eerily reminiscent of past arguments by the tobacco industry, researchers with pharmaceutical company connections insist that the case reports of aggression, thoughts of suicide, or other
psychiatric symptoms that have been associated with varenicline are not sufficient proof that the drug is dangerous. Instead, they call for more research.)[58]
The calculus of when and how to give a potentially harmful medication to a
psychiatric patient already at risk for mental symptoms is difficult. Yet those
who are invested (professionally if not also financially) stress the greater harm
for smoking and minimize a risk of taking medicine.[59]

In the last fifteen years, with increasing awareness of the high rate of smoking among mentally ill patients, researchers and practitioners have attempted

to address smoking in this population.[60] But there has also emerged a dispute about whether mentally ill smokers are different in terms of what works for smoking cessation. As I explore in the next chapter, some within the public-health community have insisted that existing methods to promote change in smokers will work in the mentally ill—it just requires more will and effort by providers to engage this population. For those in mental health who note the specific patterns of smoking behaviors among mentally ill individuals and are interested in the complex neurochemical interactions, it makes sense to approach the issue from a different framework.[61] And so researchers and providers have formulated approaches to this issue that have consequences—both positive and negative—for the mentally ill who are the subjects of these interventions and policies.

Interventions and Consequences

Most of the medical literature today presents dire warnings about the terrible mental and physical consequences that await any user of tobacco. Few acknowledge that this way of understanding consumption of tobacco products is shaped by our social, economic, and political circumstances. In fact, there is nothing inevitable about the idea that smoking represents a disease in need of treatment. It could have been treated much like obesity—as the result of a behavior that has medical consequences but not a psychiatric illness itself.[62] Influential psychiatrist Stanton Peele, who was engaged in some of the disputes around *DSM-III,* argued in 1981 that reductionist theories around biology and mental illness (including behaviors such as smoking) had waxed and waned over the decades. The potential harm of such theories was that they could lead to inappropriate uses of medication for any and all behaviors.[63] Peele's criticism anticipated issues with the application of a medical model of smoking.

The shift in conversation in the 1980s and 1990s from discussions of smoking to descriptions of problems with nicotine reinforced the idea that the problem was about brain chemicals, not behavior. And treatment was focused primarily on medication. Relatively few of the published studies on smoking cessation among the mentally ill relied on behavioral interventions in groups.[64] Many—if not most—of the investigators who discussed smoking cessation in this population pushed interventions offered to individual patients (designed by pharmaceutical companies). Researchers used medicinal remedies within a theoretical model that implied that there was a disease that could be externalized from a patient's life or behavior and successfully treated with a medication. This model of disease, though, removed agency from patients and focused on an external cause. In contrast, a team of Israeli researchers—who commented on the lack of literature on nonmedication interventions for smoking cessation—used an intervention group for smokers in a psychiatric hospital that encouraged active engagement. Many of the smokers (who were still allowed to smoke in the hospital) were able to reduce their cigarette use and had a sense of accomplishment.[65]

A medical model of smoking in the mentally ill was framed by psychiatrists as a way to reduce blame for patients who could not alter their behavior. By emphasizing the disease of nicotine dependence, psychiatrists and mental-health researchers in theory offered patients more treatment and less stigma.[66] But at the same time, the medical model promoted yet more use of medications. The rise of the pharmaceutical industry in the area of nicotine replacement reinforced the idea that smoking was a problem to be managed, not a normal variant of behavior. As Ian Stolerman and Martin Jarvis argued in 1995, the fact that nicotine replacement helped smokers quit was "evidence [that] clearly identifies nicotine as a powerful drug of addiction, comparable to heroin, cocaine and alcohol."[67] The use of medicine to define addiction allowed these researchers to avoid the messier issue of the social and economic contexts, as well as the law enforcement aspects, of substance abuse in general.[68]

But a medical model for nicotine addiction did not eradicate all of the negative connotations that typically accompanied substance abusers. One of the consequences of including smoking as a psychiatric diagnosis was that individuals who already carried a diagnosis of schizophrenia or other serious mental illness were identified as "dual diagnosis"—that is, as having both a thought (or mood) disorder and a problem with substance abuse.[69] This framework implied that these patients had many more difficulties than those who were just diagnosed with one disorder. Further, as a New Jersey treatment expert explained, they should be understood as "drug-dependent individuals" for whom other kinds of treatments (such as potentially addictive medications) should be avoided.[70] Thus even though cigarettes did not have the immediate impact on psychiatric symptoms that were typical for psychoactive substances such as cocaine or opiates (or even marijuana), mentally ill individuals who smoked were lumped in with others as dually diagnosed.

At the same time, though, there was conflict in the field about how far to push the similarities between nicotine and drugs of abuse for which users faced social and legal penalties. As tobacco use disorder pioneer Jerome Jaffe commented in 1995, "It is important for public policy to recognize the powerful dependence potential of nicotine, but blurring the distinctions among the drugs that have this potential may come back, some day, to haunt us."[71] How then to manage the complications of mentally ill individuals and their cigarette smoking? Did the nature of nicotine itself require a different way to approach the situation? What about the effect of other kinds of psychiatric treatment?

Some within psychiatry suggested that one way to approach nicotine was to use the concept of harm reduction, the idea that a small degree of change was better than none and that the needs of the patient might be different from those of the provider. For its advocates, a harm-reduction approach meant that they accepted patients for where they were and understood that they used substances for a particular reason, not just because they were addicted.[72] In the case of mentally ill smokers, the harm-reduction perspective recognized that cigarettes had a role in helping with side effects of medications, promoting cognition, or relieving stress or boredom. In treating smoking in this population, therefore, researchers suggested that issues such as cognitive effects with and without smoking needed to be addressed in order to help patients to quit.[73]

A few leaders on the topic of smoking and mental illness postulated that harm reduction in the psychiatric population might mean long-term nicotine replacement or indefinite use of medications such as buproprion and varenicline. As Jack Henningfield and Stephen Heisman explained in 1995, if nicotine did have positive effects in the brain, "then every effort should be made to develop nontobacco nicotine medications that maximize the benefits and minimize the adverse effects of nicotine."[74] In 1996, three Cornell University psychiatrists pointed out in an editorial in the *American Journal of Psychiatry* that there was a risk in throwing out nicotine along with cigarettes: "From a policy point of view one must ask: Are we allowing a carry-over 'treatment Puritanism' about the maladaptive effects of other substances of abuse to influence our perception of the proper approach to treatment of nicotine dependence?"[75] Many of the researchers who promoted the use of medicinal nicotine argued that it was not the chemical that was dangerous, but rather its delivery vehicle in cigarettes.

Vermont psychiatrist John Hughes wrote in 2001 that there were brain changes as a result of nicotine that both promoted addiction and served a purpose. He pointed out that nicotine did have benefits to the smoker and argued that tobacco-control policy should be shaped by the recognition that nicotine does something for people.[76] Several investigator teams searched for a formulation of nicotine that would be acceptable to mentally ill smokers for whom the nicotine patch was a poor substitute for smoking. These researchers, including University of California, San Francisco psychiatrist Neal Benowitz, argued that nicotine was better than cigarettes, even with the risk of addiction.[77]

So is nicotine just like other drugs of abuse? Does its form matter? Does it make a difference whether users have a mental illness? While some mental-health professionals advocated for long-term nicotine maintenance, others reacted more negatively, just as many did regarding methadone maintenance for heroin decades ago.[78] Psychiatrists' views on nicotine as a medicine (in some forms) has also put them at variance with public-health advocates who worked on the smoking problem in the general population. In 2005, the National Institute of Mental Health convened a panel of experts on the issue of psychiatric disorders and smoking, and the panel raised the question about whether current policies to reduce smoking had a positive effect on the mentally ill: "In these populations, cigarette taxes may not discourage smoking initiation and encourage cessation, as they do in the general population; they may have a negative effect on these populations. Smoking bans discourage smoking and protect nonsmokers from environmental smoke, but do they also encourage more social isolation in mentally ill smokers already predisposed to isolation?"[79] Should smoking in this population be approached with different goals and different tools than the general population? And should long-term planning and abstinence be key elements for the mentally ill smoking cessation programs?

The most recent trend among mental-health providers on the issue of smoking is to be cognizant of the special circumstances that affect mentally ill smokers—and to treat them accordingly, usually with medications. Researchers, many with ties to pharmaceutical companies, have pushed the aggressive use of treatments, including nicotine replacement, buproprion, and the controversial varenicline.[80] Basic science investigators increasingly describe nicotine in terms of its effects on the acetylcholine receptor, while drug developers try to target that receptor for a variety of illnesses. The pharmaceutical industry has embraced the idea of nicotine dependence with enthusiasm, as have its collaborators. And while tobacco-control advocates worry that availability of nicotine products will discourage people from quitting nicotine entirely, some mental-health researchers advocate loosening up limits on pharmaceutical marketing and testing so companies can effectively compete with makers of combustible tobacco products.[81]

The medical model for smoking is indebted to the pharmaceutical industry. While analysts are continuing to uncover new and disturbing ways in which the tobacco industry has affected current research and policy about smoking and mental illness, the role of the pharmaceutical industry has gone virtually unnoticed among tobacco-control experts.[82] Nicotine replacement has been a boon to drug companies. Further, as a medical reporter for *JAMA* happily pointed out in 2006, pharmaceutical companies are trying to develop products to harness potential therapies around any possible self-medicating role of nicotine use among the mentally ill.[83] Even compounds that were developed through cigarette-company research and development, such as RJR-2403, appear to be fair to use to try to alleviate symptoms of mental illness because they fall under the umbrella of pharmaceuticals rather than tobacco.[84] The growing visibility of the mentally ill among remaining smokers has increased the pressure on both patients and mental-health providers to push toward smoking cessation in this population. Although it makes sense (given what we know about the dangers of smoking) to encourage the mentally ill to give up their cigarettes, the environment of mental-health treatment and the biology of mental illness make this a very complicated issue.

But while researchers and analysts who approached smoking from the perspective of mental illness and psychiatric treatment primarily used a medical model—treatment of nicotine dependence with medication—those from the tobacco-control perspective recently began to address the high rate of smoking among the mentally ill with different priorities. As public-health academics, voluntary health organization leaders, and anti-tobacco activists discovered the problems of smoking and mental illness, their ideas about steps to take were shaped by ongoing disclosures about the malfeasance of the tobacco industry. While treatment of nicotine dependence was tied to the pharmaceutical industry, the tobacco-control approach to the "hidden epidemic" of mentally ill smokers was to expose and root out all possible connections to the tobacco industry.

Chapter 7

Tobacco Control and the Mentally Ill

In a widely cited *JAMA* article in 2000, Harvard researcher Karen Lasser and her colleagues analyzed data from the National Comorbidity Survey (a series of questionnaires given to a sample of the population in the early 1990s) that had determined that almost 50 percent of the United States population had a mental illness, including nicotine dependence, at some point in their lives. Lasser's team found that those who had both a psychiatric disorder (such as schizophrenia, depression, or bipolar disorder) and nicotine dependence composed a majority of the cigarette consumers in the country. And, in an interesting twist on the relationship between smoking and mental illness, the group not only suggested that smoking was harmful for all, but also that smoking preceded and might be a risk factor for mental illness.[1] Instead of smoking as something that was part of the lives of the mentally ill, it was the first step on a road to a bad life.

Other researchers picked up this thread, and it was repeated frequently in both medical and popular settings. In 2000, the *Dallas Morning News* reported that teenagers who smoked were more likely to become depressed, though teenagers who were already depressed were not more likely to start smoking. Thus, as the reporter concluded, teens should be educated about the dangers of smoking, including that it might make them "crazy."[2] And Mayo Clinic investigators suggested that there was a connection between the likelihood of committing suicide and smoking, maybe so much so that smoking was a risk factor for suicide.[3] From a historical point of view, it does not make sense that smoking could cause serious mental illness or suicide if for no other reason than that the rates of both have remained steady even as the prevalence of smoking in the general population has declined. But the recent trend in the tobacco-control literature has been to suggest that the strong relationship between smoking and mental illness is not just correlation, it may be that smoking causes mental illness.[4]

Though this conclusion is not supported by historical evidence, it is perhaps not surprising that research and policy directed toward the problem of mentally ill smokers lacks much long-term perspective since tobacco-control investigators have only recently become aware of the issue. As the general rate of cigarette consumption declined, the group that remained (dubbed by public-policy analyst Kenneth Warner as "hard core smokers") included the mentally ill, who had not been particularly visible to groups trying to reduce smoking prior to that time.[5] The surgeon general's reports on smoking had not specifically mentioned mentally ill populations, nor did the surgeon general's report on mental illness address smoking.[6] But in the last couple of decades, the expanding collections of individuals and groups interested in reducing tobacco use in the United States and other countries have become increasingly aware of the connection between smoking and mental illness.

By the beginning of the twenty-first century, the successes of the various efforts to control tobacco use in the general population, pushed by a fluid and eclectic tobacco-control movement, made it obvious for the first time that the mentally ill did not seem to respond to the same measures that had been effective for everyone else. Enthusiasts for controls and limits on tobacco—including a wide range of policy analysts, public-health professionals, health-care providers, and members of voluntary health associations—subsequently took this on as an important public-health problem. But it was not just the numbers of mentally ill smokers that created a sense of urgency among tobacco control advocates. The dramatic revelations about tobacco-industry malfeasance in the 1990s and the continued expansion of scholarship (based on the tobacco-industry documents) fueled a zeal in the public-health community to eradicate the influence of the industry. This animosity toward tobacco companies is understandable given their history.[7] But the anti-tobacco stance of many investigators and policy analysts was different from many who had done research on the brain effects of nicotine, and the emphasis on elimination of tobacco left out consideration for the role smoking might be playing in the lives of the mentally ill.[8] Instead of accepting the relationship between the mentally ill and their cigarettes as a problem to be understood, many tobacco control activists have had an explicit goal of removing all tobacco and nicotine. This has particularly affected psychiatric populations. The overlap between mental illness and smoking exposed rifts in policy approaches to vulnerable populations and highlighted the ways that assumptions about people and problems could create unintended consequences for the subjects of public-health interventions.

Rising Intolerance of Smoking

Although smoking in and among mental-health settings, patients, and personnel was once an unquestioned norm, the rising tide of concern about the health consequences of cigarette use eventually penetrated not only psychiatric facilities but also mental-health treatment in general. But though the reasons for pushing smoking cessation—which rapidly replaced smoking bans as the ideal intervention—were ostensibly about health, many individuals and organizations who backed a tobacco-control agenda inside and outside mental-health settings were just as motivated by their disgust with cigarettes and the tobacco industry. Instead of smoking as a behavior to enable staff and patient interactions, the increasing number of mental-health-care staff who had quit began to view their mentally ill patients as distant from themselves because of their addiction to smoking. And as tobacco-control messages became more mainstream within mental-health circles, it became less and less acceptable to tolerate smoking behaviors in any population—even the mentally ill.

As I discussed in chapter 4, decisions to limit (or eliminate) smoking in psychiatric hospitals in the early 1990s were complicated by conflicted attitudes toward freedom and smoking. Among hospital and outpatient staffs, some members became converts to the movement to reduce or eliminate smoking, and they carried their concerns into their workplaces and criticized the tradition of smoking in psychiatric settings. The psychiatric nursing literature led the way within mental health about the importance of smoking cessation for both patients and staff, and common themes emerged in both the United States and the United Kingdom. Though psychiatric-hospital personnel continued to smoke at higher rates than other health-care providers, many began to express ambivalence or outright concern about their patients' smoking habits. Instead of using smoking as a bridge to connect to patients, health-care professionals (especially nurses) increasingly viewed smoking behaviors as target symptoms to address.

Staff worried that their own smoking behaviors could make patients worse. As one British nurse pointed out in 1989, nurses might unconsciously project their own need for cigarettes onto patients instead of helping to set limits to promote health.[9] Other British nurse teams explained that mental-health providers were role models for patients and owed it to their patients to quit smoking.[10] And if the nurses quit smoking, they could transition to more professional interactions with patients and help to manage patients' distress.[11] A nurse at Boston's

McLean Hospital claimed in 1994 that the nurse-patient dynamic substantially improved when smoking was eliminated: "The nursing staff became more clearly perceived as patient advocates rather than jailers who withheld and bargained with cigarettes."[12] After smoking bans, nurses reported therapeutic interactions with patients in which they could attend more to patients' emotional needs. They repudiated the power dynamic around cigarettes and claimed a more therapeutic alliance, though this perception was not borne out by patients who continued to see nurses as wielding power, particularly around the issue of smoking.[13]

Like the power dynamics in psychiatric hospitals decades before, administrators and others continued to exert power over patients in part through smoking policies. But by the 1990s and into this century, the power was to eliminate smoking. Hospital leaders blamed smoking for evils within the institution. While administrators in the early 1990s worried about the potential for violence among psychiatric patients if their cigarettes were withheld, hospital executives over the next two decades concluded that cigarettes themselves were the cause of violence. Staff from a Palo Alto Veterans Administration hospital found that a smoking area in a long-term geriatric psychiatric ward seemed to cause problems, and they reported that behavioral and safety issues resolved when smoking was banned on all units.[14] Further, the behaviors associated with smoking seemed to get better with an elimination of smoking areas. As psychiatric professional leaders complained at an American Psychiatric Association Institute on Psychiatric Services meeting, "Cigarettes form the basis of a black-market economy and become a precursor to threats between patients. Anxiety rises as many patients remain in a state of withdrawal awaiting the special break times when they can go outside and smoke. That leads, in turn, to an increase in use of seclusion and restraint when they get agitated." The solution was to eliminate smoking entirely.[15]

Psychiatric hospitals in the United States moved more rapidly in the direction of smoking cessation than hospitals in some other countries.[16] For American health administrators and many researchers by the mid-1990s, smoking was an activity engaged in by individuals with varying degrees of psychiatric pathology. And for caregivers of these patients, the desire to smoke was yet another issue to manage along with other kinds of pathological behaviors exhibited by patients on psychiatric units.[17] While some practitioners recognized that mentally ill patients were particularly attached to cigarettes, they insisted that this population should have the same perspectives and priorities as anyone else.[18] One New York physician, whose hospital had banned smoking two years before the Joint Commission standard, was reported to have said, "I don't think our patients are so crazy that they don't want to live a healthier life."[19]

As public-health experts became more aware of the issue of smoking among the mentally ill, they embraced this assumption—that despite mental or emotional impairments, mentally ill smokers were able to understand and choose to quit smoking because it would be better for them. Researchers and policy analysts who examined issues around mentally ill smokers stated that these individuals had the capacity to make decisions for themselves—but only if they made the right ones. If they quit (or stated a desire to quit), that was proof that they were just like members of the general population. If mentally ill smokers did not quit, that was evidence of either psychopathology or some external restriction. In the view of public-health advocates who focused on the mentally ill in the last couple of decades, no one in his or her right mind could possibly want to smoke.

As analysts explored the issues of smoking with psychiatric populations, they claimed that mental-health providers had been lulled by the tradition of smoking into believing that mentally ill smokers did not want to quit. Smoking-cessation advocates insisted, though that the idea of entrenched mentally ill smokers who refused to quit was a myth. Through different methods, including enrolling patients in studies and surveying individuals not in treatment, investigators repeatedly stated that the only difference between mentally ill smokers and those in the general population was that it was harder for the former to give up cigarettes. But though tobacco-control researchers reported that mentally ill patients said they wanted to quit smoking, it was not clear how patients were being asked or whether everyone had the same definition of "quit." And researchers tended to interpret any idea about stopping smoking, no matter how far distant in the future or how connected to other issues such as housing or finances, as evidence that smoking cessation could and should be pushed more aggressively among mentally ill populations.[20]

While some psychiatric researchers emphasized the special biochemistry of mentally ill smokers and the consequences of smoking cessation, investigators with a tobacco-control perspective tended to argue that the mentally ill were just like everyone else and needed the same kind of intervention (though perhaps on a more intensive basis).[21] One University of Vermont team in 1999 studied behavioral variables on a population of schizophrenic patients and determined that these individuals made decisions about their behavior based on the same information as individuals with no mental illness. They concluded that smoking-cessation interventions should work just as effectively with this population. They did not comment, though, on whether their interpretation of their results should take into account that they tried to recruit twelve patients but were successful in getting only six to participate in the study.[22] (And several years later, they found that schizophrenic subjects responded better to monetary reward for smoking cessation than the nicotine patch.)[23] On the issue of whether mentally ill individuals thought differently about the process of smoking cessation, University of California, San Francisco investigator Judith Prochaska looked at depressed patients' ability to move along the stages of change model (in which they were encouraged to work from a point of precontemplation to taking action), which she insisted worked just as well for mentally ill individuals as those without illness.[24]

If psychiatric patients were just like everyone else, investigators reasoned, they should be targeted for smoking-cessation interventions whenever there was contact with a medical or mental-health provider. By the late 1990s, those contact times included inpatient hospitalizations—which in the past had been seen as times *not* to try to intervene with patients because of their acute psychiatric issues. Some of the early descriptions of efforts to get patients to address their smoking while on inpatient psychiatric units focused on education about the health risks of smoking. A University of Illinois group found in 1999 that patients appreciated the educational program, though most did not resolve to quit as a result.[25] Others suggested that the inpatient units were important because there were relatively few resources outside the hospital for mentally ill smokers to engage in cessation. As long as providers had contact with patients, they should use that opportunity to get them to quit smoking.[26]

When some anti-tobacco researchers found differences between mentally ill smokers and smokers in the general population, they attributed problems with cessation to a lack of will on the part of psychiatric providers. For example, a *Schizophrenia Bulletin* article reported that when a Swiss team of investigators compared schizophrenic smokers to those in the rest of the population, they concluded that the schizophrenic patients wanted as much to quit but were less confident they would be successful. The difference, then, came down to untested assumptions among psychiatrists who erroneously believed that their patients could not or did not want to quit.[27] And public-health analysts sharply criticized mental-health-care professionals—especially psychiatrists—for failing to aggressively push smoking cessation on their chronically mentally ill patients when they had them in the hospital.[28]

By the time that public-health researchers explored the overlap between smoking and psychiatric illness, it seemed impossible to believe that mentally ill smokers were making rational decisions (albeit with a different calculus regarding their health decisions). Instead, investigators assumed that the mentally ill were either duped by the tobacco industry into wanting to smoke or could not quit because of their addiction to nicotine.[29] Tobacco-focused researchers from medical or public-health schools increasingly used a disease model of nicotine dependence that detached behaviors from social, economic, or personal context. Instead, smoking as a disease became something to be managed through pressure on individual providers and medical systems. From this perspective, the problem represented a failure of health care.

As a result, much recent emphasis on tobacco among the mentally ill has focused on the role of health-care organizations and providers. Advocates for total smoking bans in psychiatric hospitals blamed the treatment settings for creating a culture in which smoking was accepted and, in effect, facilitating patients' addiction. Thus the widespread smoking within psychiatric units was a reflection primarily of misguided professionals, rather than choice or a biochemical adaptation for patients.[30] Some researchers argued that it was essential to offer mentally ill hospitalized patients smoking-cessation tools so that they did not interpret the smoking ban as a punishment "and themselves as unworthy of receiving intervention on this deadly addiction."[31] Even though patients did not seem to have the ability to choose whether to smoke because of their illness, investigators insisted that it was critical to avoid any implication that they should not bother to quit smoking: "such messages reinforce passivity and helplessness rather than encouraging self-care, fitness, and healthy life development, and they do not address the larger question of why the person has so many troubles and so few pleasures."[32] The tobacco-control message was consistent that mental-health-care teams needed to address patients' whole health picture by specifically focusing on smoking cessation.

In recent years, there has been growing criticism of psychiatric hospitals for failing both to address the issue of smoking adequately and to push for cessation while patients were in the hospital. The APA published guidelines in 2006 that suggested that inpatient hospitalization was a good time to address cessation, while a National Institute of Health statement the same year discussed the importance of pushing for smoking cessation in mentally ill populations. Tobacco-control advocates complained, though, that mental-health and addiction programs were not doing as much as they could, and called for changes in the culture to "denormalize" smoking in psychiatric settings.[33] The smoking culture was so denormalized among leaders in the field that United Kingdom researchers in 2009 worried that hospitals could be sued for not adequately warning patients about the dangers of smoking or providing them with smoking-cessation options.[34]

Public-health advocates have not only insisted that the mentally ill want to quit smoking, but also stressed that the health consequences have been particularly devastating in this population because of the high rate of smoking.

More than a century of observers have noted that mentally ill individuals had a higher mortality rate than the general population (even before smoking became widespread in the United States). For most of those who noted it, the reason was unclear.[35] Some epidemiologists at mid-century reported what they claimed was a lower rate of lung cancer among schizophrenics (despite their elevated smoking rate).[36] In the 1990s and 2000s, however, researchers and public-health activists began to assert that smoking was the major contributing factor to the higher mortality within the mentally ill population.

Some activists even suggested that smoking was to blame for mental illness itself. With the high rate of smoking within certain populations, researchers speculated that smoking caused mental or emotional problems, such as the high number of children with ADHD born to mothers who smoked while they were pregnant.[37] The solution has appeared clear to advocates of nicotine abstinence—public-health measures need to be shifted toward getting psychiatric patients to quit smoking.

Unintended Consequences of Tobacco Control

Anti-tobacco activists in academic settings and within lobbying and advocacy groups have done important work to decrease the smoking rate in the United States. Public and workplace smoking bans have been effective in reducing opportunities to smoke, while educational campaigns have helped to raise awareness of the health consequences of smoking. And increasing taxes on cigarettes has provided a powerful disincentive to consumers of cigarettes.[38] Further, the cultural acceptance of smoking has radically decreased over the past few decades to the point that smokers face social opprobrium and reduced employment options as some workplaces decide to not hire smokers. Yet while these changes are laudable, they have had unintended consequences for the mentally ill. Effective tobacco-control policies have pushed many mentally ill smokers to figurative and literal margins of society. As Kenneth Warner has pointed out, "Today, smoking is frowned upon in many social circles, viewed as a sign of individual weakness if not outright social pathology."[39] Individuals with mental illness are part of the social pathology, and many experience greater financial stress because more of their limited income is being devoted to increasingly expensive cigarettes. Although tobacco-control advocates intended to spread the benefits of smoking cessation to everyone, some of the effects of anti-tobacco measures reinforced the status of the mentally ill as a fringe group.

Over the last couple of decades, state mental-health and psychiatric-hospital groups across the country continued to address the issue of whether it was possible to turn back decades of precedent and create a smoke-free and violence-free inpatient psychiatric unit.[40] Most contributors to the medical literature on this issue highlighted the fears of staff before the institution of smoking bans in contrast with the usually undramatic results. For example, investigators at Dartmouth commented that long-term-hospital administrators had been afraid to impose a smoking ban because of worries about patient violence and the belief that patients deserved some kind of rewards. When the New Hampshire Hospital went smoke free, however, the only bad outcomes were a lot of complaining and some sneaking of cigarettes by staff.[41] Other hospitals reported no change in the incidence of assault or aggressive behaviors, though it was also not clear that the smoking ban particularly benefited the patients.[42] There was also some suspicion that adverse events of a smoking ban might not be reported due to a climate strongly in favor of tobacco control.[43]

But while the predicted flood of assaults and other problematic behaviors did not materialize, what did happen was an increasing gulf between the mentally ill and everyone else. As a psychologist from Central Michigan University pointed out in 1997, increasing conflict developed between nonsmokers and smokers. And with the condemnation of both the tobacco industry and smokers, "the nearly universal result is for nonsmokers to view smokers more negatively on any dimension being considered." Smokers thus became an "outgroup" whose every attribute was seen in negative terms.[44] Thus without much change in their own behavior, mentally ill smokers became doubly excluded from American society. Instead of smoking as a habit that connected them through common social interactions, smoking became a trait of a marginalized segment of the population.

In general, psychiatric patients were increasingly seen as different, aberrant in their smoking patterns as well as their mental illness. Further, tobacco-control activists may have unintentionally worsened this marginalization of the mentally ill by linking them and their advocates with cigarette companies at a time when the tobacco industry was increasingly viewed as the incarnation of evil. Public-health advocates have long critiqued corporate culture, and in some ways the condemnation of the tobacco industry fits within this longer trajectory.[45] Tobacco-control experts have speculated that the industry deliberately targeted mentally ill consumers and that advertising might strongly affect these vulnerable populations.[46] After the release of tobacco-industry documents in the late 1990s, scholars began to suspect that the industry had been specifically looking for consumers based on psychological profiles. Thus the remaining smokers might be those who were specially selected by the tobacco industry for their high likelihood of becoming dependent.[47] It seemed impossible to exaggerate the depths to which the tobacco companies might stoop to retain their products and protect their markets. But as a result, smokers appeared to be poor dupes, distasteful by their association with cigarette companies.

Further, fantastic revelations within the tobacco-industry documents led some researchers to conclude that anyone mentioned within the archives was part of the tobacco-industry conspiracy. For example, a tobacco-control advocacy group accused social workers Michael Greeman and Thomas McClellan (who suggested that smoking bans in psychiatric hospitals were not as easy as most represented) as well as Helen Konopka (the FAMI advocate who organized a drive to allow smoking at New York Hospitals) of being allies of the tobacco industry because copies of their materials were found within the tobacco archives.[48] There was no evidence (even within the archives) that these individuals had any connections to the industry, but the tobacco-control group evidently thought that their agendas were so close to tobacco company interests that they were suspicious.[49] A physician commenting on the efforts of Konopka and FAMI observed that though the patient advocates were likely sincere, "the ancient argument espousing the inhumanity and hopelessness affecting the tobacco group among certain populations sounds as though it has been scripted by the tobacco industry!"[50] At a time of unprecedented animosity toward cigarette companies, those who argued for the right of psychiatric patients to smoke faced hostility by association.

Mentally ill smokers have been not only tarnished by perceived connection with the tobacco industry, but also marginalized by health-care-access issues. Many mentally ill individuals have experienced limited or inferior medical care, both because of their illness and because of their lower socioeconomic status.[51] But according to some anti-tobacco activists, the problem is even worse because mentally ill patients' primary contact with physicians takes place with their psychiatrists, who according to these activists ignore their physical health and tolerate their smoking behaviors. One tobacco-control group found that Ohio psychiatrists responded to questionnaires about smoking cessation by stating that they had other priorities with patients, including treating their mental illness or dealing with other more serious substance-abuse issues. The study team complained, "These statements seem to indicate a lack of understanding that tobacco-related diseases are the major cause of death for patients treated for alcoholism and other substances of abuse."[52] Psychiatrists are portrayed as insensitive to the physical consequences of their patients' smoking, and researchers consistently worry that psychiatrists seem oblivious to the fact that smoking changes the blood levels of some medications. Thus according to anti-tobacco investigators, the mentally ill must make do with physicians whose ability to effectively function in medicine seems limited at best.[53] Tobacco-control advocates have even designed a tobacco curriculum to bring psychiatric residents (trainees) up to speed about treatment, implying that physicians who choose to go into psychiatry require remedial education about smoking, above and beyond what is provided in medical school.[54]

And while psychiatrists and other mental-health providers have been criticized for failing to treat smoking issues adequately, psychiatric patients are blamed for the failure of treatment when it does occur both because they cannot (or will not) quit smoking. Some investigators have argued that mentally ill smokers are still ignorant of the health effects of smoking, which would suggest either a startling disengagement with mainstream society and culture or a significant lack of intelligence.[55] Further, their baseline mental condition has been blamed for the adverse effects of smoking-cessation medications. In a recent *Journal of Clinical Psychiatry* article, well-respected researchers in smoking cessation partnered with employees from Pfizer, the maker of the blockbuster smoking-cessation drug varenicline, to report on the effectiveness of the drug for patients with schizophrenia. They attributed any adverse effects to nicotine withdrawal or the baseline high rate of "neuropsychiatric adverse events" in both the populations of smokers and mentally ill.[56]

And not surprisingly, mentally ill smokers were also lumped in with all the other socioeconomically disadvantaged individuals who seemed increasingly on the margins of upwardly mobile society because of their addiction to smoking. As a number of investigators (and clinicians) commented, smokers on public assistance because of their mental illness spent a considerable amount of their monthly income (sometimes up to 30 percent) on cigarettes.[57] Further, according to a research team in Baltimore, there was a "clear connection between increased smoking severity and poorer overall self-reported subjective quality of life, as well as lower satisfaction with leisure activities, social relationships, finances, and health among persons with severe mental illness." The study team was not sure if the quality of life issues were directly caused by smoking, but it seemed clear to them that smoking did not help with leisure time or relationships.[58] Once providers might have noted that these individuals could relate to others through their smoking. Now their smoking behaviors just illustrated how marginalized they were in society. Among mentally ill populations, some researchers have claimed that smokers have a worse course of their psychiatric illness, more problems with medications, and more hospitalizations. In these accounts, even for those who are on the margins, smoking makes everything worse.[59]

In the tobacco-control literature, investigators have noted correlations between smoking and adverse social, economic, and cultural circumstances.

But recently teams have asserted that smoking is the causal factor. Behavioral health epidemiologists who analyzed data on the relationship between mental illness, low socioeconomic status in populations, and smoking declared that smoking was the primary problem. While psychiatric diagnosis might be related, these investigators said that there was not a relationship between socioeconomic status and mental illness. This kind of study would suggest that mentally ill smokers are not necessarily held back in society because of their illness, but rather because of their smoking.[60] According to another study team from the Centers for Disease Control, quitting smoking would help individuals in lower socioeconomic circumstances deal more effectively with their psychological distress.[61] For these researchers, it has been more important to focus on changing smoking behaviors than to address socioeconomic inequalities.[62]

Although it is hard to believe that smoking is the primary reason for individuals to be at a lower socioeconomic level, patients' identification as smokers has certainly affected their status in both society and in relationship to treatment providers. Power dynamics around smoking are now characterized by providers encouraging (or nagging) mentally ill smokers to quit. The use of cigarettes has been something to further set apart the mentally ill from treatment teams. And many current experts insist that providers have an obligation to use their power to push for smoking cessation, regardless of the consequences. For example, an investigator team from a forensic inpatient unit in Ontario reported on the results of a smoking ban in 2007 and focused on what they said were cardiovascular improvements in patients as a result. They skated lightly over reports of increased aggression, lower mood, and significant weight gain among some of the patients, and blamed these outcomes on occasional access to tobacco.[63]

While tobacco-control researchers insisted that smoking caused terrible physical and mental problems for the mentally ill, they defined treatment only as cessation and nicotine abstinence (rather than long-term nicotine maintenance). Many advocates for tobacco control have dismissed theories regarding the utility of nicotine in the brains of mentally ill individuals as a ploy by the tobacco industry to keep people attached to tobacco products. University of California, San Francisco analyst Judith Prochaska caricatured "harm reduction" as letting patients smoke—and castigated providers who thought this was a good idea.[64] Meanwhile, psychiatrists' version of harm reduction (substituting other forms of nicotine for cigarettes) has been met with silence or criticism by most anti-tobacco activists.[65]

The mantra that nicotine is addictive has led to predictable social and cultural disdain for the addicts themselves. Addicts have usually been viewed as either criminal or weak willed in an American society that extols individual self-control.[66] Tobacco-control advocates have worried about too easy access to nicotine-replacement options, such as nicotine nasal spray, because of the risk that users might become addicted.[67] Nicotine does not seem to cause significant health problems by itself (without the dangerous delivery vehicle of the cigarette), nor does it carry the immediate risk of death during use (as is the case for a drug such as heroin). But while confessed addicts to coffee and other caffeine-containing products are supported and encouraged, nicotine addicts are mentally ill.[68]

It would make no sense to argue at this point that the mentally ill should be allowed to smoke at will because of their illness. At the same time, though, the tobacco-control approach has not been necessarily tailored to help this population specifically (other than to push harder). And there is a moral judgment embedded in calls to emphasize smoking cessation as risk reduction for physical illness among the mentally ill. As Charles Rosenberg has pointed out, the concept of reducing risk for illness sounds objective and benign, but can engender guilt for individuals who fail to achieve standards of self-control. In turn, those who cannot control themselves have only themselves to blame.[69] The measures that have been well intended and have helped to decrease smoking in the general population have made things more difficult for some mentally ill smokers by increasing their distance from mainstream society and worsening their economic situation. Further, the assertion that quality and quantity of life would be better if the mentally ill quit smoking has been made on faith and assumption, not necessarily engagement and understanding with real populations of mentally ill smokers who struggle with a complex mix of issues beyond the comprehension of most people in the general population.

The seismic shift in American society since the 1964 surgeon general's report is rightly considered a major triumph for the modern field of public health. Activist health groups such as Action on Smoking and Health, broader health organizations such as the American Cancer Society, government bodies such as the Center for Disease Control, and schools of public health around the country have helped to drive local, state, and national limitations on smoking and increasing disincentives (such as taxes). But as with older public-health efforts around issues such as infectious disease, interventions to try to help the general population can have unintended consequences for some segments of society.[70] In a span of a few decades, mentally ill smokers moved from displaying behaviors common to most in the general population to being labeled, judged, and controlled for those same behaviors. Though improved health for all is an important goal, smokers with serious and persistent psychiatric illness have potentially faced increasing challenges in managing their mental issues because of the broad push to reduce or eliminate smoking.

So how would this issue look if we took the perspective of individuals who have dealt with mental illness? What have mentally ill individuals said and done about the growing movement toward smoking cessation? Why would they continue to smoke in the light of all the information available about both the harms of smoking and the troubling behaviors of the tobacco industry? To what extent have smokers and the mentally ill become lumped together in the popular imagination? And what would actually be helpful to mentally ill populations?

Chapter 8

Double Marginalization

In 2004, health analysts Ronald Bayer and James Colgrove pointed out that tobacco-control policies in the United States over the previous decades had succeeded by focusing on children and innocent bystanders. Even though Americans typically disliked paternalistic public-health measures, those that seemed to be protecting vulnerable populations were acceptable. Bayer and Colgrove suggested, though, that because of the major shift in how cigarettes were perceived in society, Americans were able to tolerate broader regulation and restriction on tobacco.[1] But one reason that many are more willing to accept limitations on smoking is not just that smoking is less tolerated in American society—it is that smoking is more associated with an already marginalized population, the mentally ill.

Public-health activists and scholars have recently described the mentally ill as a population vulnerable to the problems of smoking and suggested that they require special protection.[2] But the concept of the mentally ill as vulnerable has a unique cultural association that is not shared with other groups (such as children). Mentally ill individuals do not generally evoke sympathy and are often seen as a potential threat for mass violence.[3] Further, it is less clear for the group as a whole the extent to which their illnesses affect their ability to make decisions for themselves. Public policy about vulnerable individuals suggests that they are impaired in their decision-making capacity. Advocacy groups composed of mental-health consumers, however, have insisted that they are not.

Not only have tobacco-control assessments of mentally ill smokers postulated that they cannot appropriately manage their own health, the large number of mentally ill individuals within the remaining population of smokers has cast doubt on smokers at a whole. In recent years, policymakers have not necessarily made a distinction between mentally ill smokers and those without a mental illness—especially because nicotine dependence (or the new diagnosis of tobacco use disorder) is itself a diagnosis. Smokers themselves are beginning to be seen as mentally ill. Who else but someone with a mental problem would stand outside in the cold to use a product that is bad for them?[4] And if a newspaper reports a fire started by someone smoking in bed, it seems to be more likely due to a mentally ill individual who is unable to display sufficiently good judgment to avoid the danger.[5]

Although tobacco-control advocates, treatment providers, and policymakers are trying to improve the health of the population as a whole by emphasizing the addictive qualities of nicotine, the health detriments of smoking, and the importance of society-wide interventions, these measures do not have an equal impact on all members of society. Nor have interventions come about as a result of consultation with the presumed targets, especially mentally ill smokers, who as a group already face stigma and social and economic problems. As I described in the last chapter, tobacco-control efforts have had unintended consequences on mentally ill populations. The framing of smoking as an addiction, a mental disorder, or a "denormalized" behavior has resulted in the double marginalization of the mentally ill. But the mentally ill population is not monolithic, nor is it without spokespersons to advocate for a different point of view.

Mental-Health Consumer Movement

As Nancy Tomes and others have described, groups of individuals who had been treated for mental illnesses organized in the 1970s to protest psychiatric power and demand more autonomy in their lives. Initially most of these groups were opposed to any form of psychiatric intervention and identified themselves as "survivors" of encounters with the mental-health establishment.[6] Some later began to call themselves "consumers," reflecting their desire for choice and more input into their treatment. In the last two decades, organizations of mental-health consumers have been willing to engage with mental-health providers in order to make sure their perspectives are heard.[7] Most of these groups identify themselves as people living with illness, rather than patients with a diagnosis.

Mental-health consumer organizations that have arisen over the decades are part of a broader movement within disability communities to empower members to be more than the objects of treatment. Among disability groups, advocates have taken on the slogan "Nothing about us without us." Individuals with disabilities have banded together to overcome long-standing problems in integrating with the rest of society.[8] But as Nancy Tomes and Beatrix Hoffman have pointed out in the area of health care, disability groups and others who attempt to influence policy have less participation and choice than would be suggested by the language of health-care consumers.[9] Further, mental-health consumer groups have two particular ongoing concerns related to power relationships in treatment: psychiatrists' and courts' power to involuntarily hospitalize, and the power to mandate use of pharmaceutical agents to treat. Consumers have decried the use of forced treatment and insisted on autonomy in treatment decisions (even when in partnership with mental-health providers).

The issue of smoking among the mentally ill falls into a complicated nexus of power relationships between mentally ill smokers and care providers. Psychiatrists, therapists, nurses, case managers, and others within mental-health teams have power to provide services—and to dictate treatment. The mental-health consumer movement has made the argument that consumers need to be part of the process and that their concerns need to be heard, particularly about treatment choices and about nonmedication alternatives. Tobacco-control advocates have encouraged psychiatrists to use their power to denormalize smoking in the mentally ill population and to strongly push smoking cessation. But as was the case for smoking privileges earlier in the century, the issue of smoking cessation now highlights power inequalities in treatment relationships.

The widening gap between those with the power to dictate policy (usually physicians) and patients puts other health-care providers in the position of having to choose how much to ally with physicians and administrators and tell patients what is good for them, or act as advocates for patients to address their needs. Not everyone has been in agreement with a top-down policy, especially those who have been traditionally close to patients and their expressed wishes. While many nurses, for example, were early converts to a tobacco-control perspective, others worried more about the exercise of power needed to enforce smoking bans and push smoking cessation.[10] In a recent study that focused on nurses in a hospital in the United Kingdom, some participants spoke up about their concerns that a new smoke-free policy resulted in eliminating patients' abilities to cope with stress. Further, they thought that the emphasis on smoking cessation felt like bullying the patients. But though these opinions were aired in the journal article report on the hospital, the authors of the article did not suggest more attention to consumers' needs. Instead they advocated for educating the staff to bring them in line with the policy.[11]

Mental-health providers have been concerned with their patients' welfare and want to help. But in the area of smoking cessation, psychiatrists have had to maintain a delicate balance in order to avoid harm to patients. As the rise of the mental-health consumer movement illustrated, there is a long-standing issue of a disconnect between mental-health-care providers and the subjects of their interventions. It may seem to consumers that some psychiatrists have assumed the power to try to make changes in patients' behavior around smoking as a way of augmenting their professional status.[12] The most common method endorsed by psychiatrists for smoking cessation is medication—which is precisely the issue for many within the mental-health consumer movement who want to see other kinds of options rather than just pills.

Advocates within the tobacco-control movement continue to castigate psychiatrists for failing to do enough to stop smoking in their patients. But the criticism of psychiatry for not doing enough presumes that professionals are the only autonomous actors. This assumption runs through debates about the addictiveness of nicotine. During the late 1980s and 1990s, researchers and policy advocates debated with foes (especially within the tobacco industry) about what it meant to call smoking or nicotine addictive. Opponents of the addiction label for cigarettes emphasized that addiction meant major brain effects and devastating social consequences for using a drug—and that by these measures smoking could not be understood as an addiction. R. J. Reynolds psychologist John Robinson stressed that the problem with calling smoking addictive was that it diluted the meaning to the point that it "cannot distinguish the pharmacological and behavioural effects of cocaine from those of nicotine."[13] But supporters of a broad definition of addiction, such as the one used by the United States Food and Drug Administration commissioner David Kessler in 1994, argued that what addiction really meant was that individuals did not have independent agency in their use of substances. As Kessler explained, when he was working through the issues of tobacco companies' behaviors around nicotine, he came to the conclusion that addicts do not have choice to use.[14] Kessler was satisfied with this definition (though the issue of choice was not explicitly a part of psychiatric diagnoses of addiction) because he felt that this argued against the tobacco industry's claims that smoking was a free consumer behavior.

Smoking has been an area in which well-meaning health activists and mental-health providers insisted that individuals could not make informed or rational choices. But however well intended these views are, they conflict with the assertion within the mental-health consumer movements that people have autonomy to make decisions for themselves. As policy analyst David Mechanic has pointed out, the concept of autonomy in health-care decisions has depended on context and social environment.[15] In the area of preventive health, most anti-tobacco advocates assume that mentally ill individuals do not have autonomy. But individuals with mental illness might be focused on different priorities. The argument most used by public-health activists—that smoking is terribly unhealthy and can lead to a shorter life span—might seem less of a pressing issue when put into the context of the side effects of psychiatric medication (including major weight gain and metabolic effects leading to diabetes and obesity, which are also risks for a shorter life span) and the social and economic conditions experienced by many individuals with mental illness who are trying to live on limited incomes.[16]

It is possible that some are voting with their feet, as it were, and passively failing to follow smoking-cessation pushes in their community—without necessarily stating that they want to continue smoking. Much of the current cessation literature acknowledges that the numbers of individuals who actually quit is fairly small. While investigators blame addiction for the discrepancy between the reported desire to quit and the low actual cessation rate among the mentally ill, some might be using passive resistance to cessation as a way of exercising (limited) power. For example, a researcher at the University of Colorado wanted to do a study on nicotine replacement to treat agitation at a psychiatric unit at his hospital, but the patients would not agree to a twenty-four hour smoking ban to do the study. (Instead, the study was completed in Geneva, Switzerland.)[17]

And one of the driving forces for tobacco-control experts—fury with the tobacco industry for promoting their products through denials of the health effects—does not appear to have had as much of an effect on people with mental illness. In the 1990s—well after both the surgeon general's report on addiction and the disclosures of tobacco industry antics—a mental-health consumer organization used part of their budget to buy cigarettes for clients of the center who could not afford it.[18] And a number of individuals who identified themselves as mentally ill wrote to tobacco companies over the last several decades to express solidarity and support—and to request help to fight smoking bans and secure cigarette supplies.[19] While these examples do not represent the concerns of all individuals with mental illness, the contrast between mental-health consumers' strong concerns about medications and the pharmaceutical industry and their lack of public comment about the tobacco industry suggests that as a group they may have a different set of priorities and an alternative target for rage at corporate misdeeds.

Although smoking cessation in the mentally ill has become an urgent issue among tobacco-control advocates and mental-health providers, it is virtually absent among the concerns of mental-health consumer groups. In 1995, the

National Alliance for the Mentally Ill (NAMI), a the consumer and family organization, issued a position statement that the mentally ill should not be forced
to quit smoking against their will (and should be offered an opportunity to
smoke while involuntarily hospitalized).[20] NAMI backed off that statement in
recent years and instead endorsed support for smoking cessation in this population.[21] But discussion of smoking is difficult to find on their website and is
not highlighted as a special issue. And for other groups—such as the National
Coalition for Mental Health Recovery—smoking is not mentioned at all. Instead,
advocacy groups focus on recovery as a whole, to empower individuals to live
full lives and be participants in their communities.[22]

As Caroline Acker has pointed out with regard to the history of narcotics, individuals who use substances that are identified as addictive do so in
ways that make sense within their lives (however maladaptive it may appear
from the outside).[23] From the narratives written by individuals dealing with
mental-health issues, it appears that smokers who also have mental illnesses
used cigarettes at particular times and places, and for particular reasons. Even
as it became clear to the whole population that cigarette use resulted in major
health problems, individuals with mental illness have had their own relationships to smoking.

Different Perspectives on Smoking

Tobacco-control activists often talk about smoking as though it were a mind-
less activity about which patients need to be educated for its dangers. But it is
hard to believe that mentally ill individuals are not already aware of the risks.
As University of Illinois psychologists pointed out, "The current prevalence of
nonsmoking environments and media antismoking messages, coupled with the
availability of over-the-counter cessation aides, make it increasingly implau-
sible that psychiatric patients smoke because they are unaware of the risks
or lack access to cessation resources. Indeed . . . psychiatric patients appreciate the disadvantages of smoking as adequately as smokers without major
psychopathology."[24] Mentally ill smokers who wrote to the tobacco industry
in the 1990s to express support and request help to obtain cheaper cigarettes
explained that they knew about the health consequences of smoking, but also
articulated their attachment to cigarettes and their desire to make their own
decisions about purchase and use of cigarettes.[25]

Most of the tobacco-control and psychiatric literature on smoking cessation
in the mentally ill implies that patients will not quit unless they are pushed
to do so by providers. But for individuals who described their experiences
with mental illness, smoking behaviors (active or not) had more to do with

internal stress and external constraints rather than contacts with providers. In first-person narratives of mental illness, individuals did sometimes report quitting for health reasons, though it appeared very difficult. Times of emotional stress made it next to impossible to quit, and trying to cut down ran the risk of exacerbating psychiatric symptoms.[26] As one writer explained about her experience of living in Paris under a great deal of stress, she acted out because she was not smoking: "I found myself increasingly unable to deal with any kind of social contrariety. Whereas previously I had subjugated all negative emotions by drawing furiously on a cigarette, I now let rip, often behaving with inappropriate and unreasonable aggressiveness."[27] The writer did not resume smoking, though she chewed up and ate a cigarette as her sign that she was beginning to get worse in her emotional stress. Others found that they needed to keep smoking in order to avoid relapse to their psychiatric symptoms.[28]

Smoking also remained tied to mental-illness experiences. One young man explained that he began to smoke when he was having trouble sorting out what was real and what was not during a psychotic episode: "While I was sucking on a cigarette, I would forget about the turmoil in my mind. The effect never lasted longer than the cigarette, but it was a few minutes of calm, or at least a reduced state of anxiety. I was putting my future health in jeopardy, but those cigarettes tasted so damn good."[29] He was not able to give up the cigarettes, even when his mental health improved.

Psychologist and mental-health consumer Patricia Deegan described her experience with overwhelming grief as a teenager when she was first given the diagnosis of schizophrenia. She framed this devastation to a social work audience in 1995 as an imagined conversation with her much younger self who was sitting and smoking cigarette after cigarette. Deegan explained that her younger self was sad, hurt, and angry about losing hope for her future. And while she noted that her younger self was smoking, she addressed the feelings and the needs symbolized by the cigarettes, not the cigarettes themselves.[30]

Even with changes in mental-health locations and increasing smoking bans, cigarettes continued to have a role for many individuals. When they were in treatment settings, they found that rooms where they could congregate were still important. And smoking could be part of the way they related to one another.[31] As British social-service workers explained about a smoking room in Birmingham, England, "life in the smoking room goes on. It is a tolerant place, one in which people seem to feel free to be themselves even if attempts at communication bypass others in the room. Relationships form in here."[32] A patient in the hospital explained to another British social scientist that conversation inside the smoking room seemed to be the most genuine of any setting in the hospital.[33] Even the most mentally disturbed were able to recognize that a smoking room offered a space in which it was possible to connect with others, if in no other way than in the pursuit of cigarettes.[34] And the existence of smoking spaces provided an entry point for patients to connect with peer support networks that allowed them to gain more control and independence in their lives.[35]

In the last twenty years the glamour of smoking within the general population has pretty much disappeared. Those who smoked, though, recognized in each other kindred spirits. On a constructive level, smoking allowed a way for women from disparate economic and educational backgrounds to reach a common understanding, even when they recognized that smoking was a habit that was not socially desirable.[36] For individuals struggling with mental illness, including the desperate sense of being alone that accompanied symptoms invisible to anyone else, smoking provided a possible way to relate to others. And in the community of mentally ill smokers, there was no judgment for needing to smoke.

But even more than their relationship to others, individuals with mental illness explained their attachment to cigarettes. A man who shared his experience with readers of the psychiatric journal *Schizophrenia Bulletin* described an episode of psychosis in which he thought he had to quit smoking because it would result in someone getting hit by a car. He measured his recovery by his ability to smoke normally again.[37] One British man described a low point in his life in which he was seriously contemplating suicide. While once in his life he cared about people, at his lowest all he cared about were cigarettes.[38] While this was obviously not a positive connection, it was a meaningful relationship and a significant attachment for this individual.

Even for those who acknowledged that they were unable to give up cigarettes, many said that in the grand scheme of things, smoking was not their biggest problem. Some expressed amazement that other people seemed to think it was. One journalist described her battle with alcoholism and the stress that some of her behavior caused her family. But as she relayed it, her family focused on the wrong things. She went to visit her parents while her mother was dying and went outside to sneak a drink and to smoke. Her mother chastised her about her smoking rather than her drinking: "Two months after she died, I enrolled in a smoking-cessation program at a local hospital, aware on some level that I was tackling the wrong substance." She quit the smoking-cessation group, but eventually realized that she needed to stop being self-destructive by drinking.[39]

Among individuals with mental illness, smoking has been a way to relate to others, a relationship with an object (when interpersonal relationships are

too hard), and just one behavior amid a host of other difficulties. It is perhaps not surprising, then, that smoking cessation looks different from this perspective. Relatively few treatment providers stop and ask the objects of their
interventions what they want.[40] When they have, investigators have found that
individuals with mental illness do not approach smoking with the same calculus of risk and benefit that is promoted by tobacco-control educators. Instead,
as one academic nursing team found in 2008, smokers who participated in
focus groups (whether or not they expressed a desire to quit) discussed their
intense relationships with cigarettes and their fears that they would not find an
adequate substitute if they were to quit. Further, these smokers "indicated that
having the autonomy to decide to smoke or not to smoke was very important
to them."[41]

Living on the Margins

In 1999, the film *Girl, Interrupted* was released, from the 1993 book of the same
name by author and former mental-health consumer Susanna Kaysen. The
story of the film was largely faithful to the broad outline of the book in which
the main character (Kaysen) experienced difficulties with social interactions
and had a lengthy hospitalization at a psychiatric hospital in Boston. Since the
book explored events from the 1960s, it would be quite realistic to see psychiatric patient characters in the film smoking. As in the book, the film portrayed
a wild sociopath named Lisa who followed her own rules and appeared to be
smoking at will. In the film, Kaysen herself was smoking at the beginning and
at times of intense emotional crisis. But she was not shown with a cigarette
after she reached an epiphany in the film and began to recover. In the taxi ride
home at the end the film, she appeared calm and without a need to smoke, in
contrast to her desperate smoking while she was still ill. Recovery meant that
she had joined everyone else and did not need to smoke. In the film, cigarettes
provided a nice marker showing her progress from illness to serene mental
health—though in the book, Kaysen remained a smoker and embraced her
identity as a smoking writer.[42]

   One of the early signs of successful tobacco-control measures in popular
culture was a significant decline in glamorous or positive smoking representations in media (especially movies). But though smoking disappeared from most
films in the last two decades, occasionally movie characters smoked as a sign of
severe distress or mental illness. Fortunately, smoking did not appear as a desirable behavior. Unfortunately, the correspondence between mental derangement
and smoking helped to reinforce the idea that only a mentally unstable person
would smoke. And popular representations of mental illness used smoking as

a sign of illness or symptoms. Patients portrayed in films smoked only when they were ill—they seemed to quit smoking (or at least were not shown as smoking) as they recovered. And as representations of mental illness in films became more popular, descriptions of smoking in books were absent in their movie versions, especially when the main characters appeared heroic in their quest for mental health.[43]

For the movie version of *A Beautiful Mind,* filmmakers used cigarettes to help track mathematician John Nash's descent into mental illness. While the way they chose to use cigarettes generally mapped onto the narrative of Sylvia Nasar's biography of Nash, the film's creative team highlighted Nash's smoking for dramatic effect. At the beginning of the film, although many around Nash were smoking (as would have been expected in the 1950s), Nash himself did not appear to begin smoking until after he had his first psychotic break. In the scene in which it was revealed that Nash had stopped taking psychiatric medications, he was smoking with great intensity. When he arrived back at Princeton after decades of struggle with his illness, others watched him pacing around and smoking on campus while attending to what seemed to be voices in his head. But when he was finally approached by the Nobel Prize committee about receiving public recognition for his theories in mathematics, he was not shown smoking, nor did he appear to smoke for the rest of his triumphant return to society.[44]

While movie magic let patients appear to recover from their mental illness and join the mainstream, the reality for most psychiatric patients was that they had to remain on the margins of society. Both inside and outside Hollywood, smoking marked people as mentally ill. One woman, who wrote a memoir about life with her mentally ill mother, described a point when she went to the hospital to meet her mother and heard laughing: "Peering over toward those laughs, I could see a vague knot of lady patients in blue nightgowns sitting at a large round table in a low gray cloud of cigarette smoke. It struck me that those were the other crazy people."[45] The daughter's memories of her mother were all shaped by her mother's constant and absorbed relationship with her cigarettes. For psychotherapist Martha Manning, who experienced her own problems with depression, smoking behaviors set apart both her patients and her fellow patients when she was in a psychiatric hospital.[46]

As the rest of society dramatically decreased their smoking behaviors, mentally ill individuals' absorption with cigarettes became more and more apparent. A New York writer in the 1990s described his attempts to connect with his schizophrenic brother Robert, and many of their interactions revolved around Robert's desire for cigarettes. Robert was constantly asking his brother to bring him cigarettes in the hospital, and Robert judged his psychiatrist by how well he could tolerate being in a room with him while he smoked. Though their father had a heart attack after a lifetime of being a three-pack-a-day smoker, Robert remained preoccupied by cigarettes and structured his concept of money around the cost of cigarettes.[47]

Families and advocates noted how much of a role smoking played in the lives of the mentally ill, but it was not always clear how to deal with it. Some families found that it was easier to quietly accommodate smoking at home. One man described the agony that he and his wife went through with their adult daughter in her struggles with serious mental illness. They allowed her to sit on the stoop of their building to smoke, describing it as "a habit she acquired in the hospital, and one that under normal circumstances we would insist she give up. In comparison with Sally's other woes, however, it seems of little importance."[48] Not only were families often accepting of their mentally ill loved one's behavior, sometimes parents could relate to their mentally ill children by smoking together.[49]

In recent decades, parents and other family members have more often complained to care providers that their schizophrenic children were doing nothing but sitting around the house all day smoking cigarettes,[50] concluding that mentally ill individuals used their cigarettes to avoid interpersonal interactions.[51] When individuals were distressed and feeling intense emotion, others noticed that they isolated themselves and chain-smoked rather than engaging in social interactions.[52] And the cigarettes seemed to have a stronger pull on the affections of some mentally ill individuals than on others. Poet Anne Sexton told her daughter Linda that she was too sick to be her mother while intensely engaging with her cigarette. Sexton later went on to commit suicide.[53] Other daughters reported similar experiences of feeling second to their mothers' cigarettes.[54]

And families have had a hard time accepting that their mentally ill relatives approached smoking differently than other members of society. New York journalist Paul Raeburn struggled to understand his children's experiences with mental illnesses. At one point, Raeburn became distressed at the fact that his daughter was smoking cigarettes. He had done some investigation of the shenanigans of the tobacco industry and hated the idea that, as he framed it, his daughter was in thrall to the cigarette companies. But he could not get his daughter's therapist to make that a priority—the therapist wanted the daughter to focus on her other maladaptive habits of abusing alcohol, cutting herself, and using marijuana. As soon as she recovered from the acute risk of suicide, Raeburn became obsessed with this issue: "Smoking was emerging as a greater risk, and I could not give up on it. I couldn't put out of my mind a vision of Alicia getting better after a long, difficult, and courageous struggle, leading a productive life, and then being cut down in her fifties by a stroke or a heart attack, a consequence of smoking. Wasn't her physical health as important as her mental health? It was an argument I could not win. Alicia is still a smoker." Raeburn was also critical of his son's experience of being given cigarettes as rewards for good behavior, though he did understand his son's agitation when he was not allowed to smoke (due to policy changes) on a repeat visit to a drug-treatment center.[55]

Psychiatrist and advocate E. Fuller Torrey addressed family distress about smoking in the most recent edition of his textbook, *Surviving Schizophrenia,* by emphasizing what smoking meant to the mentally ill. Torrey counseled families that attempting to forbid smoking was not necessarily the best thing to do: "We should be careful about taking away such pleasures unless we are certain that the gains from doing so are worth it. The ban on smoking in hospitals by the Joint Commission on Health Care Organizations did not take into account the fact that for some individuals with schizophrenia these hospitals are their homes. It also does not take into account studies suggesting that the abrupt cessation of smoking may exacerbate the symptoms of schizophrenia."[56] Although many psychiatrists and most tobacco-control activists would disagree with Torrey that mentally ill people should not be forced to quit, Torrey understood that individuals with illness might have a different perspective than others.

One of the arguments that anti-tobacco professionals have used regarding mentally ill smokers is that they have been socially isolated, but if they quit smoking they would no longer have that problem. Addiction psychiatrist Jill Williams argued in 2008 that because smokers were marginalized in society, mentally ill smokers faced further isolation.[57] Smoking cessation leaders Steven Schroeder and Chad Morris elaborated in 2010, "Already facing severe economic hardship and societal stigma, smokers with behavioral health disorders also find it increasingly difficult to integrate into communities and workplaces that no longer condone smoking."[58] They suggested that it was ultimately beneficial to mentally ill smokers to keep them from smoking whenever possible (such as on inpatient units) because it would give them a better long-term chance to blend in with general society. The implication was that quitting smoking would decrease or eliminate psychiatric patients' social isolation.

But individuals with mental illness may have had a different perspective on cause and effect with regard to being on the margins. A social worker in San Francisco conducted interviews with mentally ill patients to understand more about why they continued to smoke. She found that they were all aware of the health risks, and some were thinking about quitting. For those who continued to smoke, they articulated a feeling of frustration with the limited number of things they could do and felt that smoking helped them exercise their rights. One participant explicitly addressed the feeling of being marginalized through mental illness: "Well, if you don't fit in with the general population anymore, then you look for what the fringe population is doing, and the fringe population is smoking."[59] She found that patients had clear patterns of weighing the benefits and drawbacks of smoking and that for many the feeling of control and belonging to their own community was more desirable than the health benefits of quitting.

Though individuals might have made choices about their smoking, they had few options around their mental illness. While some individuals groups actually argued that psychotic experiences had a meaning and a significance beyond the pathological, most individuals who experienced times of losing touch with reality, hearing voices, or becoming paranoid or isolated in their own worlds have in recent years lived within a revolving system of hospitalization alternating with living on the street or in dingy quarters.[60] Smoking marked these individuals in their space. Author Nathaniel Lachenmeyer described his effort to uncover information about his schizophrenic father Charles through contacts his father might have had on the street. He found a man who had sat with Charles and was able to have a conversation with him when he offered him cigarettes. As Lachenmeyer tried to discover his father's life, he described himself as an "outsider," though it was clear that Charles was really the outsider as he was part of a class of men who would sit outside and smoke alone.[61]

Another man narrated his brother Michael's descent into deeper and darker levels of unreality, as signaled by his progressively intense engagement with cigarettes. At the time of his first psychotic break, Michael sat and smoked three packs a day without sleeping or bathing. His appearance in public identified him as someone with major problems: "Michael was smoking a cigarette like a prisoner on death row, as if it were his last, always his last, inhaling with exaggerated need. The skin between his fingers was yellow." Michael eventually set fire to the family's house when he was forced to go out to the garage and smoke—because the father was inside dying of lung cancer.[62]

In the last decade, the move away from smoking—at the same time that people with mental illness were strongly associated with smoking—has reified the idea that anyone who smokes is mentally ill, which tobacco-control advocates suggest people can avoid by quitting smoking. But while smoking undoubtedly complicates both the health and the finances of individuals already struggling with social, occupational, interpersonal, and economic problems, the paradigm of smoking cessation has not been as meaningful to many of

them. As the term suggests, quitting means giving up something that has meaning and value, even if it is not all positive or if we would dispute its meaning.
Many individuals with mental-health issues have already had to give up a lot,
including economic security, relationships, and prospects for a future career
or educational opportunities. The language of cessation might not be the most
effective for these individuals.

What happens to the issue of smoking cessation if we look at it from the
perspective of mental-health consumers? A few investigators have taken as a
point of departure that they may not know what will work best for mentally ill
individuals and that maybe they should ask the individuals themselves. One
research group in Minneapolis reported in the early 1990s on their efforts to get
substance-abusing veterans to give up cigarettes along with alcohol and other
drugs. They compared cohorts who were undergoing treatment in two different conditions—one on a unit with smoking opportunities and the other with
a smoking ban. They did not find much success in smoking cessation, but they
interviewed the patients afterwards and found out that many did not appreciate
being made to quit cigarettes with their other drugs. They also did not like having to make a commitment to stop smoking and insisted that nicotine was different from other substances. As a result of input from their subject population,
the research team changed their approach and provided education and support
rather than restrictions to help patients make their own decisions about when
and how to quit.[63] Even within treatment programs, sometimes mentally ill
consumers have had different perspectives on how to frame assistance. A group
of nurses from London, Ontario, found to their surprise that schizophrenic
smokers said that they wanted to learn more distraction techniques rather than
the relaxation tools that are usually the focus of smoking cessation programs.[64]
Other research groups have incorporated peer support into programs so that
consumers feel that they can connect with people who have similar challenges.

But it remains difficult for anti-tobacco activists to allow mental-health
consumers to deal with the issue on their own terms. For example, in the somewhat ironically named CHOICES (Consumers Helping Others Improve their
Condition by Ending Smoking) program, the title reflects the tobacco-control
perspective that individuals cannot choose to smoke because they are addicted,
but can choose to quit smoking. There is really only one choice.[65] The program
uses peer support and endeavors to motivate grassroots-advocacy groups to
become interesting in smoking cessation.[66] Jill Williams, the energetic physician lead of the program (from the Robert Wood Johnson Medical School in
New Jersey), has also written educational materials for the National Alliance
for the Mentally Ill.[67] These are important initiatives, but they emerge more

from the tobacco-control movement than the mental-health consumer movement. And although they are trying to work from the ground up, they are also pushing their agenda from the top down to change the culture of smoking in spaces occupied by the mentally ill.[68]

A consumer approach to smoking cessation may look different primarily in its emphasis. As one peer counselor for CHOICES explained in a 2012 panel discussion, consumers who have been asked about smoking cessation want to place it within a comprehensive set of interventions that include attention to housing and financial issues.[69] And economics are certainly important within this and other disadvantaged populations.[70] One study team in Arizona was able to achieve what looked like fairly good smoking-cessation outcomes with a group of seriously mentally ill patients by giving them financial rewards for remaining abstinent from cigarettes. Although it turned out that some of the smokers manipulated the reward system (they quickly figured out how long they had to avoid cigarettes in order to have a lower expired carbon monoxide level, the measure for which they got the reward), the results encouraged the team to think that there might be something to this kind of approach.[71] Unfortunately, researchers who find that financial incentives can be helpful often conclude that the answer is better pharmaceutical intervention for smoking cessation among the mentally ill.[72] But those who have consulted with the targets of their interventions—people with mental illness—can come to different kinds of conclusions about what might work. It may not be helpful to nag mental-health consumers to quit or to push cessation in the form of pills.

It has become increasingly common for researchers in both psychiatric treatments and tobacco control to focus on numbers, populations, and disease burden. But a consumer perspective on the issue of smoking and mental illness reminds us that whether or not there is a pure biological connection between smoking and mental illness, there are clearly social, cultural, economic—and historical—factors involved. Many individuals with mental illness want to quit smoking, and they definitely deserve help. But it is also important for tobacco-control measures to take into account the broader context of the lives of individuals struggling with mental illness. Efforts to denormalize behaviors in individuals may further reinforce the idea that they themselves are not normal. Further, recovery for individuals with mental illness is a much bigger issue than just their consumption of cigarettes. Solutions will be complicated, especially within the current climate of corporate mentalities and their interest in health care.

Conclusion

Corporate Squeeze

In 1999, a North Carolina man wrote to R. J. Reynolds to request that the company assist him in becoming "a purchaser of cigarettes from your powerful industry." The man, who enclosed a letter from his community mental-health clinic verifying that he was diagnosed with schizophrenia, explained that he was not asking for a handout. Instead, he was asking for administrative help as he thought it made sense for him to earn a living by selling cigarettes. He claimed that his doctor, who was also a smoker, recommended this to him as an appropriate course of action.[1] This letter, written more than a quarter century after the 1964 surgeon general's report that clearly outlined the health consequences of smoking, highlights the special connection between mentally ill individuals and their cigarettes. It also illustrates that at least some identified themselves as consumers rather than just patients or victims of tobacco industry manipulation.

At present, the remaining high number of smokers who also have a mental illness has generated concern about the need to push smoking cessation and to address any ongoing influence of the tobacco industry. Many in the public-health community have rightly pointed out that the tobacco industry has worked in front of and behind the scenes to market, distribute, and research their products, and that cigarette companies know a great deal about their customers. But the tobacco companies are not the only ones to have a business interest in the number of residual smokers. In 2007, employees at Philip Morris sent around a *Wall Street Journal* article for discussion. This article outlined all the ways in which tobacco-control advocates had ties to the pharmaceutical industry and suggested that the industry had undue influence over antismoking policies in the United States.[2] The staff member who passed around the article did not comment on its content.

As historians and policy analysts have described, health care in the United States has been governed as much—if not more—by private business interests than government action or regulation. For better and for worse, the American political climate has been more accommodating to corporate priorities than other kinds of interests. And at least partly for this reason, many within health-care reform invoke the language of the free market—including competition and consumer choice—to further improve health systems.[3] We may view this as either a triumph or a tragedy depending on our political point of view. But what it has meant is that health care is oriented around a consumer model in which individuals purchase or pursue products based on perceived benefit. Even smoking cessation in general has worked in this way. For many in the general population who quit smoking in the 1970s, for example, they substituted a consumer goal of personal fitness (with attention to new foods and gym memberships) for their smoking behaviors.[4]

But as I described in chapter 8, the concept of the mental-health consumer is complicated and does not reflect the same power in the marketplace. Instead, individuals with mental illness are constrained in their choices. Today mentally ill smokers seem to be stuck between the tobacco industry and the pharmaceutical industry. Both corporate entities stand to gain from the increasing recognition of smoking among the mentally ill, though the industries are essentially competing for customers.[5] Medical and mental-health professionals are now active in pushing smoking-related diagnoses and cessation treatments, and many of those treatments benefit the pharmaceutical industry. Mentally ill smokers are treated like social pariahs and their smoking behaviors have become suspect as the cause of many (if not all) of their problems, even as they spend large proportions of their small incomes on cigarettes. Most discussions of smoking among mentally ill populations assume that they do not have agency to make their own decisions. And few of the many passionate advocates for smoking cessation among the mentally ill are working with consumer groups on a possible solution.

Tobacco Use Disorder

In May of 2013, the American Psychiatric Association published its new diagnostic system, *DSM-5*. In it, a new diagnosis appeared, "tobacco use disorder." Although this label had been originally proposed by Jerome Jaffe in the late 1970s, the authors of the most recent *DSM* emphasized that this was a new diagnosis, more comprehensive than its predecessor, nicotine dependence. Tobacco use disorder consists of eleven criteria, only two of which need to be present in order to make the diagnosis. The criteria range from craving cigarettes to smoking in dangerous situations (such as in bed) to arguments with others about quitting.[6] They also include tolerance and withdrawal. And although critics in the tobacco-control research field had proposed a more specific definition for a tobacco-related disorder that would be meaningful for assessment and treatment, the *DSM-5* diagnosis essentially captures everyone who smokes on a regular basis.[7]

As we have seen, the psychiatric diagnosis around smoking has been shaped by social, cultural, and professional factors. Ideally, a diagnostic label would be able to accurately describe a pattern of symptoms that rise to the level of a valid mental illness. Further, this label would signal a condition that responds to treatment regardless of what else is going on. But is a diagnosis meaningful if it entirely depends on context? Some of the smokers who meet current criteria for tobacco use disorder would not have met the cutoff for *DSM-III's* tobacco dependence, or even *DSM-IV's* nicotine dependence. Did they suddenly develop a mental illness in May of 2013? Even when diagnoses remain stable, individual situations do not. Studies of high-stress environments in the United States and other parts of the world suggest that people increase their use of cigarettes in the wake of trauma or overwhelming stress.[8] And if smoking can be conceptualized as a coping mechanism for some (albeit one less than optimal), is it a disease, too? The trend toward increasing capture of a range of behaviors as psychiatric diagnoses has reinforced a narrow, pathology-based description of some aspects of life that would never have been considered diseases in the past.[9] Psychiatrists have skirted the difficult question of whether it is valid to say that someone has a disease because he or she makes choices that have potentially negative consequences.

Smoking-related diagnoses have not only put a disease frame around behavior, but also taken on a significance in public-health circles that may have an unfortunate effect on psychiatric epidemiology and policy directions in mental health. If a diagnosis such as nicotine dependence or tobacco use disorder is included among mental illnesses in epidemiological research, the already inflated statistics of the prevalence of mental illness become even more distorted. The relationships between tobacco-related disorders and serious mental illness still need to be worked out in the big picture of mental-health policy. Some researchers have become so preoccupied with tobacco-related disorders that they view mental illnesses such as depression only as risk factors for nicotine dependence. For these investigators, it becomes important to treat depression as a way of intervening in the development of nicotine dependence.[10]

This is a complete about-face from just a few decades ago in which smoking appeared understandable for mentally ill patients because of their emotional, social, occupational, and financial issues.

What does the diagnosis of tobacco use disorder do for people? And does it help individuals with mental illness to have another diagnosis? Anti-tobacco scholars use the diagnoses around smoking to reinforce the idea that people who cannot quit smoking are dealing with a real addiction. But as Allan Brandt has pointed out, the issue of addiction is complicated: on the one hand, individuals are absolved from blame because they have an illness, but on the other they are expected to take responsibility for their behavior (including the addiction).[11] A diagnosis also externalizes the problem and can actually limit individuals' feelings of empowerment to address the issue.[12] Australian psychobiologist Dale Atrens commented in 2001 that calling smoking addictive does not necessarily help people quit: "As long as smoking is portrayed as an inexorable addictive process, the success of cessation programs will be limited by a self-fulfilling prophecy."[13] While the tobacco industry has a vested interest in insisting that smoking is not addictive (and they got Atrens to testify to that effect), the pharmaceutical industry is equally invested in promoting the view that patients need assistance in pill (or patch, gum, or inhaler) form in order to overcome their dependence on nicotine.

Pharmaceutical Company Interest

As the United States Food and Drug Administration began to gear up to regulate tobacco products in 2013, officers of the agency assembled a panel to discuss research issues and evidence. As has been their practice for decades, FDA officials invited members of the industry that was going to be regulated to offer their perspective. But tobacco-control experts cried foul and refused to participate. University of California, San Francisco tobacco researcher Ruth Malone sent a passionate open letter to the FDA to explain why she (and others) could not sit at the same table as representatives from the tobacco industry.[14] Malone emphasized that the goals of the tobacco industry were an anathema to public-health objectives.

It is understandable that tobacco-control activists would have an intense, negative reaction to anything put forward by the tobacco industry after all the revelations about the its actions over the last century. As a result of the industry's history of bad behavior, the opponents of tobacco vehemently oppose arguments that there could be good that comes from anything the tobacco companies ever did. But interestingly enough, some of the same people who are harshly critical of the actions of the tobacco industry and who dismiss any suggestion that mentally ill individuals find utility in smoking apparently have no difficulty embracing a position that is clearly beneficial to a different industry—pharma.[15] Tobacco-control advocates push for cessation for mentally ill smokers and promote treatment, including pharmaceutical products. And while tobacco-control experts criticized the FDA for inviting tobacco representatives to a discussion of how their industry was to be regulated, these experts have said nothing about the pharmaceutical company representatives who regularly participate in the regulation of smoking-cessation remedies.[16]

Physicians and other mental-health providers openly advocate for significant increase of medications for smoking cessation (over other interventions), as well as reduced regulation for "medicinal" forms of nicotine since they claim that the nicotine in cigarettes is more addictive and more toxic.[17] As authors (who disclosed relationships to multiple pharmaceutical companies, and one with a financial interest in a novel nicotine replacement product) explained in 2009, "All nicotine medications may not be equally interchangeable or effective across patients. A corollary is that not all nicotine delivery systems warrant similar regulatory and marketing restrictions; those with higher risks of abuse and dependence are appropriately regulated and marketed more restrictively."[18] In other words, their business does not need as much government oversight. And use of their products is listed in *DSM-5* to modify the severity of the diagnosis of tobacco use disorder.[19]

As has been the case for decades with regard to a variety of health issues, pharmaceutical-company connections to physicians help to structure physician-patient encounters.[20] In the area of smoking cessation, pharmaceutical companies have sponsored important conferences on nicotine dependence.[21] And the relationship between smoking cessation and the pharmaceutical industry has become so intertwined in the mental-health literature that it is difficult to find serious discussion about smoking and mental illness that does not link back in some way to pharma. For example, in 2005, the National Institute of Mental Health assembled a number of experts in smoking issues among the mentally ill. The group deplored the current lack of treatment for smoking and identified future research areas. At the end of the article, the authors listed their relationships with outside interests—three of the most important thought leaders in the field had multiple ties to pharmaceutical companies, including companies that were heavily invested in smoking-cessation remedies.[22]

But the pharmaceutical solution is not necessarily always a safe option. As numerous critics have pointed out in the last few years, pharmaceutical companies have engaged in drug trials with economically vulnerable subjects, pushed physicians to promote products, cultivated thought leaders, and hidden adverse events of their drugs.[23] We have only learned about some of these behaviors as a result of litigation in which internal industry documents were made available as part of the discovery process.[24] This sounds familiar—in fact, historian and psychopharmacologist David Healy has suggested that the pharmaceutical industry modeled itself on the tobacco industry in terms of purely self-interested corporate behavior.[25] Researchers promoting pharmaceutical products use the same kind of language to minimize risk by claiming that there is not adequate proof that the medications are harmful.[26] But we cannot afford to assume that just because a substance is prescribed by a doctor means that it is safe—there is a gigantic industry with billions of dollars riding on minimizing side effects of medications, and physicians in clinical practice are not good watchdogs to uncover these effects.[27]

It is challenging to determine what pharmaceutical agents—if any—can or should be used in mentally ill populations. There are not as many studies with mentally ill individuals (due to ethical problems in subject recruitment). Further, the studies that have been done are not particularly robust in their findings. Some investigative teams have published articles in which they pooled results from several studies in order to find any significance for smoking-cessation medications in mentally ill populations, while others use open-label studies or optimistically interpret what appears to be poor efficacy data.[28] These kinds of tactics have been identified as symptomatic of reporting bias in medical research, especially in the context of excessive pharmaceutical-company investment.[29] But despite tepid results regarding medications for smoking cessation in mentally ill populations, there has not been much criticism of these interventions by the tobacco-control field. And clinicians appear to have become convinced by the research that medications for smoking cessation are safe and appropriate among mentally ill patients, and they minimize risks to the patients.[30]

As Healy has pointed out, one of the ways in which pharmaceutical companies cultivate influence is through treatment guidelines.[31] This is not a new phenomenon. Historian Jeremy Greene described the process in which thought leaders in medical fields consulted with pharmaceutical companies and helped construct guidelines for treatment in hypertension, diabetes, and hypercholesterolemia without professional or public outcry in the last forty years.[32] But it has become increasingly obvious that pharmaceutical influence privileges medication approaches over other kinds of solutions. And it is clear that the thought leaders who author review articles on treatment for tobacco dependence (and who have connections to the pharmaceutical industry) emphasize medicinal remedies. For example, a 2009 *Canadian Journal of Psychiatry* outline of the issue of smoking in mental illness highlighted the pharmaceutical options (with some minor mention of other kinds of therapy). The side effects of the medications were minimized, while the problem of smoking-induced disease was emphasized. Two of the primary authors of the review acknowledged their relationships to pharmaceutical companies, including those in the business of marketing smoking-cessation therapies.[33]

Although numerous observers and critics have pointed out in the last few years that there is a major problem with the extent to which the pharmaceutical industry is controlling medical treatment in the United States, most of the literature on smoking and mental illness gives this industry a free ride.[34] Some may argue that there is more demonstrated danger in smoking than in pharmaceutical drugs. Indeed, authors (with acknowledged connections to pharma, including stock in smoking-cessation treatments) have made precisely this argument.[35] But there is growing awareness that some of the effects of modern psychiatric medications are detrimental to health, especially in causing obesity and diabetes. (And the pharmaceutical industry has, like the tobacco industry, disputed the alleged harms of its products until after litigation.)[36] But since medication side effects are also risk factors for cardiovascular illness (and increased mortality), it is interesting that pharmaceutical companies make a point of emphasizing smoking as the primary risk factor for heart disease.

The tobacco-control reaction against the tobacco industry, tobacco-related products, or even devices that look like cigarettes, has been productive in maintaining vigilance to detect problematic industry practices. But it may also have the effect of limiting options for mentally ill smokers. A few research teams recently suggested that the new nonburning nicotine device—the electronic cigarette (or e-cigarette)—might be a useful tool to help individuals reduce their consumption of cigarettes, even for those not intending to quit.[37] A toxicology analysis of e-cigarettes suggests that they do not seem to pose a risk to others (unlike conventional cigarettes).[38] But the anti-tobacco response to the e-cigarette has ranged from extreme caution to outright horror.[39] As Kirsten Bell and Helen Keane recently pointed out, the early versions of the e-cigarette, though manufactured by (Chinese) companies with neither tobacco or pharmaceutical industry connections, challenged the public-health binary of bad nicotine (that found in cigarettes or smokeless tobacco) and acceptable medicinal nicotine used only for smoking cessation.[40] And the recent entry to the e-cigarette market by traditional tobacco companies has resulted in condemnation by those in the tobacco-control field, even though users of the new device argued that it helped make them feel less ostracized in society.[41] The contentious nature of public-health reception to the e-cigarette illustrates how much judgment is embedded in discussions of smoking—in a way that affects mentally ill populations who already face public opprobrium.

It makes sense that experts in tobacco control and smoking cessation can and should define best practices and warn against more harmful ones. But does that mean that we have a right to force these practices on individuals with mental illnesses? Yale mental-health academics pointed out in 2001 that it is difficult to know how to safeguard autonomy and at the same time protect individuals from harm when encountering people on the margins of society. A health approach that treated people as though they were incapable of managing themselves was a throwback to old notions of controlling psychiatry. On the other hand, too libertarian an approach might leave these individuals entirely alone (and potentially at risk for harm).[42] Although the Yale academics were addressing the challenge of approaching a homeless population, this dilemma rings true for our current population of mentally ill smokers. And while smoking is a major health concern, the conversation about how to intervene needs to be placed in the context of mental-health professionals' historical use of power. Psychiatry, medicine in general, and science have undergone intense scrutiny when a group of professionals make the decision that they know what is best for subjects or patients. That kind of paternalism has been consistently rejected in recent decades. So should it apply to smokers with mental illness?

Who Speaks for Individuals with Mental Illness?

In the last decade or so, advocates for aggressive tobacco control have argued that the failure of mental-health providers to treat tobacco use as a problem is stigmatizing to people with mental illness. As they point out, it sends a terrible message that providers do not talk about long-term physical health when they treat their seriously mentally ill patients. Others have insisted that the reasons that providers have traditionally given for not addressing tobacco use in the mentally ill population—that they are self-medicating, that they have other (bigger) problems, that they don't really want to quit—are all myths.[43] Many advocacy groups that speak on behalf of the mentally ill endorse smoking cessation as an important goal to improve long-term physical health (though it is not necessarily with the same sense of urgency as tobacco-control groups).

But the issue of what to do about mentally ill smokers is not just about trying to protect health, it involves issues of power. Most tobacco-control advocates see no problem with instituting policies that essentially force individuals to quit smoking—increasing taxes or restricting the locations in which they can smoke. But for some individuals with mental illness, as Australian investigators found in 2002, smoking is about asserting the power to determine

their own lives in a small way. According to Australian researchers who interviewed people with schizophrenia, "the most striking feature of their decision
to continue smoking was the sense of freedom it gave in the presence of overwhelming powerlessness to predict or decide their own future. Smoking thus
became a vehicle for gaining more autonomy and exerting more control over
their lives."[44]

The tobacco-control movement does not really acknowledge the power
dynamic in the struggle to reduce smoking. Advocates are increasingly calling
for enforced abstinence while patients are hospitalized or placed in long-term
facilities or in public-housing communities, the rationale being that people
should have the benefits of better health when there is an opportunity.[45] According to the many who are passionately concerned about the deleterious effects
of smoking, there is no right to smoke—the idea of smokers' rights has been
dismissed as a fiction promoted by the tobacco industry.[46] But as the medical
director of the Connecticut Department of Mental Health Services pointed out
in 2008, the forced smoking cessation for individuals—such as those in long-
term psychiatric facilities—essentially discriminates against a class of individuals because they are mentally disabled. (If they were not, they would be able to
smoke in their homes and able to make their own decisions about their smoking
behaviors.) In the name of health, smoking bans in some settings take advantage
of mental-health consumers' relatively powerless position in society.[47]

Part of the disconnect between tobacco-control advocates and mentally
ill populations is that smoking is a single—and critically important—issue for
those in the tobacco-control field, while individuals with mental illness face a
wide variety of social, occupational, economic, and interpersonal challenges.
Smoking is only one of many health and quality of life concerns. Many people
with serious mental illness struggle to find gainful employment, have major
challenges in housing, and often have to scramble to get adequate food. Those
who are taking psychiatric medications also have to cope with often serious
side effects (including major weight gain). It is true that they are likely more
impoverished because of the money they spend on cigarettes, but many individuals have understandable difficulty seeing how quitting smoking could significantly affect many of their of their other issues.[48]

Further, the hope of future good health may not be particularly motivat-
ing for individuals struggling with difficult circumstances and with challenging illnesses. Some testimony from mentally ill patients suggests that patients'
attachment to their cigarettes overrides any concerns about their health. For
example, a New Hampshire woman wrote to RJR in 1985 explaining that she
was manic-depressive and that she had found her own cure for lung cancer. She

was experiencing chest pains and tried to quit smoking, but then felt worse. So she explained that she found her own cure because, "I liked my cigarettes and I wasn't going to quit for anybody. I also got tired of waiting for a cure with scientist[s] that work with lung cancer."[49] Apart from what might have been psychotic interpretations of the risks of smoking, other individuals with mental illness may be making a calculus that it makes less sense to do something in hopes of avoiding a vague, future negative outcome when it means giving up something that helps them get through their day.[50]

As mental-health policy experts have pointed out, treatment of the mentally ill has become increasingly fragmented in the last few decades because of structural changes and reimbursement issues. David Mechanic observed that modern mental-health structures never adequately compensated for care after the deinstitutionalization movement transitioned patients outside long-term hospitals. Community constraints have resulted in inadequate systems for the chronically mentally ill. Mental-health policy can barely deal with slashed state budgets, escalating medication costs, the fraying social safety net, and the revolving door of psychiatric hospitalizations.[51] For better or for worse, smoking may not seem to be a high priority for mental-health workers struggling to make sure their patients have food, clothing, and shelter. And while it is laudable to not lose sight of this issue, it also makes sense that advocates for people with mental illness should be trying to help them gain some of the basics in life, not just pushing them to quit smoking.

As the tobacco-control movement has intensified its crusade against smoking, the people who may be left stranded are the mentally ill—doubly marginalized from mainstream expectations of life progress and (if experts have their way) harassed to stop behaviors that society has now deemed unacceptable. Tobacco-control advocates have important goals, and there is a great deal of passion in the movement to reduce—or even eliminate—smoking in the United States (and other countries). But the methods to go about this may need to be different for some segments of the population. For example, it is important to solicit opinions from consumers and consumer groups regarding proposed tobacco-control policies as there are few mechanisms for this particular heterogeneous population to make their voices heard.[52]

And while it is essential to remain vigilant about the actions of the tobacco industry (since their track record in looking after the health of the population is abysmal), we also need to keep a careful eye on the pharmaceutical industry. They also have shareholders who are interested in profit and have been resistant (to say the least) to efforts to get them to participate in changes to their practice for the greater good. Consumers who are struggling with weight gain and metabolic issues while taking psychiatric medication have been told that they need to work harder to maintain a healthy lifestyle, including good food choices and exercise. For those who smoke, that is one more health burden to manage. Many public-health advocates have acknowledged the self-control challenges that individuals with mental illness experience with regard to reducing risk for illness. But instead of engaging strategies to empower these people, experts have focused more attention on the role the tobacco industry played in promoting cigarettes.[53] Yes, it makes sense to continue to monitor the tobacco industry to make sure that companies do not try to exploit this population. But there are other aspects around self-control that go beyond the reach of the tobacco companies. And mental-health consumers are more likely to target a different industry if they are going to assign blame since the pharmaceutical industry's practices have had an immediate (and often unfortunate) effect on their lives.[54]

Beyond questions of industry influence, we need to attend to the consumer aspects of the issue. From the perspective of the mental-health consumer movement, we should be working with individuals and groups to engage on their terms and ask about their priorities and suggestions for solutions.[55] An overemphasis on smoking restrictions may unintentionally exclude consumers whose input is needed to develop future interventions.[56] And defining smoking behavior as disease does not help. Individuals who have experienced mental illness have denied that they are only their illness or their diagnosis. As psychologist and consumer Patricia Deegan pointed out, identifying individuals as illnesses rather than people changes human interactions in a profoundly negative way. From that point of view, labeling consumers as "addicts" or as patients with "tobacco use disorder" diminishes their humanity and reduces them to labels or statistics.[57]

The idea of relationships may turn out to be much more important for the issue of smoking than most have recognized. Consumers have argued that they resent a top-down, hierarchical system in which physicians or other care providers dictate diagnosis and treatment—they want to be partners.[58] And in order to collaborate with consumers, providers and policy makers need to understand consumers' existing relationships—including their attachment to cigarettes. Maybe instead of language that emphasizes quitting, abstinence, absence—all of which imply loss—we could use metaphors in treatment that respect the role of cigarettes, smoking, nicotine. If the goal for tobacco-control advocates is better physical health among the mentally ill, then there might be ways to achieve this without imposing priorities, dictating treatment, or invalidating important (even if dysfunctional) relationships.

We also need to attend to economic issues. Most pharmacological options for smoking cessation are equally expensive—if not more so—than cigarettes themselves. Some options are available over the counter, which increases access but also puts the cost burden on consumers. The prescription-only products (including nicotine inhalers and nasal sprays) require individuals to meet with a physician and commit to a smoking-cessation program before they can begin (under many insurance policies). And sometimes consumers can only get these products for a short period of time.[59] The cost of prescription-only products is out of reach for those who do not have insurance. And all of these products are more expensive when purchased by the day (because of the quantities in the packages) than individual packs of cigarettes.

Would it make sense to consider other options or other methods? Although there are risks, would it result in overall less harm to encourage mentally ill smokers who are not interested in quitting or unable to accomplish conventional smoking cessation to switch to e-cigarettes? What about working with mental-health consumers on short-term behaviors instead of just long-range goals? For example, is it possible to make smoking-cessation products (such as patch, gum, inhalers) available to consumers in places and quantities and at prices that would let them make day-by-day decisions about smoking? And can the products be priced in such a way that they are an economical alternative to cigarettes when purchased in the same way that most smokers buy cigarettes (including one day at a time)?

If we really want to help smokers who have mental illnesses, it is imperative that we find a way to understand and incorporate their perspectives and the priorities. And that means trying to understand what they want—not just telling them what they want or insisting that they are wrong about why they do things. It is not a coincidence that so many discussions and arguments about smoking begin with a disclosure (or disqualifier) about whether the author is a smoker—there is something about having shared an experience that helps investigators understand how and why people struggle. The mental-health consumer movement was in part based on the idea that the experience of having had a mental illness gives someone more expertise to speak about it.[60] And that expertise can turn out to be valuable.[61]

As self-identified mental-health consumers have pointed out, there is a potential disconnect between the ways that mental-health providers define treatment outcomes and the ways that treatment is conceptualized among consumers.[62] And while some consumers do identify problems with smoking and endorse smoking-cessation interventions, they are not necessarily weighted in the same way as for anti-tobacco experts.[63] We need to broaden our perspective with this population to explore issues such as economics and psychosocial rehabilitation. We need to consider the strengths and capabilities of individuals rather than just focus on their illnesses and include the perspectives of people who face the challenges of mental illness.[64] We also need to develop programs that address their priorities and issues. Whatever we as a society choose to do, we need to respect that smokers who also have mental illness need to be empowered to live better lives—and that we cannot assume that we know what is best for them. We need to start a conversation, and really listen.

Notes

Introduction: Smoking Privileges

1. See for example, Karen Lasser et al., "Smoking and Mental Illness: A Population-Based Prevalence Study," *JAMA* 284 (2000): 2606–2610.
2. Kenneth E. Warner and David M. Burns, "Hardening and the Hard-Core Smoker: Concepts, Evidence, and Implications," *Nicotine & Tobacco Research* 5 (2003): 37–48.
3. For a masterful account of the rise and fall of the tobacco industry, see Allan M. Brandt, *The Cigarette Century: The Rise, Fall, and Deadly Persistence of the Product that Defined America* (New York: Basic Books, 2007). See also, Robert N. Proctor, *Golden Holocaust: Origins of the Cigarette Catastrophe and the Case for Abolition* (Berkeley: University of California Press, 2012); Richard Kluger, *Ashes to Ashes: America's Hundred-Year Cigarette War, the Public Health, and the Unabashed Triumph of Philip Morris* (New York: Alfred A. Knopf, 1996); and Philip J. Hilts, *Smoke Screen: The Truth Behind the Tobacco Industry Cover-Up* (New York: Addison Wesley Publishing Company, Inc., 1996).
4. For an overview, see Gerald N. Grob, *The Mad among Us: A History of the Care of America's Mentally Ill* (Cambridge: Harvard University Press, 1994). See also notes 7–10.
5. Kenneth E. Warner, ed. *Tobacco Control Policy* (San Francisco: Jossey-Bass, 2006).
6. See also, B. Poland et al., "The Social Context of Smoking: The Next Frontier in Tobacco Control?," *Tobacco Control* 15 (2006): 59–63.
7. Gerald N. Grob, *Mental Institutions in America: Social Policy to 1875* (New York: Free Press, 1973); Gerald N. Grob, *Mental Illness and American Society, 1875–1940* (Princeton: Princeton University Press, 1983); and Gerald N. Grob, *From Asylum to Community: Mental Health Policy in Modern America* (Princeton: Princeton University Press, 1991).
8. Nathan G. Hale Jr., *The Rise and Crisis of Psychoanalysis in the United States: Freud and the Americans, 1917–1985* (New York: Oxford University Press, 1995).
9. See for example, Allan V. Horwitz, *Creating Mental Illness* (Chicago: University of Chicago Press, 2002); Rick Mayes and Allan V. Horwitz, "DSM-III and the Revolution in the Classification of Mental Illness," *Journal of the History of the Behavioral Sciences* 41 (2005): 249–267.
10. Herb Kutchins and Stuart A. Kirk, *Making Us Crazy: DSM, The Psychiatric Bible and the Creation of Mental Disorders* (New York: Free Press, 1997). Allen Frances, the editor of *DSM-IV* (1994), has accepted some responsibility for the diagnostic bloating but deplores the current practice of diagnostic expansion. Allen Frances, letter to the editor, *New York Times*, 20 March 2013; Allen Frances, *Saving Normal: An Insider's Revolt against Out-of-Control Psychiatric Diagnosis, DSM-5, Big Pharma, and the Medicalization of Ordinary Life* (New York: HarperCollins, 2013).
11. For the history of substance use and addiction, see for example David T. Courtwright, *Forces of Habit: Drugs and the Making of the Modern World* (Cambridge, MA: Harvard University Press, 2002); Caroline Jean Acker, *Creating the American Junkie: Addition Research in the Classic Era of Narcotic Control* (Baltimore: Johns

Hopkins University Press, 2002); and Sarah W. Tracy, *Alcoholism in America: From Reconstruction to Prohibition* (Baltimore: The Johns Hopkins University Press, 2005). For the history of how smoking became perceived as an addiction, see Allan M. Brandt, "From Nicotine to Nicotrol: Addiction, Cigarettes, and American Culture," in *Altering American Consciousness: The History of Alcohol and Drug Use in the United States, 1800–2000,* ed. Sarah W. Tracy and Caroline Jean Acker (Amherst: University of Massachusetts Press, 2004), 383–402.

12. Alfred H. Stanton and Morris S. Schwartz, *The Mental Hospital: A Study of Institutional Participation in Psychiatric Illness and Treatment* (New York: Basic Books, 1954), 169.

13. For the classic formulation on the relationship between gender and power, see Joan W. Scott, "Gender: A Useful Category of Historical Analysis," *American Historical Review* 91 (1986): 1053–1075.

14. Nancy Tomes, "From Outsiders to Insiders: The Consumer-Survivor Movement and Its Impact on U.S. Mental Health Policy," in *Patients as Policy Actors,* ed. Beatrix Hoffman et al. (New Brunswick, NJ: Rutgers University Press, 2011), 113–131.

15. For a review of experiences of disability over time, including the rise of the disability-rights movement, see Kim E. Nielsen, *A Disability History of the United States* (Boston: Beacon Press, 2012).

16. On the potentially conflicting perspectives of public health and medicine, see Allan M. Brandt and Martha Gardner, "Antagonism and Accommodation: Interpreting the Relationship between Public Health and Medicine in the United States During the 20th Century," *American Journal of Public Health* 90 (2000): 707–715. For an overview of public-health approaches in general, see Dorothy Porter, *Health, Civilization and the State: A History of Public Health from Ancient to Modern Times* (London: Routledge, 1999).

17. http://legacy.library.ucsf.edu/.

18. For the origins of the tobacco-industry archive, see Stanton A. Glantz et al., *The Cigarette Papers* (Berkeley: University of California Press, 1996). For more on techniques used to search the archives, see for example, Ruth E. Malone and Edith D. Balback, "Tobacco Industry Documents: Treasure Trove or Quagmire?," *Tobacco Control* 9 (2000): 334–338.

19. For more perspective on complicated public-health issues, see for example, James Colgrove, Gerald Markowitz, and David Rosner, eds., *The Contested Boundaries of American Public Health* (New Brunswick, NJ: Rutgers University Press, 2008); Rosemary A. Stevens, Charles E. Rosenberg, and Lawton R. Burns, eds., *History and Health Policy in the United States: Putting the Past Back In* (New Brunswick: Rutgers University Press, 2006).

Chapter 1   Ecology of Smoking in Mental Hospitals through the 1970s

1. "Proceedings of the American Medico-Psychological Association," *American Journal of Insanity* 49 (1892): 216–316, quote from 269. For background on the importance of occupational therapy in mental hospitals, see Jennifer Laws, "Crackpots and Basket-Cases: A History of Therapeutic Work and Occupation," *History of the Human Sciences* 24 (2011): 65–81.

2. Gerald N. Grob and Howard H. Goldman, *The Dilemma of Federal Mental Health Policy: Radical Reform or Incremental Change?* (New Brunswick: Rutgers University Press, 2006); Gerald N. Grob, *Mental Illness and American Society, 1875–1940*

(Princeton: Princeton University Press, 1983); Gerald N. Grob, *From Asylum to Community: Mental Health Policy in Modern America* (Princeton: Princeton University Press, 1991); and Alec Campbell, "The Invisible Welfare State: Establishing the Phenomenon of Twentieth Century Veterans' Benefits," *Journal of Political and Military Sociology* 32 (2004): 249–267.

3. See for example, Patricia Ibbotson, *Eloise: Poorhouse, Farm, Asylum, and Hospital, 1839–1984* (Charleston, SC: Arcadia Publishing, 2002), 19–21.

4. See for example, Allan and Coreen Bookout to Ronnie Price, Lorillard Tobacco Company, Legacy Tobacco Documents Library (hereafter cited as LTDL) (Bates 87789312), http://legacy.library.ucsf.edu/tid/wfh21e00; Joe Brennan, "Shortage Revealed at Mount Alto and St. Elizabeths," *Washington Post*, 15 December 1944, 1–2.

5. See for example, *Standards for Hospitals and Clinics*, (Washington, DC: American Psychiatric Association, 1958); American Hospital Association, *Mental Health Services and the General Hospital: A Guide to the Development and Implementation of Mental Health Service Plans* (Chicago: American Hospital Association, 1970).

6. See for example, "American Medico-Psychological Association: Proceedings of the Seventy-Seventh Annual Meeting," *American Journal of Psychiatry* 78 (1921): 268–269; Walter E. Barton, *Administration in Psychiatry* (Springfield, IL: Charles C. Thomas, 1962), 216; and *Consolidated Standards Manual for Child, Adolescent, and Adult Psychiatric, Alcoholism, and Drug Abuse Facilities*, (Chicago: Joint Commission on Accreditation of Hospitals, 1981). For a similar conversation in a British context, see "Doctor Says Smoking May Have 'Therapeutic Value' for Hospital Patients," *The Guardian*, 4 July 1968.

7. See for example, Leo H. Bartemeier, "Eating and Working," *American Journal of Orthopsychiatry* 20 (1950): 634–640.

8. Harry Stack Sullivan, "Peculiarity of Thought in Schizophrenia," *American Journal of Psychiatry* 82 (1925): 21–86.

9. Robert B. McElroy, "Psychoneuroses, Combat-Anxiety Type," *American Journal of Psychiatry* 101 (1945): 517–520, quote from 518–519.

10. See for example, Sydney Brown and Marie Nyswander, "The Treatment of Masochistic Adults," *American Journal of Orthopsychiatry* 26 (1956): 351–364.

11. See for example, Lenore Boling and Carl Brotman, "A Fire-Setting Epidemic in a State Mental Health Center," *American Journal of Psychiatry* 132 (1975): 946–950.

12. Lee G. Sewall and Charles W. Grady, "Utilizing the Community as a Therapeutic Resource," *American Journal of Psychiatry* 108 (1951): 456–461.

13. Clarence G. Schulz, "An Individualized Psychotherapeutic Approach with the Schizophrenic Patient," *Schizophrenia Bulletin* 1 (1975): 46–69; Otto F. Ehrentheil and Walter E. Marchand, *Clinical Medicine and the Psychotic Patient* (Springfield, IL: Charles C. Thomas, 1960), 327. Psychiatrists also noted deliberate burning with cigarettes among patients who harmed themselves to deal with overwhelming feelings. Richard J. Rosenthal et al., "Wrist-Cutting Syndrome: The Meaning of a Gesture," *American Journal of Psychiatry* 128 (1972): 1363–1368.

14. Richard Dewey, "First Aid to the Newly Arriving Patient in the Public Hospital for Mental Diseases," *American Journal of Psychiatry* 90 (1933): 299–301, quote from 301.

15. Karl M. Bowman, "A Constructive Criticism of Certain Hospital Procedures," *American Journal of Psychiatry* 94 (1938): 1141–1152, quote from 1146.

16. A. Irving Hallowell, "Shabwan: A Dissocial Indian Girl," *American Journal of Orthopsychiatry* 8 (1938): 329–340.

17. C. H. Cahn, "The Use of Drugs in Group Therapy," *American Journal of Psychiatry* 107 (1950): 135–136, quote from 135.

18. Edward A. Strecker et al., "Psychiatric Studies in Medical Education. II. Neurotic Trends in Senior Medical Students," *American Journal of Psychiatry* 93 (1937): 1197–1229.

19. Frederick C. Redlich, "The Psychiatrist in Caricature: An Analysis of Unconscious Attitudes toward Psychiatry," *American Journal of Orthopsychiatry* 20 (1950): 560–571.

20. John S. Tamerin and Richard A. Eisinger, "Cigarette Smoking and the Psychiatrist," *American Journal of Psychiatry* 128 (1972): 1224–1229, quote from 1226.

21. On the expansion of psychologists' expertise in American society, see Ellen Herman, *The Romance of American Psychology: Political Culture in the Age of Experts* (Berkeley: University of California Press, 1995). On the role of psychologists and social workers in mental hospitals, see Grob, *From Asylum to Community,* 93–123. On some of the conflicts among psychologists and psychiatrists during this time period, see Roderick D. Buchanan, "Legislative Warriors: American Psychiatrists, Psychologists, and Competing Claims over Psychotherapy in the 1950s," *Journal of the History of the Behavioral Sciences* 39 (2003): 225–249.

22. On the history of social work, see John H. Ehrenreich, *The Altruistic Imagination: A History of Social Work and Social Policy in the United States* (Ithaca: Cornell University Press, 1985); Daniel J. Walkowitz, *Working with Class: Social Workers and the Politics of Middle-Class Identity* (Chapel Hill: University of North Carolina Press, 1999).

23. For a social-work assessment of patients at home, including their smoking habits, see for example, Mary Jane Manning and Betty Ann Glasser, "The Home Visit in the Treatment of Psychiatric Patients Awaiting Hospitalization: A Pilot Study," *Journal of Health and Social Behavior* 3 (1962): 97–104.

24. James L. Mursell, "Contributions to the Psychology of Nutrition, II: The Sucking Reaction as a Determiner of Food and Drug Habits," *Psychological Review* 32 (1925): 402–415, quote from 403.

25. R. C. Cowden and L. I. Ford, "Systematic Desensitization with Phobic Schizophrenics," *American Journal of Psychiatry* 119 (1962): 214–245.

26. David Kantor, "Intervention into Multiple Patterns of Insularity in a Custodially Organized Mental Hospital" (PhD diss., Brandeis University, 1963), 185–186.

27. Morris S. Schwartz, "Patient Demands in a Mental Hospital Context," *Psychiatry* 20 (1957): 249–261.

28. Saul Scheidlinger, "Social Group Work in Psychiatric Residential Settings: Panel, 1955," *American Journal of Orthopsychiatry* 26 (1956): 709–750, quote from 713.

29. On the history of nursing, see for example Barbara Melosh, *"The Physician's Hand": Work Culture and Conflict in American Nursing* (Philadelphia: Temple University Press, 1982); Susan M. Reverby, *Ordered to Care: The Dilemma of American Nursing, 1850–1945* (New York: Cambridge University Press, 1987); and Patricia D'Antonio, *American Nursing: A History of Knowledge, Authority, and the Meaning of Work* (Baltimore: Johns Hopkins University Press, 2010).

30. Alfred H. Stanton and Morris S. Schwartz, *The Mental Hospital: A Study of Institutional Participation in Psychiatric Illness and Treatment* (New York: Basic Books, 1954), 126.

31. See for example, Marion E. Kalkman, *Introduction to Psychiatric Nursing* (New York: McGraw-Hill, 1950), 218.

32. Charlotte Green Schwartz, "Problems for Psychiatric Nurses in Playing a New Role on a Mental Hospital Ward," in *The Patient and the Mental Hospital: Contributions of Research in the Science of Social Behavior,* ed. Milton Greenblatt, Daniel J. Levinson, and Richard H. Williams (Glencoe, IL: Free Press,1957), 402–426.

33. Joan J. Kyes and Charles K. Hofling, *Basic Psychiatric Concepts in Nursing,* 3rd ed. (Philadelphia: J. B. Lippincott, 1974), 400–401.

34. Cheryl Krasnick Warsh and Penny Tinkler, "In Vogue: North American and British Representations of Women Smokers in *Vogue,* 1920s–1960s," *Canadian Bulletin of Medical History* 24 (2007): 9–47.

35. Quote from Donna Vokaty, the psychiatric nurse supervisor at the Institute of Psychiatry of the Mount Sinai Hospital in New York. In M. Ralph Kaufman, ed. *The Psychiatric Unit in a General Hospital: Its Current and Future Role* (New York: International Universities Press,1965), 99.

36. Irving Kartus and Herbert J. Schlesinger, "The Psychiatric Hospital-Physician and His Patient," in Greenblatt, Levinson, and Williams, *The Patient and the Mental Hospital,* 286–299.

37. Doris L. Collins, "Process of the One-to-One Relationship," in *Psychiatric Nursing: Theory and Application,* ed. Lucille A. Joel and Doris L. Collins (New York: McGraw-Hill,1978), 130–154, quote from 142.

38. Alice M. Robinson, *The Psychiatric Aide: A Textbook of Patient Care* (Philadelphia: J. B. Lippincott, 1964), 81–82.

39. Walter H. Baer, "The Training of Attendants, Psychiatric Aides and Psychiatric Technicians," *American Journal of Psychiatry* 109 (1952): 291–295.

40. Lucille Hudlin McClelland, *Textbook for Psychiatric Technicians* (St. Louis: C. V. Mosby, 1967), 32.

41. Dolores E. Swatsley, *A Study of the Effectiveness of the Case Method in Teaching Interpersonal Relations to Psychiatric Aides* (New York: National League for Nursing, 1964), 34.

42. Morton M. Hunt, *Mental Hospital: A Vivid Insight into the World of the Mentally Disturbed* (New York: Pyramid Books, 1961), 76.

43. John E. Freeman, "A Comparison of the Attitudes of State Hospital Attendants toward Rules Which Affect Patient Activities" (master's thesis, University of Michigan, 1964).

44. Robinson, *The Psychiatric Aide,* 208.

45. Leonard Handler and Gerald Perlman, "The Attitudes of Patients and Aides toward the Role of the Psychiatric Aide," *American Journal of Psychiatry* 130 (1973): 322–325.

46. M. G. Jacoby et al., "A Study in Non-Restraint," *American Journal of Psychiatry* 115 (1958): 114–120, quote from 116.

47. Stanton and Schwartz, *The Mental Hospital,* 442–443.

48. For a slightly later perspective on this, see RenataTagliacozzo and Sally Vaughn, "Stress and Smoking in Hospital Nurses," *American Journal of Public Health* 72 (1982): 441–448.

49. George A. Barron, Pittsburgh, Pennsylvania, to R. J. Reynolds, 1 May 1937, LTDL (Bates 500717909), http://legacy.library.ucsf.edu/tid/oqf76a00.

50. Robert B. Ellsworth, *Nonprofessionals in Psychiatric Rehabilitation: The Psychiatric Aide and the Schizophrenic Patient* (New York: Appleton-Century-Crofts, 1968), 48.

51. Milton Greenblatt, Richard H. York, and Esther Lucile Brown, *From Custodial to Therapeutic Patient Care in Mental Hospitals: Explorations in Social Treatment* (New York: Russell Sage Foundation, 1955), 127.

52. Carol S. North, *Welcome, Silence: My Triumph over Schizophrenia* (New York: Simon and Schuster, 1987), 15, 106–107.

53. I do not have unpublished accounts of patient experiences. Although some may suggest that the published accounts I use to understand the perspective of individuals with mental illness are less authentic or representative of real experience than unpublished records, historian Joan Scott has pointed out that all narratives—published or unpublished—are constructed by authors. Joan W. Scott, "The Evidence of Experience," *Critical Inquiry* 17 (1991): 773–797. For individuals who write about their experiences with mental illness, the words (published or unpublished) are only an approximation of what is going on inside them.

54. I am greatly indebted to Gail Hornstein for compiling an exhaustive list of first-person narratives of mental illness that she has made available to any interested scholars. I found smoking references in almost all of the approximately one hundred narratives I was able to locate at my university's library. Thanks to an ongoing digitization project at the University of Michigan, I could perform key-word searches on these texts—this allowed me to easily locate references to cigarettes, smoking, and tobacco. For more analysis of psychiatric autobiographies, see Femi Oyebode, "Autobiographical Narrative and Psychiatry," *Advances in Psychiatric Treatment* 9 (2003): 265–271.

55. Race is underrepresented in these narratives. Historians who have written about African American psychiatric experiences have highlighted that conditions were much worse for those patients. See Ellen Dwyer, "Psychiatry and Race during World War II," *Journal of the History of Medicine & Allied Sciences* 61 (2006): 117–143. For a mid-century complaint about poor conditions for African American psychiatric patients, see for example, Ida Coole, "Chances for Recovery Very Slim in Most Mental Hospitals," *Afro-American*, 1 February 1947.

56. See for example, Vladimir Bukovsky, *To Build a Castle—My Life as a Dissenter*, trans. Michael Scammell (New York: Viking Press, 1979); Leonid Plyushch, *History's Carnival: A Dissident's Autobiography* (New York: Harcourt Brace Jovanovich, 1979).

57. See for example, Marion King, *The Recovery of Myself: A Patient's Experience in a Hospital for Mental Illness* (New Haven: Yale University Press, 1931), 86.

58. Lara Jefferson, *These Are My Sisters: A Journal from the Inside of Insanity* (New York: Anchor Books, 1975), 153–154. See also, Barbara Findlay, "Shrink! Shrank! Shriek!," in *Women Look at Psychiatry*, ed. Dorothy E. Smith and Sara J. David (Vancouver: Press Gang, 1975), 70.

59. See Bowman, "A Constructive Criticism of Certain Hospital Procedures."

60. Marion Marle Woodson, *Behind the Door of Delusion by "Inmate Ward 8"* (New York: Macmillan, 1932), 78, 175.

61. Frances Farmer, *Will There Really Be a Morning?* (New York: G. P. Putnam's Sons, 1972), 103.

62. Alexander King, *Mine Enemy Grows Older* (New York: Simon and Schuster, 1958), 37–38.

63. See for example, Lawrence M. Jayson, *Mania* (New York: Funk & Wagnalls, 1937), 120.

64. Elsa Krauch, *A Mind Restored: The Story of Jim Curran* (New York: G. P. Putnam's Sons, 1937), 118–119.
65. See for example, Woodson, *Behind the Door of Delusion*, 50; Ellen C. Philtine, *They Walk in Darkness* (New York: Liveright, 1945), 21–22.
66. Albert Deutsch, *The Shame of the States* (New York: Harcourt, Brace and Company, 1948), 69.
67. Woodson, *Behind the Door of Delusion*, 259.
68. Krauch, *A Mind Restored*, 118–119.
69. Patients at Ypsilanti State Hospital were offered a reward of a package of cigarettes for completing a puzzle in the patient newspaper. *Ypsilanti Slants*, Autumn 1940, Bentley Historical Library, University of Michigan, Ann Arbor, MI.
70. See for example, Paul Hackett, *The Cardboard Giants* (New York: G. P. Putnam's Sons, 1952), 63–64, 110; David Reville, "Don't Spyhole Me," in *Shrink Resistant: The Struggle against Psychiatry in Canada*, ed. Bonnie Burstow and Don Weitz (Vancouver: New Star Books, 1988), 157–196.
71. See for example, Kate Millet, *The Loony-Bin Trip* (New York: Simon and Schuster, 1990), 92.
72. King, *Mine Enemy Grows Older*, 335–336.
73. Philtine, *They Walk in Darkness.* Information on Philtine's real identity from Deutsch, *The Shame of the States*, 145.
74. See for example, Margaret Gibson, *The Butterfly Ward* (New York: Vanguard Press, 1980), 7.
75. One mental hospital staff member wrote to R. J. Reynolds in 1989 to request that they lower the price of one of the brands of its cigarettes so that he could continue to buy cigarettes for patients. See Letter to R. J. Reynolds, 3 May 1989, LTDL (Bates 523521156), http://legacy.library.ucsf.edu/tid/xtr97c00.
76. On the history of inebriate hospitals in the early twentieth century, see Sarah W. Tracy, *Alcoholism in America: From Reconstruction to Prohibition* (Baltimore: The Johns Hopkins University Press, 2005). For an example of a patient who eventually landed in a psychiatric hospital, see Beth Day, *No Hiding Place* (New York: Henry Holt, 1957).
77. William Seabrook, *Asylum* (New York: Harcourt, Brace and Company, 1935).
78. Robert Thomsen, *Bill W.* (New York: Harper & Row, 1975), 230. Although Bill did not apparently discuss addiction to cigarettes as an issue, subsequent historians and tobacco analysts have been more critical. For example, biographer Susan Cheever speculated on the role of addiction to cigarettes in Bill's life and pointed out that he died from emphysema. Susan Cheever, *My Name is Bill: Bill Wilson—His Life and the Creation of Alcoholics Anonymous* (New York: Simon & Schuster, 2004).
79. Patricia Kent, *An American Woman and Alcohol* (New York: Holt, Rinehart and Winston, 1967), 44.
80. Fritz Peters, *The World Next Door* (New York: Farrar Straus, 1949), 20, 172–182.
81. King, *Mine Enemy Grows Older*, 291.
82. Joanne Greenberg, *I Never Promised You a Rose Garden* (New York: Signet, 1964), 116.
83. Barbara O'Brien, *Operators and Things: The Inner Life of a Schizophrenic* (South Brunswick: A. S. Barnes and Company, 1958), 39.
84. Sue E. Estroff, *Making It Crazy: An Ethnography of Psychiatric Clients in an American Community* (Berkeley: University of California Press, 1981), 21.

85. E. Robert Sinnett, "The Diary of a Schizophrenic Man," in *The Inner World of Mental Illness: A Series of First-Person Accounts of What It Was Like,* ed. Bert Kaplan (New York: Harper and Row, 1964), 196.

86. See for example, Elyn R. Saks, *The Center Cannot Hold* (New York: Hyperion, 2007), 31.

87. Erving Goffman, *Asylums: Essays on the Social Situation of Mental Patients and Other Inmates* (Chicago: Aldine, 1961), 281–282.

88. Frank M. LeBar, "Some Implications of Ward Structure for Enculturation of Patients," in *The Psychiatric Hospital as a Social System,* ed. Albert F. Wessen (Springfield, IL: Charles C. Thomas,1961), 5–19.

89. Robert Goulet, *Madhouse* (Chicago: J. Philip O'Hara, 1973), 44. (This is not the actor.)

90. Carol Allen and Herbert S. Lustig, *Tea with Demons* (New York: William Morrow and Company, 1985), 217.

91. Mary Jane Ward, *The Snake Pit* (New York: Random House, 1946), 76, 116–117. For biographical information on Ward, see Leslie Fishbein, "*The Snake Pit* (1948): The Sexist Nature of Sanity," *American Quarterly* 31 (1979): 641–665.

92. John White, *Ward N-1* (New York: A. A. Wyn, 1955), 26.

93. Carol Hebald, *The Heart Too Long Suppressed: A Chronicle of Mental Illness* (Boston: Northeastern University Press, 2001), 138–139.

94. Karoselle Washington, "The Killing Floors," in *In the Realms of the Unreal: "Insane" Writings,* ed. John G. H. Oakes (New York: Four Walls Eight Windows, 1991), 48–49.

95. Arthur Woolson, *Good-by, My Son* (New York: Harper & Brothers, 1960), 67, 98.

96. Janet Gotkin and Paul Gotkin, *Too Much Anger, Too Many Tears: A Personal Triumph over Psychiatry* (New York: Quadrangle, 1975), 351.

97. Peter W. Denzer, *Episode: A Record of Five Hundred Lost Days* (New York: E. P. Dutton & Co., 1954).

98. Eric Hodgins, *Episode: Report on the Accident inside My Skull* (New York: Atheneum, 1964), 235.

99. Clare Mare Wallace, *Portrait of a Schizophrenic Nurse* (London: Hammond, Hammond and Company, 1965), 43, 58, 87.

100. Gibson, *The Butterfly Ward,* 12.

101. Denzer, *Episode,* 218.

102. Sarah Ferguson, *A Guard Within* (New York: Pantheon, 1973), 113–114.

103. Catherine York, *If Hopes Were Dupes* (London: Hutchinson, 1966), 52.

104. Greenberg, *I Never Promised You a Rose Garden,* 45, 174, 185.

105. The bad psychiatrist tried to achieve rapport with Deborah in the movie by saying that he heard she was a smoker. She used the cigarettes he gave her to burn herself.

106. Gail A. Hornstein, *To Redeem One Person Is to Redeem the World* (New York: Free Press, 2000), 255–264.

107. Joyce MacIver, *The Frog Pond* (New York: George Braziller, 1961), 36.

108. Laura Rhodes and Lucy Freeman, *Chastise Me with Scorpions* (New York: G. P. Putnam's Sons, 1964), 192. See also, Hackett, *The Cardboard Giants,* 38, 255; Russell K. Hampton, *The Far Side of Despair: A Personal Account of Depression* (Chicago: Nelson-Hall, 1975), 47.

109. Sara Fraser, *Living with Depression—and Winning* (Wheaton, IL: Tyndale House, 1975), 11.

110. Al Siebert, *Peaking Out: How My Mind Broke Free from the Delusions in Psychiatry* (Portland, OR: Practical Psychology Press, 1995), 206, 212, 267.

111. Janet Frame, *Faces in the Water* (London: The Women's Press, 1980), 109.

112. Woolson, *Good-by, My Son*, 22.

113. Farmer, *Will There Really Be a Morning?*, 136.

114. See for example, Judi Chamberlin, *On Our Own: Patient-Controlled Alternatives to the Mental Health System* (New York: Hawthorn Books, 1978), 122; Hebald, *The Heart Too Long Suppressed*, 88, 225.

115. On the origins of the idealized environment in the nineteenth century, see Nancy Tomes, *The Art of Asylum-Keeping: Thomas Story Kirkbride and the Origins of American Psychiatry* (Philadelphia: University of Pennsylvania Press, 1994).

Chapter 2   Conflict and Smoking in Mental Hospitals in the 1960s and 1970s

1. Michael E. Staub, *Madness Is Civilization: When the Diagnosis Was Social, 1948–1980* (Chicago: University of Chicago Press, 2011); Norman Dain, "Psychiatry and Anti-Psychiatry in the United States," in *Discovering the History of Psychiatry*, ed. Mark S. Micale and Roy Porter (New York: Oxford University Press, 1994), 415–444. For criticism of medical authority in general in this time period, see Paul Starr, *The Social Transformation of American Medicine* (New York: Basic Books, 1982), 379–419.

2. The film *The Ninth Configuration* (1980), which is loosely based on a book by William Blatty, used smoking by inmates of the house in which the action takes place in order to help the viewer understand that the men are mental patients. The inmates of the asylum do not sit around and smoke in the book (though the main character, who becomes progressively more mentally disturbed, does). William Peter Blatty, *Twinkle, Twinkle, "Killer" Kane* (New York: Signet, 1966).

3. For the policy changes that further worsened financial issues for this population, see Gerald N. Grob, *From Asylum to Community: Mental Health Policy in Modern America* (Princeton: Princeton University Press, 1991); Gerald N. Grob, "The Paradox of Deinstitutionalization," *Society* 32 (1995): 51–59; and Gerald N. Grob and Howard H. Goldman, *The Dilemma of Federal Mental Health Policy: Radical Reform or Incremental Change?* (New Brunswick: Rutgers University Press, 2006).

4. Ken Kesey did not include the cigarette fragment interchange in the novel, though the men did bet cigarettes. Ken Kesey, *One Flew over the Cuckoo's Nest* (New York: Viking Critical Edition, 1996 [originally published in 1962]), 76–79).

5. Laura Rhodes and Lucy Freeman, *Chastise Me with Scorpions* (New York: G. P. Putnam's Sons, 1964), 20, 48.

6. Mindy Lewis, *Life Inside: A Memoir* (New York: Atria Books, 2002), 26.

7. Malcolm B. Bowers Jr., *Retreat from Sanity: The Structure of Emerging Psychosis* (New York: Human Sciences Press, 1974), 146.

8. Fritz Peters, *The World Next Door* (New York: Farrar Straus, 1949), 145–146.

9. Carney Landis and Fred A. Mettler, *Varieties of Psychopathological Experience* (New York: Holt, Rinehart and Winston, 1964), 93.

10. W. S. Stewart, *The Divided Self: The Healing of a Nervous Disorder* (New York: Hillary House, 1964), 155, 158, 164.

11. Wanda Martin, *Woman in Two Worlds: A Personal Story of Psychological Experience* (Norwalk, CT: Silvermine Publishers, 1966), 38.

12. Janet Frame, *Faces in the Water* (London: The Women's Press, 1980), 91. On Frame's explanation for how much of this novel was based on personal experience, see Janet Frame, *An Angel at My Table: An Autobiography, Volume Two* (New York: George Braziller, 1984), 73.

13. Robert Goulet, *Madhouse* (Chicago: J. Philip O'Hara, 1973), 120–121.

14. John Balt, *By Reason of Insanity* (New York: New American Library, 1966), 9, 15–16.

15. Ibid., 141–142.

16. See for example, Alton Brea, *Half a Lifetime* (New York: Vantage Press, 1968), 75, 88; Joseph J. Partyka, *Never Come Early: A Psychological Autobiographical Case History in Novel Form* (Mountain View, CA: J. Partyka, 1968), 43, 59, 83.

17. Bowers, *Retreat from Sanity*, 70.

18. See for example, Roxanne Lanquetot, "First Person Account: Confessions of the Daughter of a Schizophrenic," *Schizophrenia Bulletin* 10 (1984): 467–471; Bertha Peters Piercey, "First Person Account: Making the Best of It," *Schizophrenia Bulletin* 11 (1985): 155–157.

19. Arthur Woolson, *Good-by, My Son* (New York: Harper & Brothers, 1960), 79.

20. Sarah E. Lorenz, *And Always Tomorrow* (New York: Holt, Rinehart and Winston, 1963), 238.

21. Betty Hyland, "First Person Account: A Thousand Cloudy Days," *Schizophrenia Bulletin* 17 (1991): 539–545.

22. David Reed, *Anna* (New York: Basic Books, 1976), 49.

23. In one essay by a mentally ill man who worked at a self-help center there was a brief discussion of this. The author and some peers recalled a man who used to get into their faces about cigarettes—they heard that he died of cancer. Stephen B. Wyde, "He Was Still Alive," in *In the Realms of the Unreal: "Insane" Writings*, ed. John G. H. Oakes (New York: Four Walls Eight Windows, 1991), 6–7. This subject did not appear often, however.

24. On LSD in psychiatric research, see Erika Dyck, *Psychedelic Psychiatry: LSD from Clinic to Campus* (Baltimore: Johns Hopkins University Press, 2008).

25. Harold Massoon, "Gates of Eden," in *Exploring Madness: Experience, Theory, and Research*, ed. James Fadiman and Donald Kewman (Monterey, CA: Brooks/Cole, 1973), 45–46.

26. See for example, a letter from a man to R. J. Reynolds in which he explained that smoking helped reduce side effects from Trilafon (an antipsychotic medication). Donald Hagen to R. J. Reynolds, 15 November 1987, LTDL (Bates 507707054/7055), http://legacy.library.ucsf.edu/tid/jiy14d00.

27. Lenny Bruce, "So Who's Deviant," in *In Their Own Behalf: Voices from the Margin*, ed. Charles H. McCaghy, James K. Skipper Jr., and Mark Lefton, 2nd ed. (New York: Appleton-Century-Crofts, 1974), 7.

28. Ralph G. Walton, "Smoking and Alcoholism: A Brief Report," *American Journal of Psychiatry* 128 (1972): 1455–1456.

29. H. Brian McNamee, Nancy K. Mello, and Jack H. Mendelson, "Experimental Analysis of Drinking Patterns of Alcoholics: Concurrent Psychiatric Observation," *American Journal of Psychiatry* 124 (1968): 1063–1069.

30. John S. Tamerin and Jack H. Mendelson, "The Psychodynamics of Chronic Inebriation: Observations of Alcoholics during the Process of Drinking in an Experimental Group Setting," *American Journal of Psychiatry* 125 (1969): 886–899.

31. John S. Tamerin et al., "Alcohol and Memory: Amnesia and Short-Term Memory Function during Experimentally Induced Intoxication," *American Journal of Psychiatry* 127 (1971): 1659–1664, quote from 1660.

32. Military psychiatrists found behavioral techniques particularly useful within their highly structured settings. See for example, Arthur D. Colman and Stewart L. Baker Jr., "Utilization of an Operant Conditioning Model for the Treatment of Character

and Behavior Disorders in a Military Setting," *American Journal of Psychiatry* 125 (1969): 1395–1403.

33. See Robert Paul Liberman, "Behavioral Modification of Schizophrenia: A Review," *Schizophrenia Bulletin* 6 (1972): 37–48. For more background on the conflict in psychiatry between those with a psychoanalytic bent and those with other priorities, see Edward Shorter, *A History of Psychiatry: From the Era of the Asylum to the Age of Prozac* (New York: John Wiley & Sons, 1997).

34. Although Pavlov's classic experiments are popularly believed to involve a bell, he apparently did not actually use a bell. For a definitive account of Pavlov's work, see Daniel P. Todes, *Pavlov's Physiology Factory: Experiment, Interpretation, Laboratory Enterprise* (Baltimore: Johns Hopkins University Press, 2002). Thank you to Professor Todes for enlightening me about the bell.

35. On Skinner's debt to Pavlov, see A. Charles Catania and Victor G. Laties, "Pavlov and Skinner: Two Lives in Science," *Journal of the Experimental Analysis of Behavior* 72 (1999): 455–461.

36. For a history of behavior theorist B. F. Skinner, see Alexandra Rutherford, *Beyond the Box: B. F. Skinner's Technology of Behaviour from Laboratory to Life, 1950s–1970s* (Toronto: University of Toronto Press, 2009).

37. T. Ayllon, E. Haughton, and H. B. Hughes, "Interpretation of Symptoms: Fact or Fiction?," *Behavior Research and Therapy* 3 (1965): 1–7. The behavioral therapists were criticized in turn for not talking to their patients about what their behaviors meant. See Gerald C. Davison, "Appraisal of Behavior Modification Techniques with Adults in Institutional Settings," in *Behavior Therapy: Appraisal and Status,* ed. Cyril M. Franks (New York: McGraw-Hill, 1969), 220–278.

38. Ogden R. Lindsley, "Operant Conditioning Methods Applied to Research in Chronic Schizophrenia," *Psychiatric Research Reports* 5 (1956): 118–139. On Lindsley's debt to Skinner to set up this research, see Rutherford, *Beyond the Box,* 49–52.

39. Wayne Isaacs, James Thomas, and Israel Goldiamond, "Application of Operant Conditioning to Reinstate Verbal Behavior in Psychotics," *Journal of Speech and Hearing Disorders* 25 (1960): 8–12. One of these patients did not respond when cigarettes were waved in front of his face, but he did show some interest at the sight of gum.

40. W. C. Holz, N. H. Azrin, and T. Ayllon, "Elimination of Behavior of Mental Patients by Response-Produced Extinction," *Journal of the Experimental Analysis of Behavior* 6 (1963): 407–412.

41. Teodoro Ayllon and Nathn Azrin, *The Token Economy: A Motivational System for Therapy and Rehabilitation* (New York: Appleton-Century-Crofts, 1968).

42. Robert S. Ruskin and Roger F. Maley, "Item Preference in a Token Economy Ward Store," *Journal of Applied Behavior Analysis* 5 (1972): 373–378; John M. Atthowe Jr. and Leonard Krasner, "Preliminary Report on the Application of Contingent Reinforcement Procedures (Token Economy) on a 'Chronic' Psychiatric Ward," *Journal of Abnormal Psychology* 4 (1968): 37–43.

43. See for example, Charles A. Stenger and Cecil P. Peck, "Token-Economy Programs in the Veterans Administration," *Hospital and Community Psychiatry* 21 (1970): 371–375; Robert P. Liberman et al., "Behavior Therapy in State Hospitals," in *The Future Role of the State Hospital,* ed. Jack Zusman and Elmer F. Bertsch (Lexington, MA: Lexington Books, 1975), 157–189.

44. Thomas J. Crowley, "Token Programs in an Acute Psychiatric Hospital," *American Journal of Psychiatry* 132 (1975): 523–528.

45. Melvyn Hollander and Henry Glickman, "Cooperation Training in Schizophrenics," *Behavior Therapy* 7 (1976): 696–697.

46. See Arnold M. Ludwig, "Responsibility and Chronicity: New Treatment Models for the Chronic Schizophrenic"; T. Ayllon, "Toward a New Hospital Psychiatry," in *The New Hospital Psychiatry*, ed. Gene M. Abroms and Norman S. Greenfield (New York: Academic Press, 1971), 237–260, 275–287.

47. Stanley I. Greenspan, "The Clinical Use of Operant Learning Approaches: Some Complex Issues," *American Journal of Psychiatry* 131 (1974): 852–857.

48. Sam R. Alley et al., *Case Studies of Mental Health Paraprofessionals: Twelve Effective Programs* (New York: Human Sciences Press, 1979), 197.

49. On excessive smoking as a negative behavior to address, see for example, John Curran, Sonita Jorud, and Naomi Whitman, "Unconventional Treatment of Treatment-Resistant Hospitalized Patients," *Psychiatric Quarterly* 45 (1971): 187–208.

50. Richard L. Hagen, "Behavioral Therapies and the Treatment of Schizophrenics," *Schizophrenia Bulletin* 1 (1975): 70–96, quote from 90. Some did question the ethical issues around behavioral therapy in mental hospitals, however. See Zachary M. Schrag, *Ethical Imperialism: Institutional Review Boards and the Social Sciences, 1965–2009* (Baltimore: Johns Hopkins University Press, 2010), 39.

51. On the criticism of behavioral studies in coercive settings, see Alexandra Rutherford, "The Social Control of Behavior Control: Behavior Modification, 'Individual Rights,' and Research Ethics in America, 1971–1979," *Journal of the History of the Behavioral Sciences* 42 (2006): 203–220.

52. On behavioral therapy for smoking cessation, see for example, Douglas A. Bernstein, "Modification of Smoking Behavior: An Evaluative Review," *Psychological Bulletin* 71 (1969): 418–440; Gordon L. Paul, "Outcome of Systematic Desensitization I: Background, Procedures, and Uncontrolled Reports of Individual Treatment," in Franks, *Behavior Therapy*, 63–104.

53. Victor Milstein to Frederic Nordsiek, Council for Tobacco Research, 23 June 1972, LTDL (Bates 50196823/6824), http://legacy.library.ucsf.edu/tid/xkc79c00; R. C. Hockett Memo, 22 March 1973, LTDL (Bates 50196800/6800), http://legacy.library.ucsf.edu/tid/ylc79c00.

54. See for example, John A. Menninger, "Letter to the Editor: Tobacco Dependence and Smoke-free Psychiatric Units," *Western Journal of Medicine* 155 (1991): 519, copy in LTDL (Bates 508149688), http://legacy.library.ucsf.edu/tid/vu104d00.

55. James McGee, "Inpatient Cognitive Behavioral Therapy," in *Modern Hospital Psychiatry*, ed. John R. Lion, Wolfe N. Adler, and William L. Webb Jr. (New York: W. W. Norton, 1988), 136–168. See also, Breda Kingston, *Psychological Approaches in Psychiatric Nursing* (London: Croom Helm, 1989), 64.

56. Some within the hospital system understood that there were problems with authoritarian practices and sought to address this. See Grob, *From Asylum to Community*, 139–146.

57. Staub, *Madness Is Civilization*; Dain, "Psychiatry and Anti-Psychiatry in the United States."

58. See for example, R. D. Laing, *Wisdom, Madness and Folly: The Making of a Psychiatrist, 1927–1957* (London: Macmillan, 1985).

59. For a historian's criticism of the control of institutions, see for example, David J. Rothman, *The Discovery of the Asylum: Social Order and Disorder in the New Republic*, rev. ed. (Boston: Little, Brown and Company, 1990). For more information on Goffman and other critics in the context of the 1960s, see Gerald N. Grob, "The History

of the Asylum Revisited: Personal Reflections," in Micale and Porter, *Discovering the History of Psychiatry*, 260–281.

60. Erving Goffman, *Asylums: Essays on the Social Situation of Mental Patients and Other Inmates* (Chicago: Aldine, 1961), 44.

61. Morris S. Schwartz, "Patient Demands in a Mental Hospital Context," *Psychiatry* 20 (1957): 249–261, quote from 253.

62. Robert Perrucci, *Circle of Madness: On Being Insane and Institutionalized in America* (Englewood Cliffs, NJ: Prentice-Hall, 1974), 53.

63. Eric Hodgins, *Episode: Report on the Accident inside My Skull* (New York: Atheneum, 1964), 134–135.

64. Clare Mare Wallace, *Thank You, Mr. Freud* (London: Hammond, 1966), 50–51, 126–127.

65. Alfred H. Stanton and Morris S. Schwartz, *The Mental Hospital: A Study of Institutional Participation in Psychiatric Illness and Treatment* (New York: Basic Books, 1954), 284.

66. Goffman, *Asylums*, 141.

67. Jack R. Ewalt, "The Mental Health Message," *American Journal of Psychiatry* 121 (1964): 417–421.

68. Maryonda Scher and Merlin H. Johnson, "Divergent Staff Attitudes Spark a Ward Revolt," *Mental Hospitals* 14 (1963): 492–494.

69. Leo H. Berman, letter to the editor, *Mental Hospitals* 14 (1963): 662.

70. Paul S. Appelbaum, *Almost a Revolution: Mental Health Law and the Limits of Change* (New York: Oxford University Press, 1994); Nancy Tomes, "The Patient as a Policy Factor: A Historical Case Study of the Consumer/Survivor Movement in Mental Health," *Health Affairs* 25 (2006): 720–729.

71. Francesca Kress, "Evaluations of Dangerousness," *Schizophrenia Bulletin* 5 (1979): 211–217, quote from 212.

72. For the problematic history of Wiseman's film, see Carolyn Anderson and Thomas W. Benson, *Documentary Dilemmas: Frederick Wiseman's Titicut Follies* (Carbondale: Southern Illinois University Press, 1991).

73. Douglas P. Biklen, "Behavior Modification in a State Mental Hospital: A Participant-Observer's Critique," *American Journal of Orthopsychiatry* 46 (1976): 53–61, quote from 60.

74. Carla McKague, preface, in *Shrink Resistant: The Struggle against Psychiatry in Canada*, ed. Bonnie Burstow and Don Weitz (Vancouver: New Star Books, 1988), 17. See also, Fran Garber, "Mad Familiar Shorthand on the Wall," in *Voices From the Asylum*, ed. Michael Glenn (New York: Harper, 1974), 106–119.

75. Lewis, *Life Inside*, 119.

76. Helen Moeller, *Tornado: My Experience with Mental Illness* (Westwood, NJ: Fleming H. Revell, 1967), 68.

77. Goffman, *Asylums*, 48–54.

78. Ann Roy, "Escape," in *Madness Network News Reader*, ed. Sherry Hirsch et al. (San Francisco: Glide Publications, 1974), 21.

79. "It Was an Eighteenth Century Horror Show!," in *Women Look at Psychiatry*, ed. Dorothy E. Smith and Sara J. David (Vancouver: Press Gang, 1975), 48.

80. Bruce J. Ennis, *Prisoners of Psychiatry: Mental Patients, Psychiatrists, and the Law* (New York: Harcourt Brace Jovanovich, 1972), 112.

81. Walter C. Alvarez, *Minds That Came Back* (Philadelphia: J. B. Lippincott, 1961), 227.

82. Peters, *The World Next Door*, 282–283. See also, Robert E. Dahl, "On Entering a Mental Hospital," in McCaghy, Skipper, and Lefton, *In Their Own Behalf*, 201–210.

83. See for example, Lorenz, *And Always Tomorrow*, 98–99; Ellen Wolfe, *Aftershock: The Story of a Psychotic Episode* (New York: G. P. Putnam's Sons, 1969), 14.

84. John C. Belcher, "Background Norms of Patients and the Therapeutic Community," *Journal of Health and Human Behavior* 6 (1965): 27–35.

85. Ennis, *Prisoners of Psychiatry*, 71–72.

86. Donald N. Bersoff, "Bruce J. Ennis: A Remembrance," *Law and Human Behavior* 25 (2001): 663–665. For the broader movement to change civil commitment among the mentally ill, see Appelbaum, *Almost a Revolution*.

87. Phyllis Chesler, *Women & Madness* (New York: Avon Books, 1972). For the classic argument about the relationship between gender and power, see Joan W. Scott, "Gender: A Useful Category of Historical Analysis," *American Historical Review* 91 (1986): 1053–1075. For more on the historical overlap between women's issues and mental health, see Nancy Tomes, "Historical Perspectives on Women and Mental Illness," in *Women, Health, and Medicine in America*, ed. Rima D. Apple (New York: Garland Publishing, Inc., 1990), 143–172.

88. Janet Gotkin and Paul Gotkin, *Too Much Anger, Too Many Tears: A Personal Triumph over Psychiatry* (New York: Quadrangle, 1975), 64.

89. Barbara Field Benziger, *The Prison of My Mind* (New York: Walker and Company, 1969), 33, 84.

90. Kate Millet, *The Loony-Bin Trip* (New York: Simon and Schuster, 1990), 165, 194, 205, 227.

91. Kesey, *One Flew over the Cuckoo's Nest,* 116.

92. Joanne Greenberg's novel also included a strict head nurse who controlled patient access to cigarettes, and her narrative was not positive about this figure. Joanne Greenberg, *I Never Promised You a Rose Garden* (New York: Signet, 1964), 78.

93. For an overview of popular representations of smoking in women and its connection to elite habits, see Cheryl Krasnick Warsh and Penny Tinkler, "In Vogue: North American and British Representations of Women Smokers in *Vogue*, 1920s–1960s," *Canadian Bulletin of Medical History* 24 (2007): 9–47.

94. Only occasionally would a family member would mention their loved one's brand of cigarette. See for example, Elizabeth Swados, *The Four of Us: The Story of a Family* (New York: Farrar, Straus and Giroux, 1991), 68, 203.

95. For example, actress Lillian Roth, explained that she used to carry cigarettes in the 1920s as part of her image of sophisticated flapper—though she did not smoke. She did start smoking in the context of her battle with alcoholism. Lillian Roth, *I'll Cry Tomorrow* (New York: Frederick Fell, 1954), 29, 226.

Chapter 3 Smoker Psychology and the Tobacco
Industry through the Early 1980s

1. Surgeon General's Advisory Committee on Smoking and Health, *Smoking and Health; Report of the Advisory Committee to the Surgeon General of the Public Health Service* (Washington, DC: U.S. Department of Health, Education, and Welfare, Public Health Service, 1964). See also, Michael Housman, "Smoking and Health: The 1964 U.S. Surgeon General's Report as a Turning Point in the Anti-Smoking Movement," *Harvard Health Policy Review* 2 (2001): 118–126.

2. Christopher J. Bailey, "From 'Informed Choice' to 'Social Hygiene': Government Control of Cigarette Smoking in the US," *Journal of American Studies* 38 (2004): 41–65.

3. Surgeon General's Advisory Committee, *Smoking and Health,* 355–356.

4. Scholars have illuminated the shady dealings of the tobacco industry and its relationship to research. See Stanton A. Glantz et al., *The Cigarette Papers* (Berkeley: University of California Press, 1996); Lisa A. Bero, "Tobacco Industry Manipulation of Research," *Public Health Reports* 120 (2005): 200–208.

5. On industrial psychology as part of business innovation, see for example, Kim McQuaid, *Uneasy Partners: Big Business in American Politics, 1945–1990* (Baltimore: Johns Hopkins University Press, 1994), 94–96. On the expansion of psychology in the twentieth century, see Ellen Herman, *The Romance of American Psychology: Political Culture in the Age of Experts* (Berkeley: University of California Press, 1995). Important figures in the history of psychology, such as Jean Piaget, consulted for industry during their careers. Yeh Hsueh, "The Hawthorne Experiments and the Introduction of Jean Piaget in American Industrial Psychology, 1929–1932," *History of Psychology* 5 (2002): 163–189. See also, Laura L. Koppes, ed. *Historical Perspectives in Industrial and Organizational Psychology* (Mahway, NJ: Lawrence Erlbaum Associates, 2007).

6. The tobacco industry also funded researchers who looked at genetic differences between individuals. See Laura D. Hirshbein, "Scientific Research and Corporate Influence: Smoking, Mental Illness, and the Tobacco Industry," *Journal of the History of Medicine & Allied Sciences* 67 (2012): 374–397; Kenneth R. Gundle, Molly J. Dingel, and Barbara A. Koenig, "'To Prove This Is the Industry's Best Hope': Big Tobacco's Support of Research on the Genetics of Nicotine Addiction," *Addiction* 105 (2010): 974–983.

7. Allan M. Brandt, *The Cigarette Century: The Rise, Fall, and Deadly Persistence of the Product That Defined America* (New York: Basic Books, 2007); David T. Courtwright, "'Carry on Smoking': Public Relations and Advertising Strategies of American and British Tobacco Companies since 1950," *Business History* 47 (2005): 421–432.

8. On the broad question of industrial investment in research (even some that might not have obvious applications for the companies in question), see Nathan Rosenberg, "Why Do Firms Do Basic Research (With Their Own Money)?," *Research Policy* 19 (1990): 165–174. And tobacco companies were not the first to contract with academic researchers in response to outside threats. For an early example, see Ludy T. Benjamin, Anne M. Rogers, and Angela Rosenbaum, "Coca-Cola, Caffeine, and Mental Deficiency: Harry Hollingworth and the Chattanooga Trial of 1911," *Journal of the History of the Behavioral Sciences* 27 (1991): 42–55.

9. See, for example, O. Spurgeon English and Stuart M. Finch, *Introduction to Psychiatry,* 3rd ed. (New York: W. W. Norton & Company, 1964), 299–340. See also, Edward Shorter, *From Paralysis to Fatigue: A History of Psychosomatic Illness in the Modern Era* (New York: Free Press, 1992); Nissim Mizrachi, "From Causation to Correlation: The Story of *Psychosomatic Medicine,* 1939–1979," *Culture, Medicine & Psychiatry* 25 (2001): 317–343. For some of the challenges of this approach, especially to women patients, see Patricia Jasen, "Malignant Histories: Psychosomatic Medicine and the Female Cancer Patient in the Postwar Era," *Canadian Bulletin of Medical History* 20 (2003): 265–297.

10. For an analysis of the methods by which corporations used strategies to enhance their reputations, see Roland Marchand, *Creating the Corporate Soul: The Rise of Public Relations and Corporate Imagery in American Big Business* (Berkeley: University of California Press, 1998).

11. On Alexander's influence in psychosomatic medicine, see Erika S. Schmidt, "The Berlin Tradition in Chicago: Franz Alexander and the Chicago Institute for Psychoanalysis," *Psychoanalysis and History* 12 (2010): 69–83.

12. Geoffrey Todd, Some Scientific Opinions in the U.S.A. and Canada on Various Aspects of the Lung Cancer Problem, 18 December 1956, LTDL (Bates 950178385/8398), http://legacy.library.ucsf.edu/tid/rpf54f00.

13. For example, Minnesota physiologist Ancel Keys accepted funding by the American Heart Association, as well as the TIRC, for his coronary heart disease study. See the 1958 Report of the Scientific Director, TIRC, LTDL (Bates 105387014–105387046), http://legacy.library.ucsf.edu/tid/zei37a99.

14. D. M. Kissen Obituary, *British Medical Journal,* 23 March 1968, LTDL (Bates 1005049820/9821), http://legacy.library.ucsf.edu/tid/rk054e00.

15. G. F. Todd, Personality Traits of Lung Cancer Patients, 3 January 1961, TMSC, LTDL (Bates 105619750/105619751), http://legacy.library.ucsf.edu/tid/hab15a99.

16. D. M. Kissen, Personality Factors in Smoking and Lung Cancer, Stage III, 1 November 1962, LTDL (Bates 105630619/105630621), http://legacy.library.ucsf.edu/tid/pk064a99.

17. A Report on Personality Factors and Smoking, Part II, August 1962, LTDL (Bates 11297787/7844), http://legacy.library.ucsf.edu/tid/crv5aa00. For the published article (which does not mention its TMSC sponsor), see David M. Kissen and H. J. Eysenck, "Personality in Male Lung Cancer Patients," *Journal of Psychosomatic Research* 6 (1962): 123–127. See also, H. J. Eysenck, "Smoking, Personality and Psychosomatic Disorders," *Journal of Psychosomatic Research* 7 (1963): 107–130.

18. The CTR was also interested in Kissen, but he died before he could complete any substantial work for them. Kissen to Robert Hockett, CTR, 16 January 1967, LTDL (Bates CTRSP/FILES003321/3321), http://legacy.library.ucsf.edu/tid/fld8aa00; D. M. Kissen Obituary, *British Medical Journal,* 23 March 1968, LTDL (Bates 1005049820/9821), http://legacy.library.ucsf.edu/tid/rk054e00.

19. See Roderick D. Buchanan, *Playing with Fire: The Controversial Career of Hans J. Eysenck* (Oxford: Oxford University Press, 2010), 361–408. For an edited collection that identifies the major controversies in which Eysenck became embroiled, see Sohan Modgil and Celia Modgil, eds., *Hans Eysenck: Consensus and Controversy* (Philadelphia: Falmer Press, 1986).

20. See for example, Memo from W. L. Dunn to Dr. T. S. Osdene, "Quarterly Report—January 1–March 31, 1975," 25 March 1975, LTDL (Bates 1003287984/1003287986), http://legacy.library.ucsf.edu/tid/uoa76b00; Memo from D. H. Piehl to Mr. Alan Rodgman (RJR), "Visit with Dr. Hans J. Eysenck, University of London," 15 May 1979, LTDL (Bates 501542224/2225), http://legacy.library.ucsf.edu/tid/tzr39d00.

21. Eysenck's biographer reported that Eysenck began to twist paperclips to do something with his hands after he quit smoking. H. B. Gibson, *Hans Eysenck: The Man and His Work* (London: Peter Owen, 1981), 106.

22. See, for example, David Rice, Letter to the Editor, *British Journal of Psychiatry,* January 1979, LTDL (Bates 501729733), http://legacy.library.ucsf.edu/tid/rog23a00. Today there are many in the professional literature who insist that schizophrenics have higher rates of chronic illnesses, including cancer, while a few continue to

argue that the cancer rates are lower. V. S. Catts et al., "Cancer Incidence in Patients with Schizophrenia and Their First-Degree Relatives—A Meta-Analysis," *Acta Psychiatrica Scandinavica* 117 (2008): 323–336.

23. Proposal from David F. Horrobin to the Tobacco Research Council, 2 November 1977, LTDL (Bates 100245555/100245592), http://legacy.library.ucsf.edu/tid/dch22a99; Letter from Richard Doll to P. N. Lee, TRC, 29 December 1977, LTDL (Bates 100277623), http://legacy.library.ucsf.edu/tid/ywd22a99; and Summary of the Decisions of the TRC, 19 February–14 March 1978, LTDL (Bates 100322426–100322427), http://legacy.library.ucsf.edu/tid/zni32a99.

24. H. J. Eysenck, *The Causes and Effects of Smoking* (Beverly Hills, CA: Sage, 1980), 86. See also, C. B. Bahnson and M. B. Bahnson, "Cancer as an Alternative to Psychosis: A Theoretical Model of Somatic and Psychologic Regression," in D. M. Kissen and L. L. LeShan (eds.), *Psychosomatic Aspects of Neoplastic Disease* (Philadelphia: Lippincott, 1964), LTDL (Bates 70104587/4597), http://legacy.library.ucsf.edu/tid/ojb56d00.

25. Brandt, *The Cigarette Century*. On the history of advertising in the early twentieth century, including the increasing use of psychological insights, see Roland Marchand, *Advertising the American Dream: Making Way for Modernity, 1920–1940* (Berkeley: University of California Press, 1985). See also, Pamela E. Pennock, *Advertising Sin and Sickness: The Politics of Alcohol and Tobacco Marketing, 1950–1990* (DeKalb: Northern Illinois University Press, 2007). On the history of consumer psychology, see for example, Michael J. Pettit, "The Unwary Purchaser: Consumer Psychology and the Regulation of Commerce in America," *Journal of the History of the Behavioral Sciences* 43 (2007): 379–399.

26. For the history of psychologists' roles in employee management, see Andrew J. Vinchur, "A History of Psychology Applied to Employee Selection," in *Historical Perspectives in Industrial and Organizational Psychology*, ed. Laura L. Koppes (Mahwah, NJ: Lawrence Erlbaum Associates, 2007), 193–218. See also, Mark Pittenger, "'What's on the Worker's Mind': Class Passing and the Study of the Industrial Workplace in the 1920s," *Journal of the History of the Behavioral Sciences* 39 (2003): 143–161.

27. Thomas Frank, *The Conquest of Cool: Business Culture, Counterculture, and the Rise of Hip Consumerism* (Chicago: University of Chicago Press, 1997).

28. See for example, Richard D. Hurt and Channing R. Robertson, "Prying Open the Door to the Tobacco Industry's Secrets about Nicotine: The Minnesota Tobacco Trial," *JAMA* 280 (1998): 1173–1181.

29. William L. Dunn Jr., "Visual Discrimination of Schizophrenic Subjects as a Function of Stimulus Meaning," *Journal of Personality* 23 (1954): 48–64.

30. Deposition of William Dunn, PhD, 24 June 1998, LTDL (Bates 3990137048/3990137517), http://legacy.library.ucsf.edu/tid/zsz82i00.

31. Philip J. Hilts, *Smoke Screen: The Truth behind the Tobacco Industry Cover-Up* (New York: Addison-Wesley Publishing Company, 1996), 48–51; Brandt, *The Cigarette Century*, 340; and David Kessler, *A Question of Intent: A Great American Battle with a Deadly Industry* (New York: PublicAffairs, 2001), 229–232, 255–257.

32. On the history of marketing surveys in the United States, see Sarah E. Igo, *The Averaged American: Surveys, Citizens, and the Making of a Mass Public* (Cambridge, MA: Harvard University Press, 2007). On the origins of consumer panels, see Joe Moran, "Mass-Observation, Market Research, and the Birth of the Focus Group, 1937–1997," *Journal of British Studies* 47 (2008): 827–851.

33. W. L. Dunn Jr., Project 1600: Consumer Psychology, 7 January 1963, LTDL (Bates 1001520982/0983), http://legacy.library.ucsf.edu/tid/upy18e00.

34. W. L. Dunn Jr., Project 1600: Consumer Psychology, 28 February 1964, LTDL (Bates 1001521105), http://legacy.library.ucsf.edu/tid/hoy18e00.

35. W. L. Dunn Jr., Project 1600: Consumer Psychology, Annual Report, 18 November 1966, LTDL (Bates 85873509/3524), http://legacy.library.ucsf.edu/tid/ied70e00. See also the Project Review Committee's favorable assessment of this kind of work, Memo to Dunn, Review of Project 1600, 16 December 1966, LTDL (Bates 1003288349), http://legacy.library.ucsf.edu/tid/vac76b00.

36. F. J. Ryan, Project 1600: Consumer Psychology (Annual Report), 5 December 1968, LTDL (Bates 1000039674/9679), http://legacy.library.ucsf.edu/tid/bry64e00.

37. H. Wakeham, Smoker Psychology Research, 26 November 1969, LTDL (Bates 1000273741/1000273770), http://legacy.library.ucsf.edu/tid/xgw56b00.

38. Memo from W. L. Dunn and M. E. Johnston to Dr. P. A. Eichorn, Accomplishments in 1969—Projects 1600 and 2302, 28 January 1970, LTDL (Bates 1000837964/7966), http://legacy.library.ucsf.edu/tid/ofr54e00.

39. F. J. Ryan Jr., Project 1600: Consumer Psychology, 24 February 1970, LTDL (Bates 1001521241/1242), http://legacy.library.ucsf.edu/tid/wxy18e00.

40. William L. Dunn Jr., preface, in *Smoking Behavior: Motives and Incentives*, ed. William L. Dunn Jr. (Washington, DC: V. H. Winston & Sons, 1973), xi–xii.

41. Hans Selye, *The Stress of Life* (New York: McGraw-Hill, 1956). For Selye's role in stress research, see David S. Goldstein and Irwin J. Kopin, "Evolution of Concepts of Stress," *Stress* 10 (2007): 109–120. Selye spoke to many business organizations as a result of his theories that extolled the goals of capitalism. Russell Viner, "Putting Stress in Life: Hans Selye and the Making of Stress Theory," *Social Studies of Science* 29 (1999): 391–410.

42. H. Wakeham, Visit with Hans Selye, University of Montreal School of Medicine, 30 July 1969, LTDL (Bates 1000321445), http://legacy.library.ucsf.edu/tid/atx84e00; Letter from W. T. Hoyt to Hans Selye, 8 April 1971, LTDL (Bates CTRSP/FILES007972/7972), http://legacy.library.ucsf.edu/tid/xaf8aa00.

43. Hans Selye, "Some Introductory Remarks," in Dunn, *Smoking Behavior*, 2.

44. For more on Selye's relationship with the tobacco industry, see Mark P. Petticrew and Kelley Lee, "The 'Father of Stress' Meets 'Big Tobacco': Hans Selye and the Tobacco Industry," *American Journal of Public Health* 101 (2011): 411–418.

45. See Stanley Schachter, "Nesbitt's Paradox"; Caroline Bedell Thomas, "The Relationship of Smoking and Habits of Nervous Tension"; and Albert Damon, "Smoking Attitudes and Practices in Seven Preliterate Societies," in Dunn, *Smoking Behavior*, 147–155, 157–170, 219–230.

46. See Edward F. Domino, "Neuropsychopharmacology of Nicotine and Tobacco Smoking"; Murray E. Jarvik, "Further Observations on Nicotine as the Reinforcing Agent in Smoking"; and Walter B. Essman, "Nicotine-Related Neurochemical Changes: Some Implications for Motivational Mechanisms and Differences," in Dunn, *Smoking Behavior*, 5–31, 33–49, 51–65.

47. See Grant Proposal by Domino to the CTR, 3 August 1972, LTDL (Bates 10009329/10009340), http://legacy.library.ucsf.edu/tid/gld66b00; CTR Grant Report Regarding Jarvik's Project, 30 June 1975, LTDL (Bates ZN22548/2548), http://legacy.library.ucsf.edu/tid/thf3aa00; and Memo from D. H. Ford Regarding Essman's Work for the CTR, 11 September 1978, LTDL (Bates 50128552/8552), http://legacy.library.ucsf.edu/tid/dct59c00.

48. Judith P. Swazey, "Chlorpromazine's Entrance into Psychiatry: An Extremely Interesting Product," *Minnesota Medicine* 62 (1979): 81–85.

49. Ronald R. Hutchinson and Grace S. Emley, "Effects of Nicotine on Avoidance, Conditioned Suppression and Aggression Response Measures in Animals and Man" and Norman W. Heimstra, "The Effects of Smoking on Mood Change," in Dunn, *Smoking Behavior*, 171–196, 197–207. On Hutchinson's work with PM before the conference, see W. L. Dunn Jr., Project 1600: Consumer Psychology, Annual Report, 15 May 1970, LTDL (Bates 1003288243/1003288245), http://legacy.library.ucsf.edu/tid/hac76b00.

50. W. L. Dunn Jr., Smoker Psychology, 13 March 1973, LTDL (Bates 1001521309/1313), http://legacy.library.ucsf.edu/tid/pwy18e00.

51. See Philip Morris Research Center, Technical Newsletter, May 1973, LTDL (Bates 1003368157/8164), http://legacy.library.ucsf.edu/tid/xgq38e00. The newsletter discusses an article by Tamerin and Neumann. John S. Tamerin and Charles P. Neumann, "Casualties of the Antismoking Campaign," *Comprehensive Psychiatry* 14 (1973): 35–40.

52. For the idea regarding tracking psychiatric patients, see Project 1600: Consumer Psychology, Outline for Annual Report, 10 June 1969, LTDL (Bates 1000852085/2089), http://legacy.library.ucsf.edu/tid/fvg12a00. On the proposed study tracking hyperkinetic children, see W. L. Dunn Jr., Smoker Psychology, 10 June 1974, LTDL (Bates 1003288122–1003288124), http://legacy.library.ucsf.edu/tid/jjs76b00. Dunn explicitly stated that they were not planning to give cigarettes to children but rather to follow the children to see if they became smokers in the future.

53. I.C.O.S.I. Working Party on Smoking Behaviour, 1–3 September 1977, LTDL (Bates USX461298-USX461302), http://legacy.library.ucsf.edu/tid/vny36b00.

54. Raymond E. Thornton, ed. *Smoking Behaviour: Physiological and Psychological Influences* (Edinburgh: Churchill Livingstone, 1978).

55. Memo from D. H. Piehl to Dr. Alan Rodgman, Re: Justification for Research Behavioral Scientist, RJR, 23 May 1979, LTDL (Bates 502982883/2884), http://legacy.library.ucsf.edu/tid/tmt68d00.

56. Spielberger's CV, http://psychology.usf.edu/faculty/data/cspielberger_cv.pdf, accessed 28 May 2013.

57. Elizabeth Siegel Watkins, "An Investigation into the Medicalization of Stress in the Twentieth Century," *Medicine Studies* (2013) DOI: 10.1007/s12376–013–0082-7, published online 14 June 2013; Andrea Tone, *The Age of Anxiety: A History of America's Turbulent Affair with Tranquilizers* (New York: Basic Books, 2008).

58. Charles Spielberger, *Understanding Stress and Anxiety* (New York: Harper & Row, 1979), 94–95.

59. Spielberger to Edwin Jacobs, 8 August 1984, LTDL (Bates 508455895), http://legacy.library.ucsf.edu/tid/apn93d00.

60. See Arthur Stevens to Edwin Jacob, 28 August 1981, blind copy to Mr. Judge and Dr. Spears, LTDL (Bates 03754250), http://legacy.library.ucsf.edu/tid/njs88c00. For more on tobacco attorney facilitation of connections between external researchers and RJR, see for example, Letter from Charles Spielberger to Mr. H. C. Roemer, Vice President and General Counsel, RJR, 5 July 1978, LTDL (Bates 504311800), http://legacy.library.ucsf.edu/tid/jpi58d00.

61. Packet from Samuel D. Chilcote Jr., Tobacco Institute, to Dr. Charles W. Humphreys Jr., 15 March 1982, Statement by Charles D. Spielberger, 8 March 1982, LTDL (Bates TI12320566-TI12320920), http://legacy.library.ucsf.edu/tid/vin03b00.

62. The pharmaceutical industry also did this. See Dominique A. Tobbell, *Pills, Power, and Policy: The Struggle for Drug Reform in Cold War America and Its Consequences* (Berkeley: University of California Press, 2012).

63. Memo from Gilbert, Re: Annual Meeting of the Society for Psychophysiological Research, 2 November 1982, LTDL (Bates 500888801/8802), http://legacy.library .ucsf.edu/tid/qww59d00.

64. Memo from John H. Reynolds and David G. Gilbert, Re: Biobehavioral R&D Subject Pool, 3 December 1980, LTDL (Bates 502835320/5322), http://legacy.library.ucsf .edu/tid/yna78d00.

65. Gilbert was only one of the tobacco industry researchers to use EEG in consumer studies. See Vincent C. Panzano et al., "Human Electroencephalography and the Tobacco Industry: A Review of Internal Documents," *Tobacco Control* 19 (2010): 153–159.

66. Memo from Gilbert to Dr. A. Wallace Hayes, Re: Report of Trip and Presentation of Paper to the Society of Behavioral Medicine, 17 May 1985, LTDL (Bates 504789948/9949), http://legacy.library.ucsf.edu/tid/oup55d00.

67. While Gilbert was bound with a confidentiality agreement, he appeared to have parted with RJR on a cordial footing and was able to publish a dozen papers with data gathered while a company employee. See Letter from August J. Borschke, Associate Counsel, to David Gilbert, 7 August 1985, LTDL (Bates 505046952/6953), http://legacy.library.ucsf.edu/tid/fwe35d00. On Gilbert's continued work with RJR, see Letter from RJR to David Gilbert, 26 August 1985, LTDL (Bates 515860666/0669), http://legacy.library.ucsf.edu/tid/bwe92d00; Letter from Gilbert to John H. Reynolds, 10 January 1986, LTDL (Bates 504231530/1533), http://legacy.library.ucsf.edu/ tid/rfc86a00.

68. See Memo from J. H. Reynolds to Dr. A. W. Hayes, Status Report Biobehavioral Research Division, 12 December 1986, LTDL (Bates 506215473/5476), http:// legacy.library.ucsf.edu/tid/tld84d00.

Chapter 4 Psychiatry Engages Smoking

1. One article, for example, discussed anxiety and mood symptoms associated with efforts to quit smoking. Jerome L. Schwartz and Mildred Dubitzky, "Changes in Anxiety, Mood, and Self-Esteem Resulting from an Attempt to Stop Smoking," *American Journal of Psychiatry* 124 (1968): 1580–1584.

2. See Caroline Jean Acker, *Creating the American Junkie: Addition Research in the Classic Era of Narcotic Control* (Baltimore: Johns Hopkins University Press, 2002).

3. David F. Musto and Pamela Korsmeyer, *The Quest for Drug Control: Politics and Federal Policy in a Period of Increasing Substance Abuse, 1963–1981* (New Haven: Yale University Press, 2002); Jeremy Kuzmarov, *The Myth of the Addicted Army: Vietnam and the Modern War on Drugs* (Amherst: University of Massachusetts Press, 2009).

4. See for example, Seymour Fisher and Alfred M. Freedman, eds., *Opiate Addiction: Origins and Treatment* (Washington, DC: V. H. Winston & Sons, 1973). See also, Laura D. Hirshbein, "Looking Back to the Future of Psychopharmacology," *Journal of Nervous and Mental Disease* 200 (2012): 1109–1112.

5. On the shifts in conceptualization of smoking as addiction, see Allan M. Brandt, "From Nicotine to Nicotrol: Addiction, Cigarettes, and American Culture," in *Altering American Consciousness: The History of Alcohol and Drug Use in the United*

States, 1800–2000, ed. Sarah W. Tracy and Caroline Jean Acker (Amherst: University of Massachusetts Press, 2004), 383–402.

6. Peter H. Knapp, Charles Michael Bliss, and Harriet Wells, "Addictive Aspects in Heavy Cigarette Smoking," *American Journal of Psychiatry* 119 (1963): 966–972, quote from 969.

7. John S. Tamerin, "The Psychodynamics of Quitting Smoking in a Group," *American Journal of Psychiatry* 129 (1972): 589–594, quote from 591.

8. For the influence of psychodynamic approaches in psychiatry through much of the century, see Nathan G. Hale Jr., *The Rise and Crisis of Psychoanalysis in the United States: Freud and the Americans, 1917–1985* (New York: Oxford University Press, 1995).

9. Memo from Leonard Zahn, Smoking Paper at Meeting of the American Psychiatric Association, Washington, DC, 29 April 1971, LTDL (Bates ZN16396/6396), http://legacy.library.ucsf.edu/tid/eza3aa00.

10. Memo from Leonard Zahn to W. T. Hoyt, TI, May 3–7, 1971, LTDL (Bates 1005094700/4703), http://legacy.library.ucsf.edu/tid/jbv38e00.

11. John S. Tamerin and Richard A. Eisinger, "Cigarette Smoking and the Psychiatrist," *American Journal of Psychiatry* 128 (1972): 1224–1229, quote from 1226.

12. Nat Hentoff, *A Doctor among the Addicts* (New York: Rand McNally, 1968). See also, David T. Courtwright, "The Prepared Mind: Marie Nyswander, Methadone Maintenance, and the Metabolic Theory of Addiction," *Addiction* 92 (1997): 257–265.

13. R. Gordon Bell, *Escape from Addiction* (New York: McGraw-Hill, 1970), 152.

14. Harrison Pope Jr., *Voices from the Drug Culture* (Cambridge, MA: The Sanctuary, 1971), 16.

15. On Jaffe's work in Nixon's administration, see Kuzmarov, *The Myth of the Addicted Army*.

16. Jerome H. Jaffe, "Cigarette Smoking as an Addiction," *American Lung Association Bulletin* 62 (1976): 10–12. See also Murray E. Jarvik et al., eds., *Research on Smoking Behavior* (Washington, DC: Department of Health, Education, and Welfare, 1977).

17. M. D. Neuman, A. Bitton, and S. A. Glantz, "Tobacco Industry Influence on the Definition of Tobacco Related Disorders by the American Psychiatric Association," *Tobacco Control* 14 (2005): 328–337. For more context on the battles to construct *DSM-III*, see Hannah S. Decker, *The Making of DSM-III: A Diagnostic Manual's Conquest of American Psychiatry* (New York: Oxford University Press, 2013).

18. American Psychiatric Association, *Diagnostic and Statistical Manual of Mental Disorders*, 3rd ed. (Washington, DC: American Psychiatric Association, 1980), 176–178, quote from 178.

19. American Psychiatric Association, *Diagnostic and Statistical Manual of Mental Disorders*, 3rd rev. ed. (Washington, DC: American Psychiatric Press, 1987), 181–182.

20. On Freedman's role with regard to homosexuality, see Ronald Bayer, *Homosexuality and American Psychiatry: The Politics of Diagnosis*, rev. ed. (Princeton: Princeton University Press, 1987). For Freedman's statements regarding psychiatric overreach, see Alfred M. Freedman et al., eds., *Issues in Psychiatric Classification: Science, Practice and Social Policy* (New York: Human Sciences Press, 1986). On Freedman's funding by the tobacco industry, see Neuman, Bitton, and Glantz, "Tobacco Industry Influence on the Definition of Tobacco Related Disorders."

21. On the history of mental-health policy, see for example, Gerald N. Grob and Howard H. Goldman, *The Dilemma of Federal Mental Health Policy: Radical Reform or Incremental Change?* (New Brunswick: Rutgers University Press, 2006).

22. See for example, Marion R. Meyers and Hazel M. Cushing, "Types and Incidence of Behavior Problems in Relation to Cultural Background," *American Journal of Orthopsychiatry* 6 (1936): 110–116; Joseph J. Michaels, "The Incidence of Enuresis and Age of Cessation in One Hundred Delinquents and One Hundred Sibling Controls," *American Journal of Orthopsychiatry* 8 (1938): 460–465; and Ben Karpman, "Conscience in the Psychopath: Another Version," *American Journal of Orthopsychiatry* 18 (1948): 455–491. For the broader context of professional approaches to problematic children, see Kathleen W. Jones, *Taming the Troublesome Child: American Families, Child Guidance, and the Limits of Psychiatric Authority* (Cambridge: Harvard University Press, 1999).

23. Joseph D. Noshpitz, "A Smoking Episode in a Residential Treatment Unit," *American Journal of Orthopsychiatry* 32 (1962): 669–681, quote from 679.

24. See for example, Steve Stapleton, "Close Encounters of the Worst Kind," in *Shrink Resistant: The Struggle against Psychiatry in Canada,* ed. Bonnie Burstow and Don Weitz (Vancouver: New Star Books, 1988), 242–245.

25. Sue E. Estroff, *Making It Crazy: An Ethnography of Psychiatric Clients in an American Community* (Berkeley: University of California Press, 1981), 163.

26. See Letter from Max Crohn to H. R. Kornegay, 28 August 1980, LTDL (Bates TI17931385/TI17931386), http://legacy.library.ucsf.edu/tid/aot09a00; Letter from Crohn to Torrey, 3 October 1980, LTDL (Bates 502358644), http://legacy.library.ucsf.edu/tid/aim18c00.

27. Craig Diaz to R. J. Reynolds, 24 August 1987, LTDL (Bates 505915047/5048), http://legacy.library.ucsf.edu/tid/xhe94d00.

28. Laura D. Hirshbein, "'We Mentally Ill Smoke a Lot': Identity, Smoking, and Mental Illness in America," *Journal of Social History* 44 (2010): 7–21.

29. John R. Hughes et al., "Prevalence of Smoking among Psychiatric Outpatients," *American Journal of Psychiatry* 143 (1986): 993–997.

30. Thomas H. Lewis, "Staff Smoking on the Ward: Iatrogenic Addiction, Iatrogenic Cancer," *Hospital and Community Psychiatry* 32 (1981): 502–503.

31. Renata Tagliacozzo and Sally Vaughn, "Stress and Smoking in Hospital Nurses," *American Journal of Public Health* 72 (1982): 441–448.

32. Edward H. Gaston, "Solving the Smoking Problem on a Chronic Ward," *Journal of Psychiatric Treatment and Evaluation* 4 (1982): 397–401, quote from 398.

33. Vladimir F. Yegorov, "And How Is It over There, across the Ocean?," *Schizophrenia Bulletin* 18 (1992): 7–14.

34. Tomer Levin, "A Psychiatric Resident's Journey through the Closed Ward," *Schizophrenia Bulletin* 27 (2001): 539–547. This article does not mention when Levin did his rotation. He described a unit in Israel that sounded very similar to American inpatient units from the 1970s and 1980s.

35. E. Fuller Torrey, *Surviving Schizophrenia: A Family Manual,* rev. ed. (New York: Harper & Row, 1988), 296. For Torrey's suggestion that families avoid fighting about cigarettes, see 296–297. For the first edition, see *Surviving Schizophrenia: A Family Manual* (New York: Harper & Row, 1983).

36. Sheldon B. Cohen, "Are Physicians to Blame if Patients Smoke?," *New York State Journal of Medicine* 83 (1983): 1295.

37. AMA Council on Scientific Affairs, "Nonsmoking in Hospitals," *Connecticut Medicine* 48 (1984): 297–305. Physicians tended to point the finger at smoking nurses who interfered with nonsmoking policies at the hospital. See for example, letter to the editor, *New York State Journal of Medicine* 84 (1984): 165.

38. Ellen R. Gritz et al., "Prevalence of Cigarette Smoking in VA Medical and Psychiatric Hospitals," *Bulletin of the Society of Psychologists in Addictive Behaviors* 4 (1985): 151–165. See also, Hughes et al., "Prevalence of Smoking among Psychiatric Outpatients."

39. Letter to the editor, *Hospital and Community Psychiatry* 38 (1987): 413–414.

40. See for example, Harold H. Dawley Jr., "The Control, Discouragement, and Cessation of Smoking in a Hospital Setting," *International Journal of the Addictions* 22 (1987): 477–485.

41. Michael Resnick and Eric Bosworth, "A Survey of Smoking Policies in Oregon Psychiatric Facilities," *Hospital and Community Psychiatry* 39 (1988): 313–315.

42. Patricia Dingman et al., "A Nonsmoking Policy on an Acute Psychiatric Unit," *Journal of Psychosocial Nursing* 26 (1988): 12–14.

43. Michael Resnick, Rebecca Gordon, and Eric E. Bosworth, "Evolution of Smoking Policies in Oregon Psychiatric Facilities," *Hospital and Community Psychiatry* 40 (1989): 527–529.

44. See for example, Harold H. Dawley Jr. et al., "Smoking Control in a Psychiatric Setting," *Hospital and Community Psychiatry* 40 (1989): 1299–1301.

45. See for example, Frederick J. Fuoco et al., *Behavioral Procedures for a Psychiatric Unit and Halfway House* (New York: Van Nostrand Reinhold, 1985). See also, Second Draft, Office of Mental Health Policy on Patient Smoking, [New York City], [1987], LTDL (Bates 522128467/8470), http://legacy.library.ucsf.edu/tid/fkj51c00.

46. Raanan Gillon, "Health Education and Health Promotion," *Journal of Medical Ethics* 13 (1987): 3–4; Irma Kurtz, "Health Educators—The New Puritans," *Journal of Medical Ethics* 13 (1987): 40–41, 48.

47. Louise P. Baenninger and Weizhen Tang, "Teaching Chronic Psychiatric Inpatients to Use Differential Attention to Change Each Other's Behaviors," *Hospital and Community Psychiatry* 41 (1990): 425–429.

48. Letter to the editor, *Hospital and Community Psychiatry* 39 (1988): 317.

49. Wayne R. Smith and Brian L. Grant, "Effects of a Smoking Ban on a General Hospital Psychiatric Service," *Hospital and Community Psychiatry* 40 (1989): 497–502, quote from 497. See also, Michael P. Resnick, "A Smoke-Free Psychiatric Unit," *Hospital and Community Psychiatry* 40 (1989): 525–527.

50. See for example, Lois Biener et al., "A Comparative Evaluation of a Restrictive Smoking Policy in a General Hospital," *American Journal of Public Health* 79 (1989): 192–195.

51. Roland D. Maiuro et al., "Patient Reactions to a No Smoking Policy in a Community Mental Health Center," *Community Mental Health Journal* 25 (1989): 71–77.

52. "Hospitals Act to Curb Cigarette Sales, Smoking," *New York Times*, 9 February 1964.

53. At the University of Michigan Hospital, for example, the decision to stop selling cigarettes in the gift shop in 1971 generated controversy because the proceeds from the shop supported children's programs. Lower revenue with no cigarette sales translated to fewer children's activities. David R. Stutz, President of the Galens Honorary Medical Society, to the Editor of the *Michigan Daily*, 26 January 1971, Folder—Officers' Records and Reports, 1970–1971, Box 2, Galens Medical Society Records, Bentley Historical Library, University of Michigan, Ann Arbor, MI.

54. Not surprisingly, the tobacco industry closely followed these developments. "Daily Synopsis of Press, Radio and Television Coverage for Wednesday, 23 March 1983," Campbell-Johnson Limited, London [British division of Hill and Knowlton], LTDL (Bates 303673660/303673662), http://legacy.library.ucsf.edu/tid/llk87a99.

55. Similar concerns were raised in other countries, though there were other mechanisms for regulation. On concern about smoking among staff in hospitals in the UK, see for example, S. F. Hussain et al., "Attitudes to Smoking and Smoking Habits among Hospital Staff," *Thorax* 48 (1993): 174–175.

56. Joe B. Tye, David G. Altman, and Andrew McGuire, "Duty Calls: Hospitals' Responsibility for Controlling the Tobacco Epidemic," *Hospital and Health Services Administration* 34 (1989): 445–455.

57. See for example, "Tobacco Not Hazardous to the AMA Pocketbook," editorial from Yuma, Arizona, 12 June 1981, LTDL (Bates TI54470934), http://legacy.library.ucsf.edu/tid/bpi09b00.

58. Rosemary Stevens, *In Sickness and in Wealth: American Hospitals in the Twentieth Century* (New York: Basic Books, 1989), 246–251.

59. "Smoking Standard Clarified," *Joint Commission Perspectives,* November/December 1991. Copy in LTDL (Bates 2024726896/6898), http://legacy.library.ucsf.edu/tid/gdx23e00.

60. Interview with Paul Schuyve, 10 November 2009. Some did interpret smoking bans as an opportunity to push cessation, though. For an example within general medicine, see Adam A. Goldstein et al., "Hospital Efforts in Smoking Control: Remaining Barriers and Challenges," *Journal of Family Practice* 34 (1992): 729–734.

61. For several decades, the Joint Commission had published a separate standards volume for behavioral health facilities. These were produced every few years. See for example, *Consolidated Standards Manual for Child, Adolescent, and Adult Psychiatric, Alcoholism, and Drug Abuse Facilities and the Facilities Serving the Mentally Retarded/Developmentally Disabled,* (Chicago: Joint Commission on Accreditation of Hospitals, 1985). The 1991 edition was the last separate volume for these kinds of facilities. After this, the Joint Commission expected all types of hospitals to use the general standard. *Consolidated Standards Manual,* (Chicago: Joint Commission, 1991).

62. Kathryn M. Connell, "Smoking at Central State," *Indianapolis Star,* 15 January 1989, LTDL (Bates TI26570231-TI26570232), http://legacy.library.ucsf.edu/tid/flp10g00; Howard M. Smulevitz, "Lawsuit Challenges Ban on Smoking at Central State Hospital," *Indianapolis Star,* 28 January 1989, LTDL (Bates TI26570257-TI26570258), http://legacy.library.ucsf.edu/tid/llp10g00.

63. Gerald N. Grob, "World War II and American Psychiatry," *Psychohistory Review* 19 (1990): 41–69.

64. "Letter to the editor, *Hospital and Community Psychiatry* 40 (1989): 1301–1302.

65. "Letter to the editor, *Hospital and Community Psychiatry* 41 (1990): 806; Michael Lavin, "Let the Patients Smoke: A Defense of a Patient Privilege," *Journal of Medical Ethics* 16 (1990): 136–140.

66. For an early example of conflict over a limitation on cigarettes in a mental hospital, see Glenn Rutherford, "State Mental Hospital in Indiana Decides to Snuff Out Cigarette Sales," 16 March 1979, LTDL (Bates TI26042080-TI26042081), http://legacy.library.ucsf.edu/tid/nae10g00.

67. Tim Golden, "One More Anxiety for a Psychiatric Ward: No Smoking," *New York Times,* 3 March 1990.

68. Peter Allebeck, "Schizophrenia: A Life-Shortening Disease," *Schizophrenia Bulletin* 15 (1989): 81–89.

69. James D. Wright, "Poor People, Poor Health: The Health Status of the Homeless," *Journal of Social Issues* 46 (1990): 49–64.

70. Tori A. Bronaugh and Richard J. Frances, "Establishing a Smoke-Free Inpatient Unit: Is It Feasible?," *Hospital and Community Psychiatry* 41 (1990): 1303–1305, quote from 1303.

71. Andrzej B. Koczapski et al., "Multisubstance Intoxication among Schizophrenic Inpatients: Reply to Hyde," *Schizophrenia Bulletin* 16 (1990): 373–375.

72. Michael Greeman and Thomas A. McClellan, "Negative Effects of a Smoking Ban on an Inpatient Psychiatry Service," *Hospital and Community Psychiatry* 42 (1991): 408–412, quote from 412.

73. Donald C. Goff, David C. Henderson, and Edward Amico, "Cigarette Smoking in Schizophrenia: Relationship to Psychopathology and Medication Side Effects," *American Journal of Psychiatry* 149 (1992): 1189–1194.

74. "Smoking Standard Clarified," *Joint Commission Perspectives,* November/December 1991. Copy in LTDL (Bates 2024726896/6898), http://legacy.library.ucsf.edu/tid/gdx23e00.

75. See for example, JoAnne Young, "City's Hospitals to Be Smoke Free," *Lincoln Journal-Star,* 14 December 1991, LTDL (Bates TI26891331), http://legacy.library.ucsf.edu/tid/sns10g00.

76. Carolyn Acker, "Smoke-Free Psychiatric Wards," *Washington Post,* 21 January 1992. For the new Joint Commission standards, see *Accreditation Manual for Hospitals,* (Chicago: Joint Commission, 1992).

77. See letter to the editor, *New York Times,* 13 July 1992, LTDL (Bates TI02681551), http://legacy.library.ucsf.edu/tid/rti19a00. On the evolution of the VA smoking policy, see Anne M. Joseph and Patricia J. O'Neil, "The Department of Veterans Affairs Smoke-Free Policy," *JAMA* 267 (1992): 87–90.

78. Letter to the editor, *JAMA* 267 (1992): 3286–3287.

79. Elizabeth Fee and Theodore M. Brown, "Hospital Smoking Bans and Their Impact," *American Journal of Public Health* 94 (2004): 185. On the reaction of hospitals in traditional tobacco territory, see for example, Memo from T. L. Ogburn, Jr. (R. J. Reynolds), Re: Forsyth Memorial Hospital/Hospital Accreditation, 3 May 1991, LTDL (Bates 512565155/5157), http://legacy.library.ucsf.edu/tid/bmk33d00.

80. Stephen N. Kales, "Smoking Restrictions at Boston-Area Hospitals, 1990–1992: A Serial Survey," *Chest* 104 (1993): 1589–1591. Kales specifically excluded psychiatric and substance facilities from his review.

81. Report in *Tobacco Weekly,* a publication of the Tobacco Merchants Association of the United States, 3 January 1992, LTDL (Bates 517391400/1407), http://legacy.library.ucsf.edu/tid/uos03a00.

82. Shook, Hardy & Bacon, "Report on Recent ETS and IAQ Developments," 24 April 1992, LTDL (Bates 2050751036/1069), http://legacy.library.ucsf.edu/tid/lgn32d00.

83. Lisa W. Foderaro, "Battling Demons, and Nicotine," *New York Times,* 19 February 1995, LTDL (Bates 502553322), http://legacy.library.ucsf.edu/tid/twx86a99.

84. Michael W. Miller, "Mental Patients Fight to Smoke in the Hospital," *Wall Street Journal,* 11 October 1994, LTDL (Bates 2071540458), http://legacy.library.ucsf.edu/tid/thc60c00.

85. Elizabeth Gardner and John Burns, "Joint Commission Modifies, Expands Smoking Regulations," *Modern Healthcare,* 25 January 1993, 12, LTDL (Bates TI03051671), http://legacy.library.ucsf.edu/tid/hu079b00. See also, *Accreditation Manual for Hospitals,* (Chicago: Joint Commission, 1996).

86. Joseph J. Parks and Diane D. Devine, "The Effects of Smoking Bans on Extended Care Units at State Psychiatric Hospitals," *Hospital and Community Psychiatry* 44

(1993): 885–886. For popular press coverage of this study, see Sandra G. Boodman, "Smoking Bans Work in Psychiatric Hospitals," *Washington Post Health,* 11 January 1994, 5, LTDL (Bates TI27072278-TI27072288), http://legacy.library.ucsf.edu/tid/cat33b00.

87. Jamie Talan, "Psychiatric Units Fume over Rule," *New York Newsday,* 2 April 1994, LTDL (Bates 2071540459/0460), http://legacy.library.ucsf.edu/tid/shc60c00.

88. "Mental Illness Advocacy Group Battling Hospital Smoking Ban in New York," *Psychiatric News,* 16 September 1994, LTDL (Bates 2071540461), http://legacy.library.ucsf.edu/tid/rhc60c00. See also, Hearing Report/Bill Signing Report, 12 January 1995, LTDL (Bates 2070110763/0766), http://legacy.library.ucsf.edu/tid/zki47d00.

89. AMI/FAMI, Campaign to Bring Discrete Smoking Areas to City Hospitals, [1994], LTDL (Bates 2071540436), http://legacy.library.ucsf.edu/tid/mic60c00.

90. AMI/FAMI pamphlet, [1995], LTDL (Bates 2071540440), http://legacy.library.ucsf.edu/tid/iic60c00.

91. Shook, Hardy & Bacon, "Ongoing Overview of ETS Cases Not Involving Cigarette Manufacturers" 2 September 1994, LTDL (Bates 71002511), http://legacy.library.ucsf.edu/tid/prz17b00. See also, Paul S. Appelbaum, "Do Hospitalized Psychiatric Patients Have a Right to Smoke?," *Psychiatric Services* 46 (1995): 653–654, 660.

92. Albert J. Solnit, Commissioner, State of Connecticut Department of Mental Health, to Edward Mattison, Connecticut Legal Rights Project, 12 January 1993, LTDL (Bates TI25260223), http://legacy.library.ucsf.edu/tid/nyh45b00.

93. Mattison to Representative Robert Farr, 19 March 1993, LTDL (Bates TI25260199), http://legacy.library.ucsf.edu/tid/yxh45b00.

94. Shook, Hardy & Bacon, "Ongoing Overview of ETS Cases Not Involving Cigarette Manufacturers." 2 September 1994, LTDL (Bates 71002511), http://legacy.library.ucsf.edu/tid/prz17b00.

95. "AMI/FAMI Policy Paper on Nicotine Addiction and Psychiatric Patients," 28 March 1995, LTDL (Bates 2071540455), http://legacy.library.ucsf.edu/tid/vhc60c00.

96. Alexander H. Glassman, "Cigarette Smoking: Implications for Psychiatric Illness," *American Journal of Psychiatry* 150 (1993): 546–553.

97. Douglas M. Ziedonis et al., "Nicotine Dependence and Schizophrenia," *Hospital and Community Psychiatry* 45 (1994): 204–206.

Chapter 5 The Many Faces of Nicotine

1. Martin Tolchin, "Surgeon General Asserts Smoking Is an Addiction," *New York Times,* 17 May 1988.

2. U.S. Department of Health and Human Services, *Nicotine Addiction: The Health Consequences of Smoking, a Report of the Surgeon General* (Rockville, MD: U.S. Department of Health and Human Services, Public Health Service, Centers for Disease Control, Center for Health Promotion and Education, Office on Smoking and Health, 1988), iii–vii.

3. Ibid., 7.

4. Ibid.

5. John M. Pinney, preface, in *Cigarette Smoking as a Dependence Process,* ed. Norman A. Krasnegor, (Rockville, MD: Department of Health, Education, and Welfare, 1979), viii. In 1994, Pinney founded a consulting organization, Pinney Associates, to advise the pharmaceutical industry. See http://www.pinneyassociates.com/1090.xml, accessed 21 July 2013.

6. Gina Bari Kolata, "New Drugs and the Brain," *Science*, 24 August 1979 (copy from LTDL [Bates 10408548/8550], http://legacy.library.ucsf.edu/tid/rwd4aa00).

7. On Jarvik's work with pharmaceutical companies, see chapter 6. His paper in the NIDA volume was, "Tolerance to the Effects of Tobacco," in Krasnegor, *Cigarette Smoking as a Dependence Process*, 150–157.

8. L. G. Abood, K. Lowy, and H. Booth, "Acute and Chronic Effects of Nicotine in Rats and Evidence for a Noncholinergic Site of Action," in Krasnegor, *Cigarette Smoking as a Dependence Process*, 136–149.

9. On the importance of innovation and its effect on business structure, see Louis Galambos and Jane Eliot Sewell, *Networks of Innovation: Vaccine Development at Merck, Sharp & Dohme, and Mulford, 1895–1995* (New York: Cambridge University Press, 1995); Louis Galambos and Jeffrey L. Sturchio, "Pharmaceutical Firms and the Transition to Biotechnology: A Study in Strategic Innovation," *Business History Review* 72 (1998): 250–278.

10. This is consistent with a number of industries at the time that were innovating using high-tech knowledge and methods. See Sandro Mendonca, "Brave Old World: Accounting for 'High-Tech' Knowledge in 'Low-Tech' Industries," *Research Policy* 38 (2009): 470–482.

11. Allan M. Brandt, "From Nicotine to Nicotrol: Addiction, Cigarettes, and American Culture," in *Altering American Consciousness: The History of Alcohol and Drug Use in the United States, 1800–2000*, ed. Sarah W. Tracy and Caroline Jean Acker (Amherst: University of Massachusetts Press, 2004), 383–402.

12. David T. Courtwright, *Forces of Habit: Drugs and the Making of the Modern World* (Cambridge, MA: Harvard University Press, 2002).

13. U.S. Department of Health and Human Services, *Nicotine Addiction*, 334.

14. On the importance of rhetoric and conceptual frames in substance-abuse policy, see William L. White, "The Lessons of Language: Historical Perspectives on the Rhetoric of Addiction," in Tracy and Acker, *Altering American Consciousness*, 33–60.

15. See Walter Pritchard, Report on the Second Comparative Substance Abuse Workshop, 17–19 October 1991, LTDL (Bates 516551103/1107), http://legacy.library.ucsf.edu/tid/ncv03a00. See also, David M. Warburton, *Pleasure, the Politics and the Reality* (New York: John Wiley & Sons, 1994).

16. David M. Warburton, ed. *Addiction Controversies* (New York: CRC Press, 1992).

17. John H. Robinson and Walter S. Pritchard, "The Role of Nicotine in Tobacco Use," *Psychopharmacology* 108 (1992): 397–407, quote from 406.

18. Robert West, "Nicotine Addiction: A Re-Analysis of the Arguments," *Psychopharmacology* 108 (1992): 408–410.

19. John H. Robinson and Walter S. Pritchard, "The Meaning of Addiction: Reply to West," *Psychopharmacology* 108 (1992): 411–416.

20. John R. Hughes, "Smoking Is a Drug Dependence: A Reply to Robinson and Pritchard," *Psychopharmacology* 113 (1993): 282–283.

21. "Cigarette Smoking and Addiction," Transcript of TV Commercial, BATCo, [1994], LTDL (Bates 500851262/500851268), http://legacy.library.ucsf.edu/tid/fpd30a99.

22. Murray E. Jarvik, "Commentary," *Psychopharmacology* 117 (1995): 18–20.

23. Jack E. Henningfield and Stephen J. Heisman, "The Addictive Role of Nicotine in Tobacco Use," *Psychopharmacology* 117 (1995): 11–13.

24. Saul Shiffman, "Comments on Nicotine Addiction," *Psychopharmacology* 117 (1995): 14–15.

25. See for example, Torgny Svensson, Progress Report, Cellular Basis of Smoking Behavior, May 1988 to May 1989, CTR, LTDL (Bates 50348892/8898), http://legacy .library.ucsf.edu/tid/qot00d00. See also, CTR Notice of Research Grant, Svensson, Nicotine Dependence in Psychiatric Illness: An Experimental Study, 30 October 1996, LTDL (Bates 516887083), http://legacy.library.ucsf.edu/tid/zdg11d00.

26. D. C. Tasher et al., "Introduction of a New Type of Psychotropic Drug: Cyclopenti-mine," *Journal of Neuropsychiatry* 1 (1960): 266–273.

27. See for example, memo from JM Brady to Clarence Little, CTR, 15 January 1965, LTDL (Bates 50025256/5256), http://legacy.library.ucsf.edu/tid/pva8aa00.

28. Elliot S. Valenstein, *The War of the Soups and the Sparks: The Discovery of Neu-rotransmitters and the Dispute over How Nerves Communicate* (New York: Colum-bia University Press, 2005).

29. See Report of the Council for Tobacco Research-USA, Inc., 1985, LTDL (Bates 946009271/9487), http://legacy.library.ucsf.edu/tid/auu11a00.

30. The Role of Receptors in Biology, CTR-Sponsored meeting, 11 June 1985, LTDL (Bates 508453348/3349), http://legacy.library.ucsf.edu/tid/ug093d00.

31. See for example, Gerry Nixon, PM, to Dr. Hans-Juergen Haussmann, INBIFO, 27 April 1994, LTDL (Bates 2029040810/0813), http://legacy.library.ucsf.edu/tid/ obv59e00.

32. 1984 Report of the Smokeless Tobacco Research Council, LTDL (Bates 2546007–6030), http://legacy.library.ucsf.edu/tid/cji21b00. The board of directors of the STRC was composed of representatives from the various smokeless tobacco companies, including Conwood Corporation, Culbro, Helme Tobacco Company, as well as U.S. Tobacco. See for example, STRC Board of Directors Meeting, 5 October 1990, LTDL (Bates USTC3031952-USTC3031964), http://legacy.library.ucsf.edu/tid/wsg45b00.

33. On changes in public perception of Alzheimer's, as well as evolution in medical thinking about the illness, see Jesse F. Ballenger, *Self, Senility, and Alzheimer's Dis-ease in Modern America: A History* (Baltimore: Johns Hopkins University Press, 2006).

34. See for example, New Business Opportunities, RJR, 6 October 1993, LTDL (Bates 509806864/6865), http://legacy.library.ucsf.edu/tid/mlw63d00.

35. For the classic description of Alzheimer's disease, see Peter J. Whitehouse, Konrad Maurer, and Jesse F. Ballenger, eds., *Concepts of Alzheimer Disease: Biological, Clin-ical, and Cultural Perspectives* (Baltimore: Johns Hopkins University Press, 2000).

36. Peter J. Whitehouse et al., "Nicotinic Acetylcholine Binding Sites in Alzheimer's Disease," *Brain Research* 371 (1986): 146–151. Although there was a copy of this paper in the tobacco company archives ([Bates 2023230460/0465], http://legacy .library.ucsf.edu/tid/fqd78e00) the research does not appear to have been spon-sored by the industry. See also, P. J. Whitehouse and K. J. Kellar, "Nicotinic and Muscarinic Cholinergic Receptors in Alzheimer's Disease and Related Disorders," *Journal of Neural Transmission* 24 (1987): 175–182. Copy located in LTDL (Bates 2023230466/0473), http://legacy.library.ucsf.edu/tid/bqd78e00.

37. Memo from Carr Smith and Sam Simmons to Dr. G. R. DiMarco, Re: September 2 Conversation with Dr. Ezio Giacobini, LTDL (Bates 506770727), http://legacy.library .ucsf.edu/tid/upj44d00. Giacobini apparently had a conversation with a Dr. Levy who made the comment about the tobacco industry being happy about lowered Alzheimer's incidence among smokers. On the Premier development process, see Alpha Project, September 19–20, 1988, RJR, LTDL (Bates 510220288/0298), http:// legacy.library.ucsf.edu/tid/yvg13a00.

38. Margaret Glynn to A. Wallace Hayes, R. J. Reynolds, 11 September 1989, LTDL (Bates 508236036), http://legacy.library.ucsf.edu/tid/cqc04d00.

39. See Minutes from BAT Meeting, 10 February 1992, LTDL (Bates USX473448-USX473451), http://legacy.library.ucsf.edu/tid/evz36b00.

40. Gray, while much less controversial than his predecessor Eysenck, was similarly influential in the field of psychology, particularly physiological methods within psychology. Philip J. Corr and Adam M. Perkins, "The Role of Theory in the Psychophysiology of Personality: From Ivan Pavlov to Jeffrey Gray," *International Journal of Psychophysiology* 62 (2006): 367–376.

41. Jeffrey A. Gray to Dr. R. E. Thornton, BATCo, 11 April 1988, LTDL (Bates 300555923/300555930), http://legacy.library.ucsf.edu/tid/sex67a99.

42. Memo from Dr. R. E. Thornton to Mr. E. A. A. Burell, BAT, 1 March 1988, LTDL (Bates 300555955), http://legacy.library.ucsf.edu/tid/afx67a99. Based on the dates of these two pieces of correspondence, it appears that BAT had conversations with and about Gray before he submitted the formal application.

43. See CTR Progress Report, Gray and Dr. S. N. Mitchell, January 1991 to December 1993, LTDL (Bates 50305138/5139), http://legacy.library.ucsf.edu/tid/jiz99c00.

44. David St. James, "Take Two Marlboros and Call Me in the Morning," *New York Monthly,* October 1988, LTDL (Bates 2024300823), http://legacy.library.ucsf.edu/tid/wbg34e00.

45. Tony Reid, Associate Director of Eurofi, to Dr. Ray Thornton, BAT Manager, 31 August 1992, LTDL (Bates 300530482/300530496), http://legacy.library.ucsf.edu/tid/qgu97a99.

46. Susan Wonnacott, "The Paradox of Nicotinic Acetylcholine Receptor Upregulation by Nicotine," *Trends in Pharmacological Sciences* 11 (1990): 216–219, quote from 218. Copy located in LTDL (Bates 508283852/3856), http://legacy.library.ucsf.edu/tid/xky93d00. Wonnacott reviewed grants for BAT. See Wonnacott to Annalisa Westergreen, BATCo, 20 October 1997, LTDL (Bates 325308570–325308572), http://legacy.library.ucsf.edu/tid/nne44a99.

47. Roundtable Discussion, RJR, 14 December 1990, LTDL (Bates 515973449/3515), http://legacy.library.ucsf.edu/tid/iec92d00. Participants in the roundtable included Jed Rose, Charles Meliska, David Gilbert, Elliott Vessell, Allan Collins, Jeffrey Gray, George Lunt, Susan Wonnacott, Samuel Deadwyler, as well as researchers within RJR.

48. See Pritchard, Psychophysiology of Smoking, 2 January 1991, RJR, LTDL (Bates 515431979), http://legacy.library.ucsf.edu/tid/fkw92d00.

49. Group Conference on Smoking Issues, BAT, 29 March 1988, LTDL (Bates 301127229/301127240), http://legacy.library.ucsf.edu/tid/drn20a99.

50. See for example, Science & Technology Report, Philip Morris Europe/Neuchatel, 22 August 1994, LTDL (Bates 2048366755–6789), http://legacy.library.ucsf.edu/tid/hty20h00.

51. See for example, Annabel Ferriman, "Is Smoking Good for You?," *Weekly Telegraph,* 28 September 1994, LTDL (Bates 2046532877), http://legacy.library.ucsf.edu/tid/gkn57d00.

52. See for example, Application to Philip Morris USA for research funding from Dr. Gordon L. Mangan, University of Auckland, New Zealand, November 1994, LTDL (Bates 2051517545/7551), http://legacy.library.ucsf.edu/tid/nmw14c00; Edna F. R. Pereira et al., "Physostigmine and Galanthamine: Probes for a Novel Binding Site on the alpha4beta2 Subtype of Neuronal Nicotinic Receptors Stably Expressed in

Fibroblast Cells," *Journal of Pharmacology and Experimental Therapeutics* 270 (1994): 768–778. Copy in LTDL (Bates PUBLICATIONS045045/5055), http://legacy.library.ucsf.edu/tid/tzw00a00.

53. See for example, Thomas Maugh, "Scientists Smoke Out Nicotine's Power: Benefits Are Seen for Cigarette Addicts and Alzheimer Victims," *International Herald Tribune*, 23 September 1995, LTDL (Bates 800128795), http://legacy.library.ucsf.edu/tid/eyj73a99.

54. See for example, Jeff S. Kim and Edward D. Levin, "Nicotinic, Muscarinic and Dopaminergic Actions in the Ventral Hippocampus and the Nucleus Accumbens: Effects on Spatial Working Memory in Rats," *Brain Research* 725 (1996): 231–240. The authors acknowledged support of the CTR for this research. Copy of paper in LTDL (Bates 2063120791/0800), http://legacy.library.ucsf.edu/tid/jig33e00.

55. Press release, Duke University, Nicotine Research at Duke University Medical Center, 23 August 1996, LTDL (Bates 2070157462/7466), http://legacy.library.ucsf.edu/tid/gqy08d00. Duke had been endowed by tobacco in the first place. See Richard Kluger, *Ashes to Ashes: America's Hundred-Year Cigarette War, the Public Health, and the Unabashed Triumph of Philip Morris* (New York: Alfred A. Knopf, 1996), 52–53.

56. Edward D. Levin, "Nicotinic Agonist and Antagonist Effects on Memory," *Drug Development Research* 38 (1996): 188–195. This research was supported by the CTR, as well as other funding sources such as the National Science Foundation. Copy in LTDL (Bates 2063603450/3452), http://legacy.library.ucsf.edu/tid/lsn67e00.

57. Alfonso Gambardella, *Science and Innovation: The US Pharmaceutical Industry During the 1980s* (New York: Cambridge University Press, 1995).

58. Report from Gilbert, Twenty-Second Annual Meeting of the Society for Psychophysiological Research, 2 November 1982, RJR, LTDL (Bates 502853492), http://legacy.library.ucsf.edu/tid/yoz68d00. For some history of the Society for Psychophysiological Research, see Frances H. Gabbay and Robert M. Stern, "A Quiet Voice: Roland Clark Davis and the Emergence of Psychophysiology," *Psychophysiology* 49 (2012): 443–453; Chester W. Darrow, "Psychophysiology, Yesterday, Today, and Tomorrow," *Psychophysiology* 1 (1964): 4–7.

59. For more context on the use of EEG within the tobacco industry, see Vincent C. Panzano et al., "Human Electroencephalography and the Tobacco Industry: A Review of Internal Documents," *Tobacco Control* 19 (2010): 153–159.

60. For a broader consideration of the connections between psychology and pharmacology, see Lori A. Schmied, Hannah Steinberg, and Elizabeth A. B. Sykes, "Psychopharmacology's Debt to Experimental Psychology," *History of Psychology* 9 (2006): 144–157.

61. Memo from J. H. Reynolds, Third Quarter Status Report, Biobehavioral Research Division, 8 October 1986, RJR, LTDL (Bates 506804310/4326), http://legacy.library.ucsf.edu/tid/fbu54d00.

62. Memo from J. H. Robinson to Dr. A. W. Hayes, Nicotine Conference, 3 November 1986, LTDL (Bates 512051685/1688), http://legacy.library.ucsf.edu/tid/rqf43d00.

63. Biobehavioral Research Division, 1987 Action Plan, LTDL (Bates 506221890/1897), http://legacy.library.ucsf.edu/tid/nnc84d00.

64. See for example, Letter from Dr. Michael M. Harpold, Vice President of Scientific Planning, SIBIA, to Dr. Wallace Hayes, Biochemical and Biotechnological Research and Development, RJR, 8 August 1988, LTDL (Bates 506792238/2239), http://legacy.library.ucsf.edu/tid/egv54d00. On the SIBIA receptor technology program, see

Outline, 29 July 1988, LTDL (Bates 506792240/2250), http://legacy.library.ucsf.edu/tid/fgv54d00.

65. Objectives of RJR in Any Relationship with Hoechst, August 1989, RJR, LTDL (Bates 507063521), http://legacy.library.ucsf.edu/tid/dcn34d00.

66. Memo from P. M. Lippiello to G. R. DiMarco, Subject: Progress in RJRT/HRPI Collaboration, 25 October 1990, LTDL (Bates 515656150/6153), http://legacy.library.ucsf.edu/tid/dyq92d00.

67. Slide Show Regarding RJRT and HPRI Collaboration, 1991, LTDL (Bates 508035041/5058), http://legacy.library.ucsf.edu/tid/mdv04d00.

68. See for example, Memo from Jim Wilson, Benefits of Smoking, RJR, 3 March 1994, LTDL (Bates 513049818/9819), http://legacy.library.ucsf.edu/tid/wh023d00.

69. See for example, Merouane Bencherif and Patrick M. Lippiello, Report on Nicotine Pharmacology and Neurodegenerative Diseases Program (NPND)/Positive Aspects of Nicotine, 25 June 1994, RJR, LTDL (Bates 510282818/2819), http://legacy.library.ucsf.edu/tid/pwg63d00.

70. See for example, Contract Information, Dr. Ezio Giacobini, RJR, 31 December 1994, LTDL (Bates 515859466), http://legacy.library.ucsf.edu/tid/wqe92d00.

71. Memo from Carr Smith to Layten Davis, Preliminary Outline of Article on How Nicotine Works in the Brain, RJR, 12 February 1993, LTDL (Bates 510662857/2858), http://legacy.library.ucsf.edu/tid/xcy53d00. He planned to publish this article but this apparently did not happen. Memo to Layten Davis et al., RJR, 21 May 1993, LTDL (Bates 510662850/2851), http://legacy.library.ucsf.edu/tid/qcy53d00.

72. Nicotine Pharmacology and Neurodegenerative Disease Team Functions, April 1994, RJR, LTDL (Bates 508802210/2211), http://legacy.library.ucsf.edu/tid/qsw83d00.

73. Presentation, Positive Aspects ("Benefits") of Smoking, RJRT, 1994, LTDL (Bates 400446517/400446525), http://legacy.library.ucsf.edu/tid/ycx83a99.

74. Newspaper reports in the mid-1990s suggested that tobacco companies were considering spinning off different parts of the companies in the wake of ongoing legal difficulties. See for example, "Philip Morris, RJR May Quit Cigarettes," *Investor's Business Daily,* 18 April 1994, copy in LTDL (Bates 513595721/5724), http://legacy.library.ucsf.edu/tid/hds13d00.

75. Corporate Overview of Pharmaceutical Related Technologies of the R. J. Reynolds Tobacco Company, March 1997, LTDL (Bates 516889375/9378), http://legacy.library.ucsf.edu/tid/gxh56d00.

76. Targacept, Inc., May 1997, LTDL (Bates 530230635/0643), http://legacy.library.ucsf.edu/tid/toh25a00.

77. Summary Document, IBC Conference, 29 July 1997, RJR, LTDL (Bates 519419746/9747), http://legacy.library.ucsf.edu/tid/tte50d00. See also, Stephen P. Arneric, Mark Halladay, and Michael Williams, "Neuronal Nicotinic Receptors: A Perspective on Two Decades of Drug Discovery Research," *Biochemical Pharmacology* 74 (2007): 1092–1101.

78. Press Release by Targacept and Rhone Poulenc Rorer, 8 February 1999, LTDL (Bates 2072685314), http://legacy.library.ucsf.edu/tid/zkh42c00. This particular copy of the press release was located within the Philip Morris files. Rhone-Poulenc was the company responsible for the widespread introduction of Thorazine (chlorpromazine) in psychiatric hospitals in the 1950s and 1960s. David Healy, *The Creation of Psychopharmacology* (Cambridge: Harvard University Press, 2002).

79. Press Release, Targacept, 21 August 2000, LTDL (Bates 527824503/4505), http://legacy.library.ucsf.edu/tid/ahv96a00.

80. Kenneth E. Warner, John Slade, and David T. Sweanor, "The Emerging Market for Long-Term Nicotine Maintenance," *JAMA* 278 (1997): 1087–1092.

81. Usha Lee McFarling, "Nicotine Can Improve Memory, Study Says," *Charlotte Observer*, 8 November 1998, LTDL (Bates 522544096/4098), http://legacy.library.ucsf .edu/tid/lkd60d00. See also, John Schwartz, "A Cigarette Chemical Packed with Helpful Effects?," *Washington Post*, 9 November 1998, LTDL (Bates 520766513/6514), http://legacy.library.ucsf.edu/tid/dxc30d00.

82. Some analysts have focused on the tobacco industry's development of analogs and suspected that the cigarette companies would be making covert use of them to addict more customers. The primary beneficiaries of the analog programs were pharmaceutical companies, however. For a concerned perspective about nicotine analogs, see Rosemary Vagg and Simon Chapman, "Nicotine Analogues: A Review of Tobacco Industry Research Interests," *Addiction* 100 (2005): 701–712.

83. Daniel Q. Haney, "Nicotine May Help Brain Disease," *Associated Press Online*, 21 February 2000, LTDL (Bates 522544058/4059), http://legacy.library.ucsf.edu/tid/ ikd60d00; Lee Bowman, "Nicotine Might Reduce Symptoms of Brain Diseases," *Columbus Dispatch (Scripps Howard News Service)*, 22 February 2000, LTDL (Bates 2083518973/8974), http://legacy.library.ucsf.edu/tid/xdz35c00; and Ulysses Torassa, "Scientists Studying Benefits of Nicotine," *San Francisco Examiner*, 22 February 2000, LTDL (Bates 2083518975/8976), http://legacy.library.ucsf.edu/tid/ ydz35c00.

84. "Great Drug, Shame about the Delivery System," *The Economist*, 23 September 2000, LTDL (Bates 2078881595A/1597), http://legacy.library.ucsf.edu/tid/gjn86c00.

Chapter 6   From Tolerance to Treatment

1. Gregory W. Dalack and Alexander H. Glassman, "A Clinical Approach to Help Psychiatric Patients with Smoking Cessation," *Psychiatric Quarterly* 63 (1992): 27–39, quote from 34. Dalack subsequently moved to the University of Michigan, where he has been the chair of the psychiatry department since 2007.

2. Babalola Faseru et al., "Prevalence and Predictors of Tobacco Treatment in an Academic Medical Center," *Joint Commission Journal on Quality and Patient Safety* 35 (2009): 551–557.

3. This was true for proposed *DSM-III* diagnoses in general. Hannah Decker pointed out that an early draft version of what would become *DSM-III* was originally presented at a conference sponsored by the Squibb pharmaceutical company. Hannah S. Decker, *The Making of DSM-III: A Diagnostic Manual's Conquest of American Psychiatry* (New York: Oxford University Press, 2013), 144. As historians have pointed out, physicians in many fields had established relationships with pharmaceutical companies in the twentieth century. See John P. Swann, *Academic Scientists and the Pharmaceutical Industry: Cooperative Research in Twentieth-Century America* (Baltimore: Johns Hopkins University Press, 1988); Dominique A. Tobbell, *Pills, Power, and Policy: The Struggle for Drug Reform in Cold War America and Its Consequences* (Berkeley: University of California Press, 2012).

4. David Healy, *The Creation of Psychopharmacology* (Cambridge: Harvard University Press, 2002), 109.

5. For an overview on the shifts in psychiatry from a psychoanalytic to a biological perspective, see Gerald N. Grob, *The Mad Among Us: A History of the Care of America's Mentally Ill* (Cambridge: Harvard University Press, 1994); Edward Shorter, *A History*

of Psychiatry: From the Era of the Asylum to the Age of Prozac (New York: John Wiley & Sons, 1997).

6. The ACNP continues to promote relationships with the pharmaceutical industry. See http://www.acnp.org/aboutus/default.aspx, accessed 26 July 2013. For the origins of psychopharmacology, including relationships to the pharmaceutical industry, see Lori A. Schmied, Hannah Steinberg, and Elizabeth A. B. Sykes, "Psychopharmacology's Debt to Experimental Psychology," *History of Psychology* 9 (2006): 144–157.

7. Jerome H. Jaffe and Murray E. Jarvik, "Tobacco Use and Tobacco Use Disorder," in *Psychopharmacology: A Generation of Progress*, ed. Morris A. Lipton, Alberto DiMascio, and Keith F. Killam (New York: Raven Press, 1978), 1665–1676.

8. See for example, Daniel Goleman, "Who's Mentally Ill?," *Psychology Today*, January 1978, 34–41; William T. McReynolds, "*DSM-III* and the Future of Applied Social Science," *Professional Psychology* 10 (1979): 123–132.

9. Nina G. Schneider et al., "The Use of Nicotine Gum during Cessation of Smoking," *American Journal of Psychiatry* 134 (1977): 439–440.

10. "Conversation with Murray Jarvik," *Addiction* 96 (2001): 1241–1252.

11. David Healy has cited the 1962 Kefauver-Harris amendments as the origin of the FDA requirement that pharmaceutical companies must have a diagnosis as an indication for a new drug application. David Healy, *The Antidepressant Era* (Cambridge: Harvard University Press, 1997), 26–28.

12. Advertisement printed in *JAMA*, 2 March 1984, LTDL (Bates 505016789), http://legacy.library.ucsf.edu/tid/szk35d00. Merrell's caution in this advertisement might have been due in some part to its difficulty with the FDA when it attempted to bring Kevalon—thalidomide—to market in the United States. in the early 1960s. Daniel Carpenter, *Reputation and Power: Organizational Image and Pharmaceutical Regulation at the FDA* (Princeton: Princeton University Press, 2010).

13. "Calls for an Active Antismoking Role for Psychiatrists," *Clinical Psychiatry News*, March 1986, LTDL (Bates 506635726), http://legacy.library.ucsf.edu/tid/snw44d00.

14. William A. Check, "New Knowledge about Nicotine Effects," *JAMA* 247 (1982): 2333–2338.

15. Murray E. Jarvik and Dorothy K. Hatsukami, "Tobacco Dependence," in *Smoking and Human Behavior*, ed. Tara Ney and Anthony Gale (New York: Wiley, 1989), 57–67.

16. American Psychiatric Association, *Diagnostic and Statistical Manual of Mental Disorders*, 3rd rev. ed. (Washington, DC: American Psychiatric Press, 1987).

17. *DSM* criteria were based on research criteria from investigators at Washington University in St. Louis and the New York State Psychiatric Institute. See John P. Feighner et al., "Diagnostic Criteria for Use in Psychiatric Research," *Archives of General Psychiatry* 26 (1972): 57–63; Robert L. Spitzer, Jean Endicott, and Janet B. W. Williams, "Research Diagnostic Criteria," *Archives of General Psychiatry* 36 (1979): 1381–1383.

18. For a comparison of different kinds of measures, see for example, John R. Hughes, Steven W. Gust, and Terry F. Pechacek, "Prevalence of Tobacco Dependence and Withdrawal," *American Journal of Psychiatry* 144 (1987): 205–208.

19. Karl-Olov Fagerström, "Measuring Degree of Physical Dependence to Tobacco Smoking with Reference to Individualization of Treatment," *Addictive Behaviors* 3 (1978): 235–241.

20. Karl-Olov Fagerström and Nina G. Schneider, "Measuring Nicotine Dependence: A Review of the Fagerström Tolerance Questionnaire," *Journal of Behavioral Medicine* 12 (1989): 159–182.

21. Executive Profile: Karl-Olov Fagerström, http://investing.businessweek.com/research/stocks/private/person.asp?personId=26959017&privcapId=25290342&previousCapId=2231152&previousTitle=Sj%C3%A4tte%20AP-fonden, accessed 12 February 2013. See also Fagerström's 2009 review, funded by Pfizer. Karl Fagerström and Henri-Jean Aubin, "Management of Smoking Cessation in Patients with Psychiatric Disorders," *Current Medical Research & Opinion* 25 (2009): 511–518.

22. American Psychiatric Association, *Diagnostic and Statistical Manual of Mental Disorders,* 4th ed. (Washington, DC: American Psychiatric Association, 1994), 243.

23. For an example of the widespread acceptance of psychiatric diagnosis and medication, see Peter D. Kramer, *Listening to Prozac* (New York: Penguin Books, 1993).

24. American Psychiatric Association, *Practice Guidelines for Treatment of Patients with Substance Use Disorders: Alcohol, Cocaine, Opioids* (Washington, DC: American Psychiatric Association, 1995). The exclusion of nicotine was noted and criticized in Barbara S. McCrady and Douglas Ziedonis, "American Psychiatric Association Practice Guidelines for Substance Use Disorders," *Behavior Therapy* 32 (2001): 309–336.

25. American Psychiatric Association, "Position Statement on Nicotine Dependence," *American Journal of Psychiatry* 152 (1995): 481–482; "New APA Position Statement Urges Actions to Reduce High Rates of Nicotine Dependence," *Psychiatric Services* 46 (1995): 194–195.

26. American Psychiatric Association, *Practice Guideline for the Treatment of Patients with Nicotine Dependence* (Washington, DC: American Psychiatric Association, 1996).

27. American Psychiatric Association, *Practice Guidelines for Treatment of Patients with Substance Use Disorders: Alcohol, Cocaine, Opioids.*

28. John R. Hughes, "Treating Nicotine Dependence in Mental Health Settings," *Journal of Practical Psychiatry and Behavioral Health,* July 1997, LTDL (Bates 2081911947/1951), http://legacy.library.ucsf.edu/tid/goy81c00.

29. See John Hughes CV, http://www.uvm.edu/~psych/faculty/cv/Hughes_cv.pdf, accessed 12 February 2013.

30. Stephen J. Heishman, Lynn T. Koslowski, and Jack E. Henningfield, "Nicotine Addiction: Implications for Public Health Policy," *Journal of Social Issues* 53 (1997): 13–33.

31. Theodore E. Keeler et al., "The Benefits of Switching Smoking Cessation Drugs to Over-the-Counter Status," in *Tobacco Control Policy,* ed. Kenneth E. Warner (San Francisco: Jossey-Bass, 2006), 417–438.

32. See for example, J. Taylor Hays, Jon O. Ebbert, and Amit Sood, "Efficacy and Safety of Varenicline for Smoking Cessation," *American Journal of Medicine* 121 (2008): S32–S42. Pfizer, the maker of varenicline, had a relationship with the lead author of this study and also paid for an editorial consultant to produce the article.

33. On the history of the changing views of schizophrenia, see Sander L. Gilman, "Constructing Schizophrenia as a Category of Mental Illness," in *History of Psychiatry and Medical Psychology,* ed. Edwin R. Wallace IV and John Gach (New York: Springer, 2008), 461–483.

34. Arvid Carlsson, "Mechanism of Action of Neuroleptic Drugs," in *Psychopharmacology: A Generation of Progress,* ed. Morris A. Lipton, Alberto DiMascio, and Keith F. Killam (New York: Raven Press, 1978), 1057–1070.

35. International teams had also looked at similar tests in Alzheimer's disease. See for example, E. Gordon et al., "The Differential Diagnosis of Dementia Using P300 Latency," *Biological Psychiatry* 21 (1986): 1123–1132.

36. Robert Freedman et al., "Neurobiological Studies of Sensory Gating in Schizophrenia," *Schizophrenia Bulletin* 13 (1987): 669–678; Lawrence E. Adler et al., "Normalization by Nicotine of Deficient Auditory Sensory Gating in the Relatives of Schizophrenics," *Biological Psychiatry* 32 (1992): 607–616. Tobacco-company researchers were closely following this research and had copies of the Freedman group's work. See for example, copy located in LTDL (Bates 2050236458/6467), http://legacy.library.ucsf.edu/tid/tun86e00.

37. Not surprisingly, the tobacco industry tracked this research, though they do not seem to have funded most of it. See for example, Sherry Leonard et al., "Nicotinic Receptor Function in Schizophrenia," *Schizophrenia Bulletin* 22 (1996): 431–445; Lee Bowman, "Nicotine May Give Short-Lived Relief of Symptoms. Gene Defect Linked to Schizophrenics' Heavy Smoking," *Scripps Howard News Service*, 21 January 1997, LTDL (Bates 2073480711/0713), http://legacy.library.ucsf.edu/tid/zpq80b00; and Thomas Maugh, "New Study Links Defect in Brain Gene to Schizophrenia," *Seattle Times*, 21 January 1997, LTDL (Bates 770006515), http://legacy.library.ucsf.edu/tid/ooi45a99.

38. See for example, E. D. Levin et al., "Nicotine Effects on Adults with Attention-Deficit/Hyperactivity Disorder," *Psychopharmacology* 123 (1996): 55–63. Copy in LTDL (Bates 2063120782/0790), http://legacy.library.ucsf.edu/tid/kug33e00.

39. See for example, Joseph McEvoy et al., "Clozapine Decreased Smoking in Patients with Chronic Schizophrenia," *Biological Psychiatry* 37 (1995): 550–552. Copy in LTDL (Bates 2065399878/9881), http://legacy.library.ucsf.edu/tid/tiw43a00.

40. See for example, Jose De Leon, "Smoking and Vulnerability for Schizophrenia," *Schizophrenia Bulletin* 22 (1996): 405–409.

41. See for example, email from Don deBethizy, 25 February 1997, RJR, LTDL (Bates 528807501/7503), http://legacy.library.ucsf.edu/tid/zzf96a00.

42. Edward D. Levin, William Wilson, Jed E. Rose, Joseph McEvoy, "Nicotine-Haloperidol Interactions and Cognitive Performance in Schizophrenics," *Neuropsychopharmacology* 15 (1996): 429–436. No tobacco funding was mentioned for this study. Copy of article in LTDL (Bates 2063120815/0822), http://legacy.library.ucsf.edu/tid/mig33e00.

43. See for example, Shawn R. Currie et al., "Outcome from a Community-Based Smoking Cessation Program for Persons with Serious Mental Illness," *Community Mental Health Journal* 44 (2008): 187–194.

44. On psychiatric diagnosis and pharmaceuticals, see Healy, *The Creation of Psychopharmacology*; Laura D. Hirshbein, *American Melancholy: Constructions of Depression in the Twentieth Century* (New Brunswick, NJ: Rutgers University Press, 2009).

45. See for example, Douglas M. Ziedonis and Tony P. George, "Schizophrenia and Nicotine Use: Report of a Pilot Smoking Cessation Program and Review of Neurobiological and Clinical Issues," *Schizophrenia Bulletin* 23 (1997): 247–254.

46. Roman Kotov et al., "Smoking in Schizophrenia: Diagnostic Specificity, Symptom Correlates, and Illness Severity," *Schizophrenia Bulletin* 36 (2010): 173–181.

47. Amy L. Copeland, Magdalena Kulesza, and Gerald S. Hecht, "Pre-Quit Depression Level and Smoking Expectancies for Mood Management Predict the Nature of Smoking Withdrawal Symptoms in College Women Smokers," *Addictive Behaviors* 34 (2009): 481–483. This was also true for older adults with drinking problems. See

Brent A. Kenney et al., "Depressive Symptoms, Drinking Problems, and Smoking Cessation in Older Adults," *Addictive Behaviors* 34 (2009): 548–553.

48. Annette K. McClave et al., "Associations between Smoking Cessation and Anxiety and Depression," *Addictive Behaviors* 34 (2009): 491–497.

49. See for example, Richard A. Brown et al., "Effects on Substance Use Outcomes in Adolescents Receiving Motivational Interviewing for Smoking Cessation during Psychiatric Hospitalization," *Addictive Behaviors* 34 (2009): 887–891; Andrea H. Weinberger et al., "Gender Differences in Associations between Lifetime Alcohol, Depression, Panic Disorder, and Posttraumatic Stress Disorder and Tobacco Withdrawal," *American Journal on Addictions* 18 (2009): 140–147; and Erin C. Marshall et al., "Reasons for Quitting Smoking Prior to a Self-Quit Attempt among Smokers with and without Posttraumatic Stress Disorder or Other Anxiety/Mood Psychopathology," *American Journal on Addictions* 18 (2009): 309–315.

50. Francisco J. Diaz et al., "Tobacco Smoking Behaviors in Bipolar Disorder: A Comparison of the General Population, Schizophrenia, and Major Depression," *Bipolar Disorders* 11 (2009): 154–165.

51. On the lack of clarity in psychiatric diagnoses, see Allan V. Horwitz, *Creating Mental Illness* (Chicago: University of Chicago Press, 2002); Allen Frances, *Saving Normal: An Insider's Revolt against Out-of-Control Psychiatric Diagnosis, DSM-5, Big Pharma, and the Medicalization of Ordinary Life* (New York: HarperCollins, 2013).

52. Sandra Baker Morissette et al., "Anxiety, Anxiety Disorders, Tobacco Use, and Nicotine: A Critical Review of Interrelationships," *Psychological Bulletin* 133 (2007): 245–272.

53. See for example, Stephen L. Dewey et al., "A Pharmacologic Strategy for the Treatment of Nicotine Addiction," *Synapse* 31 (1999): 76–86.

54. Stephen P. Arneric, Mark Halladay, and Michael Williams, "Neuronal Nicotinic Receptors: A Perspective on Two Decades of Drug Discovery Research," *Biochemical Pharmacology* 74 (2007): 1092–1101.

55. Bridget M. Kuehn, "Studies Linking Smoking-Cessation Drug with Suicide Risk Spark Concerns," *JAMA* 301 (2009): 1007–1008.

56. Alain Dervaux and Xavier Laqueille, "Letter to the Editor: Antidepressant Treatment and Smoking Cessation in Bipolar Disorder," *JAMA* 301 (2009): 2093.

57. On the black-box warning (and marketing despite the warning), see Laura Eggertson, "Pfizer Advertises Smoking Cessation Drug despite Health Warnings," *Canadian Medical Association Journal* 184 (2012): E127–E128. On the alleged benefits of the drug for depression, see Noah S. Philip et al., "Varenicline Augmentation in Depressed Smokers: An 8-Week, Open-Label Study," *Journal of Clinical Psychiatry* 70 (2009): 1026–1031.

58. See for example, Jennifer B. McClure et al., "Mood, Side-Effects and Smoking Outcomes among Persons with and without Probable Lifetime Depression Taking Varenicline," *Journal of General Internal Medicine* 24 (2009): 563–569; Joan Arehart-Treichel, "Several Medications Linked to Violent Acts," *Psychiatric News*, 4 February 2011, 16, 24.

59. See for example, Neal L. Benowitz, "Pharmacology of Nicotine: Addiction, Smoking-Induced Disease, and Therapeutics," *Annual Review of Pharmacology and Toxicology* 49 (2009): 57–71. For this article, Benowitz disclosed that he acted as a paid consultant to several pharmaceutical companies about smoking-cessation medications.

60. Karen Lasser et al., "Smoking and Mental Illness: A Population-Based Prevalence Study," *JAMA* 284 (2000): 2606–2610.

61. For a nice review of the complicated neurobiology of schizophrenia, see Edward F. Domino, Diana Mirzoyan, and Hideo Tsukada, "N-methyl-D-aspartate Antagonists as Drug Models of Schizophrenia: A Surprising Link to Tobacco Smoking," *Progress in Neuro-Psychopharmacology & Biological Psychiatry* 28 (2004): 801–811. On some of the different patterns of smoking behaviors among mentally ill individuals, see for example, Jennifer W. Tidey et al., "Cigarette Smoking Topography in Smokers with Schizophrenia and Matched Non-Psychiatric Controls," *Drug and Alcohol Dependence* 80 (2005): 259–265; Jill M. Williams et al., "Increased Nicotine and Cotinine Levels in Smokers with Schizophrenia and Schizoaffective Disorder Is Not a Metabolic Effect," *Schizophrenia Research* 79 (2005): 323–335.

62. The American Medical Association recently made the newsworthy assertion that obesity was actually a disease. See Andrew Pollock, "A.M.A. Recognizes Obesity as a Disease," *New York Times,* 18 June 2013. It is still not considered a psychiatric disorder, however.

63. Stanton Peele, "Reductionism in the Psychology of the Eighties: Can Biochemistry Eliminate Addiction, Mental Illness, and Pain?," *American Psychologist* 36 (1981): 807–818.

64. See for example, Jean Addington, "Group Treatment for Smoking Cessation among Persons with Schizophrenia," *Psychiatric Services* 49 (1998): 925–928.

65. Marc Gelkopf et al., "Nonmedication Smoking Reduction Program for Inpatients with Chronic Schizophrenia: A Randomized Control Design Study," *Journal of Nervous and Mental Disease* 200 (2012): 142–146.

66. Nora D. Volkow, "Celebrating the History of NIDA (2003–present)," *Drug and Alcohol Dependence* 107 (2010): 106–107.

67. Ian P. Stolerman and Martin J. Jarvis, "The Scientific Case That Nicotine Is Addictive," *Psychopharmacology* 117 (1995): 2–10, quote from 2.

68. As Musto and Korsmeyer have pointed out, most substance-abuse policy over the last four decades has hinged on both law enforcement and medical treatment. David F. Musto and Pamela Korsmeyer, *The Quest for Drug Control: Politics and Federal Policy in a Period of Increasing Substance Abuse, 1963–1981* (New Haven: Yale University Press, 2002).

69. For a recent statement of this, see Nora D. Volkow, "Substance Use Disorders in Schizophrenia—Clinical Implications of Comorbidity," *Schizophrenia Bulletin* 35 (2009): 469–472.

70. James Cocores, "Nicotine Dependence: Diagnosis and Treatment," *Psychiatric Clinics of North America* 16 (1993): 49–60.

71. Jerome H. Jaffe, "Commentary on the Nicotine IS/IS Not Addictive Debate," *Psychopharmacology* 117 (1995): 21–22, quote from 22.

72. Patt Denning, *Practicing Harm Reduction Psychotherapy: An Alternative Approach to Addictions* (New York: Guilford, 2000).

73. See for example, Taryn G. Moss et al., "Prefrontal Cognitive Dysfunction Is Associated with Tobacco Dependence Treatment Failure in Smokers with Schizophrenia," *Drug and Alcohol Dependence* 104 (2009): 94–99.

74. Jack E. Henningfield and Stephen J. Heisman, "The Addictive Role of Nicotine in Tobacco Use," *Psychopharmacology* 117 (1995): 11–13, quote from 12.

75. John P. Docherty, Peter M. Marzuk, and Jack D. Barchas, "Editorial: Nicotine Dependence: Perspectives on a New Guideline from APA," *American Journal of Psychiatry* 153 (1996): 1247–1248.

76. John R. Hughes, "Why Does Smoking So Often Produce Dependence? A Somewhat Different View," *Tobacco Control* 10 (2001): 62–64.

77. Benowitz, "Pharmacology of Nicotine." See also, Jill M. Williams, Douglas M. Ziedonis, and Jonathan Foulds, "A Case Series of Nicotine Nasal Spray in the Treatment of Tobacco Dependence among Patients with Schizophrenia," *Psychiatric Services* 55 (2004): 1064–1066.

78. For a description of hostility to opiate maintenance in the early twentieth century, see Caroline Jean Acker, *Creating the American Junkie: Addition Research in the Classic Era of Narcotic Control* (Baltimore: Johns Hopkins University Press, 2002).

79. Douglas Ziedonis et al., "Tobacco Use and Cessation in Psychiatric Disorders: National Institute of Mental Health Report," *Nicotine & Tobacco Research* 10 (2008): 1691–1715, quote from 1708.

80. See for example, Katrina Lising-Enriquez and Tony P. George, "Treatment of Comorbid Tobacco Use in People with Serious Mental Illness," *Journal of Psychiatry and Neuroscience* 34 (2009): E1–E2; E. L. M. Ochoa, "Varenicline Reduced Smoking Behaviour in a Mentally Ill Person," *Journal of Psychopharmacology* 23 (2009): 340–341; and Jon O. Ebbert et al., "Combination Treatment with Varenicline and Nicotine Replacement Therapy," *Nicotine & Tobacco Research* 11 (2009): 572–576.

81. Mitchell Zeller, Dorothy K. Hatsukami, and Strategic Dialogue on Tobacco Harm Reduction Group, "The Strategic Dialogue on Tobacco Harm Reduction: A Vision and Blueprint for Action in the US," *Tobacco Control* 18 (2009): 324–332.

82. This is despite a growing literature on the problems with the pharmaceutical industry regarding mental-illness treatments. See for example, Robert Whitaker, *Anatomy of an Epidemic: Magic Bullets, Psychiatric Drugs, and the Astonishing Rise of Mental Illness in America* (New York: Crown, 2010).

83. Bridget M. Kuehn, "Link Between Smoking and Mental Illness May Lead to Treatments," *JAMA* 295 (2006): 483–484.

84. See for example, J. T. Andreasen et al., "Antidepressant-Like Effects of Nicotinic Acetylcholine Receptor Antagonists, But Not Agonists, in the Mouse Forced Swim and Mouse Tail Suspension Tests," *Journal of Pharmacology* 23 (2009): 797–804.

Chapter 7 Tobacco Control and the Mentally Ill

1. Karen Lasser et al., "Smoking and Mental Illness: A Population-Based Prevalence Study," *JAMA* 284 (2000): 2606–2610.

2. Steve Blow, "Data Show Smoking's Mental Toll," *Dallas Morning News,* 26 November 2000, LTDL (Bates 531638437/8444), http://legacy.library.ucsf.edu/tid/vjp55a00.

3. Timothy W. Lineberry et al., "Population-Based Prevalence of Smoking in Psychiatric Inpatients: A Focus on Acute Suicide Risk and Major Diagnostic Groups," *Comprehensive Psychiatry* 50 (2009): 526–532. See also, Ineke Keizer et al., "Smoking in Psychiatric Inpatients: Association with Working Status, Diagnosis, Comorbid Substance Abuse and History of Suicide Attempts," *Addictive Behaviors* 34 (2009): 815–820; and Joan Arehart-Treichel, "Smoking High on List of Suicide-Risk Factors," *Psychiatric News,* 4 February 2011, 16–17.

4. For a study that pointed out that it was unlikely that smoking caused schizophrenia, see for example, Mark Weiser et al., "Higher Rates of Cigarette Smoking in Male

Adolescents before the Onset of Schizophrenia: A Historical-Prospective Cohort Study," *American Journal of Psychiatry* 161 (2004): 1219–1223.

5. Kenneth E. Warner and David M. Burns, "Hardening and the Hard-Core Smoker: Concepts, Evidence, and Implications," *Nicotine & Tobacco Research* 5 (2003): 37–48.

6. For the report on mental illness, see U.S. Department of Health and Human Services, *Mental Health: A Report of the Surgeon General* (Rockville, MD: U.S. Department of Health and Human Services, Substance Abuse and Mental Health Services Administration, Center for Mental Health Services, National Institutes of Health, National Institute of Mental Health, 1999).

7. Allan M. Brandt, *The Cigarette Century: The Rise, Fall, and Deadly Persistence of the Product That Defined America* (New York: Basic Books, 2007).

8. For a powerful statement about the need to attend to social context in smoking (including power relationships), see B. Poland et al., "The Social Context of Smoking: The Next Frontier in Tobacco Control?," *Tobacco Control* 15 (2006): 59–63.

9. Breda Kingston, *Psychological Approaches in Psychiatric Nursing* (London: Croom Helm, 1989), 99–100.

10. See for example, Enric Batlle et al., "Tobacco Prevention in Hospitals: Long-Term Follow-Up of a Smoking Control Programme," *British Journal of Addiction* 86 (1991): 709–717.

11. See for example, Scott Erwin and Diana Biordi, "A Smoke-Free Environment: Psychiatric Hospitals Respond," *Journal of Psychosocial Nursing* 29 (1991): 12–18.

12. Melanie Richardson, "Nursing Implementation of Smoking Bans on Psychiatric Wards," *Journal of Psychosocial Nursing and Mental Health Services* 32 (1994): 17–19, quote from 17.

13. See Paulette M. Gillig et al., "A Comparison of Staff and Patient Perceptions of the Causes and Cures of Physical Aggression on a Psychiatric Unit," *Psychiatric Quarterly* 69 (1998): 45–60.

14. Gary Hartz and Gloria Kuhlman, "Smoking Cessation for Geropsychiatric Patients in Long-Term Care," *Psychiatric Services* 55 (2004): 454.

15. Aaron Levin, "State Hospitals Struggle to Give Up Smoking," *Psychiatric News*, 16 November 2007, 4.

16. Psychiatric administrators in Israel at the same time period noted that the culture of smoking was still quite entrenched and that staff felt that there were benefits to smoking for the mentally ill on the unit. Roberto Mester et al., "Survey of Smoking Habits and Attitudes of Patients and Staff in Psychiatric Hospitals," *Psychopathology* 26 (1993): 69–75. A similar situation existed in Australia. See Sharon Lawn and Judith Condon, "Psychiatric Nurses' Ethical Stance on Cigarette Smoking by Patients: Determinants and Dilemmas in Their Role in Supporting Cessation," *International Journal of Mental Health Nursing* 15 (2006): 111–118. For smoking among all kinds of hospitalized patients in Finland, see Antti Tanskanen et al., "Smoking among Psychiatric Patients," *European Journal of Psychiatry* 11 (1997): 179–188.

17. See for example, Normal L. Keltner, "Developing the Therapeutic Environment," in *Psychiatric Nursing*, ed. Norman L. Keltner, Lee Hilyard Schwecke, and Carol E. Bostrom, 2nd ed. (St. Louis: Mosby, 1995), 313–328.

18. Letter to the editor, *Hospital and Community Psychiatry* 41 (1990): 454–455.

19. Tim Golden, "One More Anxiety for a Psychiatric Ward: No Smoking," *New York Times*, 3 March 1990.

20. See for example, Douglas M. Ziedonis and Kimberlee Trudeau, "Motivation to Quit Using Substances among Individuals with Schizophrenia: Implications for a Motivation-Based Treatment Model," *Schizophrenia Bulletin* 23 (1997): 229–238.

21. See for example, Stephen Kisely and Leslie Anne Campbell, "Use of Smoking Cessation Therapies in Individuals with Psychiatric Illness: An Update for Prescribers," *CNS Drugs* 22 (2008): 263–273.

22. Jennifer W. Tidey, Suzanne C. O'Neill, and Stephen T. Higgins, "Effects of Abstinence on Cigarette Smoking among Outpatients with Schizophrenia," *Experimental and Clinical Psychopharmacology* 7 (1999): 347–353.

23. Jennifer W. Tidey, Suzanne C. O'Neill, and Stephen T. Higgins, "Contingent Monetary Reinforcement of Smoking Reductions, with and without Transdermal Nicotine, in Outpatients with Schizophrenia," *Experimental and Clinical Psychopharmacology* 10 (2002): 241–247.

24. Judith J. Prochaska et al., "Depressed Smokers and Stages of Change: Implications for Treatment Interventions," *Drug and Alcohol Dependence* 76 (2004): 143–151. In 2011, James Prochaska, one of the principal architects of the stages of change model, accepted a public-health award for his work. He noted that he was pleased to see that an investigator—who happened to be his daughter—was able to use the stages of change model with psychiatric patients. See "URI's James Prochaska and First Lady Michelle Obama to Be Honored for Contributions to Improve Public Health," press release from the University of Rhode Island, 27 October 2011, http://www.uri .edu/news/releases/?id=6020, accessed 5 March 2013. Boston University researchers, while sympathetic to the stages of change model, did not find it predictive for their sample of mentally ill individuals. E. Sally Rogers et al., "Assessing Readiness for Change among Persons with Severe Mental Illness," *Community Mental Health Journal* 37 (2001): 97–112.

25. Cherise Rosen-Chase and Vida Dyson, "Treatment of Nicotine Dependence in the Chronic Mentally Ill," *Journal of Substance Abuse Treatment* 16 (1999): 315–320.

26. Brian Hitsman et al., "Treatment of Tobacco Dependence in Mental Health and Addictive Disorders," *Canadian Journal of Psychiatry* 54 (2009): 368–377; Ranita Siru, Gary K. Hulse, and Robert J. Tait, "Assessing Motivation to Quit Smoking in People with Mental Illness: A Review," *Addiction* 104 (2009): 719–733. This had been an argument used on medical units decades before. See for example, Victor J. Stevens et al., "A Smoking-Cessation Intervention for Hospital Patients," *Medical Care* 31 (1993): 65–72.

27. Manuela Etter et al., "Stages of Change in Smokers with Schizophrenia or Schizoaffective Disorder and in the General Population," *Schizophrenia Bulletin* 30 (2004): 459–468.

28. See for example, Judith J. Prochaska, Patricia Gill, and Sharon M. Hall, "Treatment of Tobacco Use in an Inpatient Psychiatric Setting," *Psychiatric Services* 55 (2004): 1265–1270.

29. See for example, letter to the editor, *New York Times,* 22 August 1996; "Mentally Ill Make Up Nearly Half of U.S. Tobacco Market, Are Twice as Likely to Smoke, Study Says," Press Release from Harvard University, 21 November 2000, LTDL (Bates 431113759/3760), http://legacy.library.ucsf.edu/tid/xyj21c00; and Norman Hymowitz et al., "Cigarette Smoking among Patients with Mental Retardation and Mental Illness," *Psychiatric Services* 48 (1997): 100–102.

30. Taryn G. Moss et al., "A Tobacco Reconceptualization in Psychiatry: Toward the Development of Tobacco-Free Psychiatric Facilities," *American Journal on Addictions* 19 (2010): 293–311.

31. Judith J. Prochaska, Stephen E. Hall, and Sharon M. Hall, "Stage-Tailored Tobacco Cessation Treatment in Inpatient Psychiatry," *Psychiatric Services* 60 (2009): 848.

32. Alicia Lucksted, Lisa B. Dixon, and Joseph B. Sembly, "A Focus Group Pilot Study of Tobacco Smoking among Psychosocial Rehabilitation Clients," *Psychiatric Services* 51 (2000): 1544–1548, quote from 1548.

33. Sharon M. Hall and Judith J. Prochaska, "Treatment of Smokers with Co-Occurring Disorders: Emphasis on Integration in Mental Health and Addiction Treatment Settings," *Annual Review of Clinical Psychology* 5 (2009): 409–431.

34. Paula M. Wye et al., "Smoking Restrictions and Treatment for Smoking: Policies and Procedures in Psychiatric Inpatient Units in Australia," *Psychiatric Services* 60 (2009): 100–107.

35. Emil Kraepelin noted the higher mortality of mentally ill individuals. Emil Kraepelin, *Clinical Psychiatry*, trans. A. Ross Diefendorf (New York: Macmillan, 1907). For American studies over the century, see for example, Benjamin Malzberg, "Mortality among Patients with Involutional Melancholia," *American Journal of Psychiatry* 93 (1937): 1231–1238; Ming T. Tsuang, Robert F. Woolson, and Jerome A. Fleming, "Premature Deaths in Schizophrenia and Affective Disorders: An Analysis of Survival Curves and Variables Affecting the Shortened Survival," *Archives of General Psychiatry* 37 (1980): 979–983.

36. See for example, Dilip V. Jeste et al., "Medical Comorbidity in Schizophrenia," *Schizophrenia Bulletin* 22 (1996): 413–430.

37. See Carolyn Chambers Clark and Wailua Brandman, "Complementary Therapies and Practices," in *Advanced Practice Nursing in Psychiatric and Mental Health Care*, ed. Carol A. Shea et al. (St. Louis: Mosby, 1999), 243–270.

38. Tobacco interventions have been so successful that they can provide a model for other health behaviors. See Kenneth E. Warner, "Tobacco Policy in the United States: Lessons for the Obesity Epidemic," in *Policy Challenges in Modern Health Care*, ed. David Mechanic et al. (New Brunswick, NJ: Rutgers University Press, 2005), 99–114. For Warner's important work in taxation for cigarettes, see Kenneth E. Warner, "Death and Taxes: Using the Latter to Reduce the Former," *Tobacco Control* (2013), epub 22 May 2013, 10.1136/tobaccocontrol-2013–051079.

39. Kenneth E. Warner, "Tobacco Policy Research: Insights and Contributions to Public Health Policy," in *Tobacco Control Policy*, ed. Kenneth E. Warner (San Francisco: Jossey-Bass, 2006), 9.

40. See for example, Joel Velasco et al., "A Two-Year Follow-up on the Effects of a Smoking Ban in an Inpatient Psychiatric Service," *Psychiatric Services* 47 (1996): 869–871.

41. Udo K. Rauter, Alexander de Nesnera, and Sylvia Grandfield, "Up in Smoke? Linking Patient Assaults to a Psychiatric Hospital's Smoking Ban," *Journal of Psychosocial Nursing* 35 (1997): 35–40.

42. Cedric M. Smith, Cynthia A. Pristach, and Maria Cartagena, "Obligatory Cessation of Smoking by Psychiatric Inpatients," *Psychiatric Services* 50 (1999): 91–94.

43. See for example, Nady el-Guebaly et al., "Public Health and Therapeutic Aspects of Smoking Bans in Mental Health and Addiction Settings," *Psychiatric Services* 53 (2002): 1617–1622.

44. Bryan Gibson, "Smoker-Nonsmoker Conflict: Using a Social Psychological Framework to Understand a Current Social Controversy," *Journal of Social Issues* 53 (1997): 97–112.

45. Nancy Tomes, "Speaking for the Public: The Ambivalent Quest of Twentieth-Century Public Health," in *The Contested Boundaries of American Public Health*, ed. James Colgrove, Gerald Markowitz, and David Rosner (New Brunswick, NJ: Rutgers University Press, 2008), 57–81.

46. Lasser et al., "Smoking and Mental Illness"; Dorie Apollonio and Ruth E. Malone, "Marketing to the Marginalised: Tobacco Industry Targeting of the Homeless and Mentally Ill," *Tobacco Control* 14 (2005): 409–415.

47. Bridget F. Grant et al., "Nicotine Dependence and Psychiatric Disorders in the United States: Results from the National Epidemiologic Survey on Alcohol and Related Conditions," *Archives of General Psychiatry* 61 (2004): 1107–1115.

48. See chapter 4.

49. Advocacy Institute, "Directory of Tobacco Industry Spokespersons, Front Groups and Their Allies," LTDL (Bates 513874590/4701), http://legacy.library.ucsf.edu/tid/oaa71d00. I could not find any evidence within the tobacco-industry documents that there was any relationship between the industry and these individuals.

50. Letter to the editor, *Psychiatric News*, 4 November 1994, LTDL (Bates 2073810915), http://legacy.library.ucsf.edu/tid/fyt85c00.

51. David Mechanic, "Mental Health Services Then and Now," *Health Affairs* 26 (2007): 1548–1550.

52. James H. Price et al., "Psychiatrists' Smoking Cessation Activities with Ohio Community Mental Health Center Patients," *Community Mental Health Journal* 43 (2007): 251–266, quote from 262.

53. Douglas Ziedonis, Jill M. Williams, and David Smelson, "Serious Mental Illness and Tobacco Addiction: A Model Program to Address This Common but Neglected Issue," *American Journal of the Medical Sciences* 326 (2003): 223–230.

54. Judith J. Prochaska et al., "Evaluation of an Evidence-Based Tobacco Treatment Curriculum for Psychiatry Residency Training Programs," *Academic Psychiatry* 32 (2008): 484–492.

55. Deanna L. Kelly et al., "Perception of Smoking Risks and Motivation to Quit among Nontreatment-Seeking Smokers with and without Schizophrenia," *Schizophrenia Bulletin* 38 (2012): 543–551.

56. Jill M. Williams et al., "A Randomized, Double-Blind, Placebo-Controlled Study Evaluating the Safety and Efficacy of Varenicline for Smoking Cessation in Patients with Schizophrenia or Schizoaffective Disorder," *Journal of Clinical Psychiatry* 73 (2012): 654–660.

57. M. L. Steinberg, J. M. Williams, and D. M. Ziedonis, "Letter to the Editor: Financial Implications of Cigarette Smoking among Individuals with Schizophrenia," *Tobacco Control* 13 (2004): 206.

58. Lisa B. Dixon et al., "Correlates of Severity among Persons with Severe Mental Illness," *American Journal on Addictions* 16 (2007): 101–110.

59. See for example, Chad D. Morris et al., "Smoking Reduction for Persons with Mental Illnesses: 6-Month Results from Community-Based Interventions," *Community Mental Health Journal* 47 (2011): 694–702.

60. Eric O. Johnson and Scott P. Novak, "Onset and Persistence of Daily Smoking: The Interplay of Socioeconomic Status, Gender, and Psychiatric Disorders," *Drug and Alcohol Dependence* 104S (2009): S50–S57.

61. Shanta R. Dube et al., "The Relationship between Smoking Status and Serious Psychological Distress: Findings from the 2007 Behavioral Risk Factor Surveillance System," *International Journal of Public Health* 54 (2009): S68–S74.

62. For some of the policy perils in focusing on individual risk factors instead of broader socioeconomic inequalities, see David R. Williams, "Patterns and Causes of Disparities in Health," in *Policy Challenges in Modern Health Care*, 115–134.

63. Grant T. Harris, Daniel Parle, and Joseph Gagne, "Effects of a Tobacco Ban on Long-Term Psychiatric Patients," *Journal of Behavioral Services & Research* 34 (2007): 43–55.

64. Judith J. Prochaska, "Failure to Treat Tobacco Use in Mental Health and Addiction Treatment Settings: A Form of Harm Reduction?," *Drug and Alcohol Dependence* 110 (2010): 177–182.

65. For conflict between the different perspectives on harm reduction and nicotine maintenance, see for example, Mitchell Zeller, Dorothy K. Hatsukami, and Strategic Dialogue on Tobacco Harm Reduction Group, "The Strategic Dialogue on Tobacco Harm Reduction: A Vision and Blueprint for Action in the US," *Tobacco Control* 18 (2009): 324–332.

66. On cultural views of addicts, see Caroline Jean Acker, *Creating the American Junkie: Addiction Research in the Classic Era of Narcotic Control* (Baltimore: Johns Hopkins University Press, 2002). See also, David T. Courtwright, *Forces of Habit: Drugs and the Making of the Modern World* (Cambridge, MA: Harvard University Press, 2002).

67. David Kessler, *A Question of Intent: A Great American Battle with a Deadly Industry* (New York: PublicAffairs, 2001).

68. Now the APA wants to include caffeine addicts, too. The *DSM-5* includes a "Caffeine Use Disorder" in a section "Conditions for Further Study." The *DSM* editors noted that it will be important to have an appropriately high cutoff "to prevent overdiagnosis of caffeine use disorder due to the high rate of habitual nonproblematic daily caffeine use in the general population." American Psychiatric Association, *Diagnostic and Statistical Manual of Mental Disorders*, 5th ed. (Arlington, VA: American Psychiatric Publishing, 2013), 792–795.

69. Charles Rosenberg, "Banishing Risk: Continuity and Change in the Moral Management of Disease," in *Morality and Health*, ed. Allan M. Brandt and Paul Rozin (New York: Routledge, 1997), 35–51.

70. See for example, Judith Walzer Leavitt, *Typhoid Mary: Captive to the Public's Health* (Boston: Beacon Press, 1996).

Chapter 8   Double Marginalization

1. Ronald Bayer and James Colgrove, "Children and Bystanders First: The Ethics and Politics of Tobacco Control in the United States," in *Unfiltered: Conflicts over Tobacco Policy and Public Health*, ed. Eric A. Feldman and Ronald Bayer (Cambridge, MA: Harvard University Press, 2004), 8–37. This argument was borne out by FDA commissioner David Kessler's move to focus on smoking as a pediatric disease in his efforts to get FDA oversight over cigarettes. David Kessler, *A Question of Intent: A Great American Battle with a Deadly Industry* (New York: PublicAffairs, 2001). See also, Christopher J. Bailey, "From 'Informed Choice' to 'Social Hygiene': Government Control of Cigarette Smoking in the US," *Journal of American Studies* 38 (2004): 41–65.

2. For a history of shifts in perceptions of classes of patients based on vulnerability, see David J. Rothman, *Strangers at the Bedside: A History of How Law and Bioethics Transformed Medical Decision Making* (New York: Basic Books, 1991).

3. In the wake of mass shootings in 2012 and 2013, many lawmakers looked to the mentally ill rather than gun control as a way of addressing the issue. See Erica Goode and Jack Healy, "Focus on Mental Health Laws to Curb Violence Is Unfair, Some Say," *New York Times*, 31 January 2013.

4. For an early articulation of this, see "More States Enforce Laws to Isolate Smokers," *Daily Record* (Baltimore), 11 January 1983, LTDL (Bates TI17531647-TI17531648), http://legacy.library.ucsf.edu/tid/yqu09a00.

5. See for example, Tim Roche, "Man Killed by Fire Started by Cigarette," *St. Petersburg Times*, 19 March 1997, LTDL (Bates 2075729136/9137), http://legacy.library .ucsf.edu/tid/zbg55c00.

6. Groups incorporated the language of psychiatry's critics. On the social context in which antipsychiatry critiques arose, see Michael E. Staub, *Madness Is Civilization: When the Diagnosis Was Social, 1948–1980* (Chicago: University of Chicago Press, 2011).

7. Nancy Tomes, "From Outsiders to Insiders: The Consumer-Survivor Movement and Its Impact on U.S. Mental Health Policy," in *Patients as Policy Actors*, ed. Beatrix Hoffman et al. (New Brunswick, NJ: Rutgers University Press, 2011), 113–131. See also, Athena Helen McLean, "From Ex-Patient Alternatives to Consumer Options: Consequences of Consumerism for Psychiatric Consumers and the Ex-Patient Movement," *International Journal of Health Services* 30 (2000): 821–847.

8. On disability perspectives, see for example, Paul K. Longmore and Lauri Umansky, eds., *The New Disability History: American Perspectives* (New York: New York University Press, 2001).

9. Nancy Tomes and Beatrix Hoffman, "Introduction: Patients as Policy Actors," in Hoffman et al., *Patients as Policy Actors*, 1–16.

10. This is evident within textbooks of psychiatric nursing, in which some authors stress abstinence from smoking while others acknowledge that schizophrenics get something from cigarettes. See for example, Norman L. Keltner, Lee Hilyard Schwecke, and Carol E. Bostrom, eds., *Psychiatric Nursing*, 4th ed. (St. Louis: Mosby, 2003).

11. Elena Ratchen et al., "Smoke-Free Policy in Acute Mental Health Wards: Avoiding the Pitfalls," *General Hospital Psychiatry* 31 (2009): 131–136.

12. This is how the issue is sometimes presented within the psychiatric press. See for example, Joan Arehart-Treichel, "Psychiatrists Can Be Crucial to Smoking Cessation," *Psychiatric News*, 1 May 2009, 14–15.

13. John Robinson, "Smoking: Habit Not Addiction," *Chemistry & Industry*, 5 September 1994, LTDL (Bates 322283246–322283248), http://legacy.library.ucsf.edu/tid/ wrz60a99.

14. Kessler, *A Question of Intent.*

15. David Mechanic, "The Social Context of Health and Disease and Choices among Health Interventions" in *Morality and Health*, ed. Allan M. Brandt and Paul Rozin (New York: Routledge, 1997), 79–98.

16. Historian and psychopharmacologist David Healy has blamed the newer generations of psychiatric medications for the higher mortality among the mentally ill, especially because of the well-known side effects of obesity and diabetes. David Healy, *Pharmageddon* (Berkeley: University of California Press, 2012).

17. Michael H. Allen et al., "Effect of Nicotine Replacement Therapy on Agitation in Smokers with Schizophrenia: A Double-Blind, Randomized, Placebo-Controlled Study," *American Journal of Psychiatry* 168 (2011): 395–399.

18. Bonnie Schell, "Mental Health Client Action Network (MHCAN), Santa Cruz, California," in *On Our Own, Together: Peer Programs for People with Mental Illness,* ed. Sally Clay (Nashville, TN: Vanderbilt University Press, 2005), 67–91.

19. Laura D. Hirshbein, "'We Mentally Ill Smoke a Lot': Identity, Smoking, and Mental Illness in America," *Journal of Social History* 44 (2010): 7–21.

20. AMI/FAMI Policy Paper on Nicotine Addiction and Psychiatric Patients, 28 March 1995, copy located in the LTDL (Bates 2071540429), http://legacy.library.ucsf.edu/tid/ric60c00.

21. Public Policy Committee of the Board of Directors and the NAMI Department of Public Policy and Legal Affairs, "Public Policy Platform of the National Alliance for the Mentally Ill" (Arlington, VA: 2008). See also, Pam Belluck, "Smoking, Once Used to Reward, Faces a Ban in Mental Hospitals," *New York Times* 6 February 2013.

22. See www.ncmhr.org, accessed 23 July 2013.

23. Caroline Jean Acker, *Creating the American Junkie: Addition Research in the Classic Era of Narcotic Control* (Baltimore: Johns Hopkins University Press, 2002).

24. Bonnie Spring, Regina Pingitore, and Dennis E. McChargue, "Reward Value of Cigarette Smoking for Comparably Heavy Smoking Schizophrenic, Depressed, and Nonpatient Smokers," *American Journal of Psychiatry* 160 (2003): 316–322.

25. Hirshbein, "'We Mentally Ill Smoke a Lot.'"

26. See for example, Tracey Dykstra, "First Person Account: How I Cope," *Schizophrenia Bulletin* 23 (1997): 697–699; Clea Simon, *Mad House: Growing Up in the Shadow of Mentally Ill Siblings* (New York: Doubleday, 1997), 194.

27. Rosie Alexander, *Folie a Deux: An Experience of One-to-One Therapy* (London: Free Association Books, 1995), 81.

28. See for example, BGW, "Graduate Student in Peril: A First Person Account of Schizophrenia," *Schizophrenia Bulletin* 28 (2002): 745–755.

29. Kurt Snyder, *Me, Myself, and Them: A Firsthand Account of One Young Person's Experience with Schizophrenia* (Oxford: Oxford University Press, 2007), 82.

30. Patricia E. Deegan, "Recovery and Empowerment for People with Psychiatric Disabilities," *Social Work in Health Care* 25 (1997): 11–24.

31. For poems written by mentally ill individuals about the day room-culture that included passionate discussion of cigarettes, see Jo Harris, "Rave On," and Kit Wright, "The Day Room," in *Beyond Bedlam: Poems Written out of Mental Distress,* ed. Ken Smith and Matthew Sweeney (London: Anvil Press Poetry, 1997), 57–58, 89–94. For a poem about smoking and a treatment center at a Native American area in South Dakota, see Debra Nystrom, "Smoke Break Behind the Treatment Center," in *Bad River Road* (Louisville, KY: Sarabande Books, 2009), 48. (Thanks to Ben Harris for calling my attention to this poem.)

32. Ken Rollason, John Stow, and Jenifer Paul, "People in the Smoke Room," *Community Care,* 14–20 December 2000, 20–21, quote from 21.

33. Juliet L. H. Foster, *Journeys through Mental Illness: Clients' Experiences and Understandings of Mental Distress* (Basingstoke: Palgrave Macmillan, 2007), 61. See also, Janey Antoniou, "Bored on the Ward," in *Experiences of Mental Health Inpatient Care: Narratives from Service Users, Carers and Professionals,* ed. Mark Hardcastle et al. (London: Routledge, 2007), 33–36.

34. See for example, Scott Zwiren, *God Head* (Normal, IL: Dalkey Archive Press, 1996), 100–103. For an analysis of the smoking room as a safe space, see A. Skorpen et al., "The Smoking-Room as Psychiatric Patients' Sanctuary: A Place for Resistance," *Journal of Psychiatric and Mental Health Nursing* 15 (2008): 728–736.

35. See for example, Helen Minth, "The St. Louis Empowerment Center, St. Louis, Missouri," in *On Our Own, Together,* 108–122.

36. See for example, Shulamith Firestone, *Airless Spaces* (New York: Semiotext(e), 1998); Meri Nana-Ama Danquah, *Willow Weep for Me: A Black Woman's Journey through Depression* (New York: One World, 1999), 80–81.

37. Thomas Campbell, "First Person Account: Falling on the Pavement," *Schizophrenia Bulletin* 26 (2000): 507–509.

38. Tim Lott, *The Scent of Dried Roses* (New York: Viking, 1996), 235.

39. Caroline Knapp, *Drinking: A Love Story* (New York: Delta, 1996), 231–232.

40. This was noted by an official from the Australian public-health department who cautioned about the problems of top-down interventions. See Kristen Moeller-Saxone, "Cigarette Smoking and Interest in Quitting among Consumers at a Psychiatric Disability Rehabilitation and Support Service in Victoria," *Australian and New Zealand Journal of Public Health* 32 (2008): 479–481.

41. Marsha Snyder, Judith McDevitt, and Susan Painter, "Smoking Cessation and Serious Mental Illness," *Archives of Psychiatric Nursing* 22 (2008): 297–304.

42. Susanna Kaysen, *Girl, Interrupted* (New York: Vintage, 1993).

43. The book version of Ned Vizzini's *It's Kind of a Funny Story* (New York: Miramax, 2006) includes a discussion of a patient smoking room on the inpatient unit. The 2010 film has only one brief mention of a cigarette to indicate that one of the characters, Bobby, is mentally ill. There are no other cigarettes in the film.

44. In contrast, Nasar relays a conversation between a Nobel committee member and Nash while he was smoking. Sylvia Nasar, *A Beautiful Mind: The Life of Mathematical Genius and Nobel Laureate John Nash* (New York: Simon & Schuster, 1998), 361.

45. Mary Karr, *The Liars' Club: A Memoir* (New York: Viking, 1995), 172.

46. Martha Manning, *Undercurrents: A Therapist's Reckoning with Her Own Depression* (San Francisco: HarperSanFrancisco, 1994).

47. Jay Neugeboren, *Imagining Robert: A Memoir* (New Brunswick, NJ: Rutgers University Press, 1997).

48. Michael Greenberg, *Hurry Down Sunshine: A Father's Story of Love and Madness* (New York: Vintage, 2008).

49. See for example, Lori Schiller and Amanda Bennett, *The Quiet Room: A Journey out of the Torment of Madness* (New York: Warner Books, 1994), 211.

50. See for example, Jeffrey R. Bedell, Peter Provet, Jeffrey A. Frank, "Rehabilitation-Oriented Multiple-Family Therapy," in *Psychological Assessment and Treatment of Persons with Severe Mental Disorders,* ed. Jeffrey R. Bedell (Washington, DC: Taylor & Francis, 1994), 215–234.

51. See for example, Linda Katherine Cutting, *Memory Slips* (New York: HarperCollins, 1997), 173.

52. See for example, Jenny Diski, *Skating to Antarctica* (London: Granta Books, 1997), 141–142; Amy Sundquist, "First Person Account: Family Psychoeducation Can Change Lives," *Schizophrenia Bulletin* 25 (1999): 619–621.

53. Linda Gray Sexton, excerpt from *Searching for Mercy Street* (1994), in *Out of Her Mind: Women Writing on Madness*, ed. Rebecca Shannonhouse (New York: Modern Library, 2000), 120–129.

54. Susan Nathiel, *Daughters of Madness: Growing Up and Older with a Mentally Ill Mother* (Westport, CT: Praeger, 2007), 31, 42, 93.

55. Paul Raeburn, *Acquainted with the Night: A Parent's Quest to Understand Depression and Bipolar Disorder in His Children* (New York: Broadway Books, 2004), 231–233.

56. E. Fuller Torrey, *Surviving Schizophrenia: A Manual for Families, Patients, and Providers*, 5th ed. (New York: Harper, 2006), 277.

57. Jill M. Williams, "Eliminating Tobacco Use in Mental Health Facilities: Patients' Rights, Public Health, and Policy Issues," *JAMA* 299 (2008): 571–573.

58. Steven A. Schroeder and Chad D. Morris, "Confronting a Neglected Epidemic: Tobacco Cessation for Persons with Mental Illnesses and Substance Abuse Problems," *Annual Review of Public Health* 31 (2010): 297–314.

59. Erica Singer Solway, "The Lived Experiences of Tobacco Use, Dependence, and Cessation: Insights and Perspectives of People with Mental Illness," *Health and Social Work* 36 (2011): 19–32, quote from 25.

60. See for example, Pete Earley, *A Father's Search through America's Mental Health Madness* (New York: G. P. Putnam's Sons, 2006). For an argument for an alternative to the psychiatric model, see, Benjamin Gray, "Hidden Demons: A Personal Account of Hearing Voices and the Alternative of the Hearing Voices Movement," *Schizophrenia Bulletin* 34 (2008): 1006–1007.

61. Nathaniel Lachenmeyer, *The Outsider: A Journey into My Father's Struggle with Madness* (New York: Broadway, 2000).

62. Greg Bottoms, *Angelhead: My Brother's Descent into Madness* (London: Headline, 2001), 109.

63. Anne M. Joseph, Kristin L. Nichol, and Hazel Anderson, "Effect of Treatment for Nicotine Dependence on Alcohol and Drug Treatment Outcomes," *Addictive Behaviors* 18 (1993): 635–644.

64. Cheryl Forchuk et al., "Schizophrenia and the Motivation for Smoking," *Perspectives in Psychiatric Care* 38 (2002): 41–49.

65. For another example of the idea that addiction means no choice, while individuals can quit smoking, see the National Association of State Mental Health Program Directors Position Statement on Smoking Policy and Treatment at State Operated Psychiatric Hospitals, 10 July 2006, http://www.nasmhpd.org/docs/publications/MDCdocs/Oct2006%20Final%20Report%20on%20Smoking%20Policy%20and%20Treatment%20atState%20Operated%20Psychiatric%20Facilities.pdf, accessed 2 June 2014.

66. Jill M. Williams et al., "Evaluation of the CHOICES Program of Peer-to-Peer Tobacco Education and Advocacy," *Community Mental Health Journal* 47 (2011): 243–251; Jill M. Williams et al., "A Comprehensive Model for Mental Health Tobacco Recovery in New Jersey," *Administration and Health Policy in Mental Health* 38 (2011): 368–383.

67. Jill Williams and Marie Verna, "Strong Advocacy Effort Needed to Help Smokers with Mental Illness," 13 March 2103, http://www.nami.org/Content/NavigationMenu/Top_Story/Strong_Advocacy_Effort_Needed_to_Help_Smokers_with_Mental_Illness.htm, accessed 8 August 2013.

68. See for example, Jill M. Williams et al., "A Tobacco Treatment Model for Persons with Serious Mental Illness," *Psychiatric Services* 57 (2006): 1210.

69. Panel Discussion, "A Hidden Epidemic," Legacy Warner Series, 31 May 2012, archived at http://www.legacyforhealth.org/what-we-do/warner-series/a-hidden-epidemic-tobacco-use-and-mental-illness.

70. Jamie Bryant et al., "A Systematic Review and Meta-Analysis of the Effectiveness of Behavioural Smoking Cessation Interventions in Selected Disadvantaged Groups," *Addiction* 106 (2011): 1568–1585.

71. Sandra M. Gallagher et al., "A Comparison of Smoking Cessation Treatments for Persons with Schizophrenia and Other Serious Mental Illnesses," *Journal of Psychoactive Drugs* 39 (2007): 487–497.

72. See for example, Jennifer W. Tidey et al., "Effects of Contingency Management and Buproprion on Cigarette Smoking in Smokers with Schizophrenia," *Psychopharmacology* 217 (2011): 279–287.

Conclusion: Corporate Squeeze

1. Letter from Michael Smith to R. J. Reynolds, 6 July 1999, LTDL (Bates 522762510/2513), http://legacy.library.ucsf.edu/tid/osm70d00.

2. Kevin Helliker, "Nicotine Fix: Behind Antismoking Policy, Influence of Drug Industry," *Wall Street Journal*, 7 February 2007, LTDL (Bates 3117185364–3117185369), http://legacy.library.ucsf.edu/tid/bou95g00.

3. See Charles E. Rosenberg, "Anticipated Consequences: Historians, History, and Health Policy," in *History and Health Policy in the United States: Putting the Past Back In*, ed. Rosemary A. Stevens, Charles E. Rosenberg, and Lawton R. Burns (New Brunswick, NJ: Rutgers University Press, 2006), 13–31; Nancy Tomes and Beatrix Hoffman, "Introduction: Patients as Policy Actors," in *Patients as Policy Actors*, ed. Beatrix Hoffman et al. (New Brunswick, NJ: Rutgers University Press, 2011), 1–16.

4. Thomas Borstelmann, *The 1970s: A New Global History from Civil Rights to Economic Inequality* (Princeton: Princeton University Press, 2012), 247.

5. Kenneth Warner pointed out the potential for this competition more than a decade ago. See Kenneth E. Warner, John Slade, and David T. Sweanor, "The Emerging Market for Long-term Nicotine Maintenance," *JAMA* 278 (1997): 1087–1092.

6. American Psychiatric Association, *Diagnostic and Statistical Manual of Mental Disorders*, 5th ed. (Arlington, VA: American Psychiatric Publishing, 2013), 571–576.

7. As far as I can tell, the work group that formulated the *DSM-5* criteria did not incorporate any suggestions by critics. Timothy B. Baker et al., "DSM Criteria for Tobacco Use Disorder and Tobacco Withdrawal: A Critique and Proposed Revisions for DSM-5," *Addiction* 107 (2012): 263–275.

8. See for example, Quinn M. Biggs et al., "Acute Stress Disorder, Depression, and Tobacco Use in Disaster Workers Following 9/11," *American Journal of Orthopsychiatry* 80 (2010): 586–592. This has been noted for many substances of abuse in general. See David R. Williams, "Patterns and Causes of Disparities in Health," in *Policy Challenges in Modern Health Care*, ed. David Mechanic et al. (New Brunswick, NJ: Rutgers University Press, 2005), 115–134.

9. For some of the problems inherent in blurring the boundary between a normal and a psychiatric condition, see for example, Allan V. Horwitz and Jerome C. Wakefield, *The Loss of Sadness: How Psychiatry Transformed Normal Sorrow into Depressive Disorder* (New York: Oxford University Press, 2007); Paula J. Caplan, *They Say*

You're Crazy: How the World's Most Powerful Psychiatrists Decide Who's Normal (Reading, MA: Addison-Wesley Publishing Company, 1995).

10. See for example, Salma M. Khaled et al., "Major Depression Is a Risk Factor for Shorter Time to First Cigarette Irrespective of the Number of Cigarettes Smoked Per Day: Evidence of a National Population Health Survey," *Nicotine & Tobacco Research* 13 (2011): 1059–1067.

11. Allan M. Brandt, "From Nicotine to Nicotrol: Addiction, Cigarettes, and American Culture," in *Altering American Consciousness: The History of Alcohol and Drug Use in the United States, 1800–2000,* ed. Sarah W. Tracy and Caroline Jean Acker (Amherst: University of Massachusetts Press, 2004), 383–402. On more of the implications regarding addiction and personal responsibility, see Caroline Jean Acker, *Creating the American Junkie: Addition Research in the Classic Era of Narcotic Control* (Baltimore: Johns Hopkins University Press, 2002).

12. One therapist in the last couple of decades wrote that she refuses to use *DSM* diagnoses in practice because it separates people and can damage them. She focuses instead on problems—and everybody has problems. See Gloria Anthony, "Resisting Diagnosis," in *Bias in Psychiatric Diagnosis,* ed. Paula J. Caplan and Lisa Cosgrove (Lanham, MD: Jason Aronson, 2004), 241–242.

13. Dale M. Atrens, "Nicotine as an Addictive Substance: A Critical Examination of the Basic Concepts and Empirical Evidence," *Journal of Drug Issues* 31(2001): 325–394. For Atrens's testimony, see LTDL (Bates 530213376/3404), http://legacy.library.ucsf.edu/tid/ufr05a00. Atrens was not a proponent of smoking, though—his book *Don't Diet* (1988) calls for simple health interventions, including quitting smoking.

14. See http://blogs.bmj.com/tc/2013/01/31/a-letter-to-the-us-fda-from-tobacco-control-editor-ruth-malone/, accessed 26 July 2013. Thanks to Gregory Dalack for alerting me to this letter.

15. See for example, Mitchell Zeller, Dorothy K. Hatsukami, and Strategic Dialogue on Tobacco Harm Reduction Group, "The Strategic Dialogue on Tobacco Harm Reduction: A Vision and Blueprint for Action in the US," *Tobacco Control* 18 (2009): 324–332. And pharmaceutical companies help cultivate positive relationships within tobacco control—in part by donating to tobacco-control organizations. In 2012, for example, GlaxoSmithKline made substantial contributions to a number of tobacco-control groups. See http://fortherecord.payments.us.gsk.com/content/dam/hcppaymenttransparency/en/documents/pdf/archive-reports/1Q-4Q%202012%20GSK%20Grants%20Report%20v3.0.pdf, accessed 26 July 2013.

16. As political scientist Daniel Carpenter pointed out, it has long been the practice for pharmaceutical-company representatives to have regular interactions with officials at the FDA. Daniel Carpenter, *Reputation and Power: Organizational Image and Pharmaceutical Regulation at the FDA* (Princeton: Princeton University Press, 2010).

17. See for example, Henri-Jean Aubin et al., "Smoking, Quitting, and Psychiatric Disease: A Review," *Neuroscience and Biobehavioral Reviews* 36 (2012): 271–284.

18. Reginald V. Fant et al., "Pharmacotherapy for Tobacco Dependence," in *Nicotine Psychopharmacology,* ed. Jack E. Henningfield, Edythe D. London, and Sakire Pogun (Berlin: Springer, 2009), 487–510, quote from 496.

19. Individuals who are in maintenance therapy (the specific drugs buproprion and varenicline are mentioned) get a different label extension with tobacco use disorder. *DSM-5,* 572.

20. For a historical perspective on this, see the Tomes's brilliant essay. Nancy Tomes, "The Great American Medicine Show Revisited," *Bulletin of the History of Medicine* 79 (2005): 627–663.

21. See for example, Jack E. Henningfield and Maxine L. Stitzer, eds., *New Developments in Nicotine-Delivery Systems: Proceedings of a Conference, Johns Hopkins University, September 24, 1990* (Ossining, NY: Cortlandt Communications, 1991).

22. Douglas Ziedonis et al., "Tobacco Use and Cessation in Psychiatric Disorders: National Institute of Mental Health Report," *Nicotine & Tobacco Research* 10 (2008): 1691–1715.

23. See for example, Robert Whitaker, *Anatomy of an Epidemic: Magic Bullets, Psychiatric Drugs, and the Astonishing Rise of Mental Illness in America* (New York: Crown, 2010); Howard I. Kushner, "The Other War on Drugs: The Pharmaceutical Industry, Evidence-Based Medicine, and Clinical Practice," *Journal of Policy History* 19 (2007): 49–70; David Healy, *Let Them Eat Prozac: The Unhealthy Relationship between the Pharmaceutical Industry and Depression* (New York: New York University Press, 2004); Jill A. Fisher, *Medical Research for Hire: The Political Economy of Pharmaceutical Clinical Trials* (New Brunswick, NJ: Rutgers University Press, 2009); and Daniel J. Carlat, *Unhinged: The Trouble with Psychiatry—A Doctor's Revelations about a Profession in Crisis* (New York: Free Press, 2010).

24. See for example, Michael A. Steinman et al., "Characteristics and Impact of Drug Detailing for Gabapentin," *PLoS Medicine* 4 (2007): e134; Michael A. Steinman et al., "Narrative Review: The Promotion of Gabapentin: An Analysis of Internal Industry Documents," *Annals of Internal Medicine* 145 (2006): 284–293.

25. David Healy, *Pharmageddon* (Berkeley: University of California Press, 2012).

26. For example, one group insisted that that the effective use of varenicline in mentally ill populations had been "hampered" by reports that it was not safe. They offered their own double-blind study to prove this—with a grand total of eight patients. See Elaine Weiner et al., "Letter to the Editor: Varenicline for Smoking Cessation in People with Schizophrenia: A Double Blind Randomized Pilot Study," *Schizophrenia Research* 129 (2011): 94–95.

27. On physicians' disinclination to report adverse events, see for example, Barry Meier, "Doctors Who Don't Speak Out," *New York Times,* 15 February 2013.

28. Andrea H. Weinberger et al., "Predictors of Abstinence and Changes in Psychiatric Symptoms in a Pooled Sample of Smokers with Schizophrenia Receiving Combination Pharmacotherapy and Behavioral Therapy for Smoking Cessation," *Journal of Clinical Psychopharmacology* 29 (2009): 601–603; Elaine Weiner et al., "Buproprion Sustained Release Added to Group Support for Smoking Cessation in Schizophrenia: A New Randomized Trial and a Meta-Analysis," *Journal of Clinical Psychiatry* 73 (2012): 95–102; and Sunny J. Dutra et al., "Varenicline as a Smoking Cessation Aid in Schizophrenia: Effects on Smoking Behavior and Reward Sensitivity," *Psychopharmacology* 219 (2012): 25–34.

29. Natalie McGauran et al., "Reporting Bias in Medical Research—A Narrative Review," *Trials* 11 (2010): 37.

30. See for example, letter to the editor, *American Journal of Psychiatry* 156 (1999): 798–799.

31. Healy, *Pharmageddon*. See also, Lisa Cosgrove et al., "Conflicts of Interest and Disclosure in the American Psychiatric Association's Clinical Practice Guidelines," *Psychotherapy and Psychosomatics* 78 (2009): 228–232.

32. Jeremy A. Greene, *Prescribing by Numbers: Drugs and the Definition of Disease* (Baltimore: Johns Hopkins University Press, 2007).

33. Brian Hitsman et al., "Treatment of Tobacco Dependence in Mental Health and Addictive Disorders," *Canadian Journal of Psychiatry* 54 (2009): 368–377. See also, Karl Fagerström and Henri-Jean Aubin, "Management of Smoking Cessation in Patients with Psychiatric Disorders," *Current Medical Research & Opinion* 25 (2009): 511–518.

34. On the problems of pharmaceutical-industry practices and mental illness, see especially Allen Frances, *Saving Normal: An Insider's Revolt against Out-of-Control Psychiatric Diagnosis, DSM-5, Big Pharma, and the Medicalization of Ordinary Life* (New York: HarperCollins, 2013); Carlat, *Unhinged*.

35. Deanna L. Kelly et al., "Cigarette Smoking and Mortality Risk in People with Schizophrenia," *Schizophrenia Bulletin* 37 (2011): 832–838.

36. See for example, Alex Berenson, "Lilly Settles with 18,000 over Zyprexa," *New York Times*, 5 January 2007.

37. Riccardo Polosa et al., "Effect of an Electronic Nicotine Delivery Device (e-Cigarette) on Smoking Reduction and Cessation: A Prospective 6-Month Pilot Study," *BMC Public Health* 11 (2011): 786–797; C. Bullen et al., "Effect of an Electronic Nicotine Delivery Device (e cigarette) on Desire to Smoke and Withdrawal, User Preferences and Nicotine Delivery: Randomised Cross-Over Trial," *Tobacco Control* 19 (2010): 98–103.

38. T. R. McAuley et al., "Comparison of the Effects of e-Cigarette Vapor and Cigarette Smoke on Indoor Air Quality," *Inhalation Toxicology* 24 (2012): 850–857.

39. For exhortations about caution, see for example, Jennifer L. Pearson et al., "e-Cigarette Awareness, Use, and Harm Perceptions in US Adults," *American Journal of Public Health* 102 (2012): 1758–1766.

40. Kirsten Bell and Helen Keane, "Nicotine Control: E-cigarettes, Smoking and Addiction," *International Journal of Drug Policy* 23 (2012): 242–247. Many public-health analysts are distressed by the idea that smokeless tobacco could be marketed as safer than conventional cigarettes. See Adrienne B. Mejia and Pamela M. Ling, "Tobacco Industry Consumer Research on Smokeless Tobacco Users and Product Development," *American Journal of Public Health* 100 (2010): 78–87.

41. Stuart Elliott, "E-Cigarette Makers' Ads Echo Tobacco's Heyday," *New York Times*, 29 August 2013.

42. Michael Rowe et al., "Clinical Responsibility and Client Autonomy: Dilemmas in Mental Health Work at the Margins," *American Journal of Orthopsychiatry* 71 (2001): 400–407.

43. Judith J. Prochaska, "Smoking and Mental Illness—Breaking the Link," *New England Journal of Medicine* 365 (2011): 196–198; Melinda Beck, "Helping the Mentally Ill to Quit Smoking," *Wall Street Journal*, 25 April 2011.

44. Sharon J. Lawn, Rene G. Pols, and James G. Barber, "Smoking and Quitting: A Qualitative Study with Community-Living Psychiatric Clients," *Social Science & Medicine* 54 (2002): 93–104, quote from 97.

45. The same kind of discussion is going on about prison populations. See for example, R. M. Kauffman, A. K. Ferketich, and M. E. Wewers, "Tobacco Policy in American Prisons, 2007," *Tobacco Control* 17 (2008): 357–360.

46. Elizabeth A. Smith and Ruth E. Malone, "'We Will Speak as the Smoker': The Tobacco Industry's Smokers' Rights Groups," *European Journal of Public Health*

17 (2007): 306–313. See also, Jill M. Williams, "Eliminating Tobacco Use in Mental Health Facilities: Patients' Rights, Public Health, and Policy Issues," *JAMA* 299 (2008): 571–573.

47. Kenneth Marcus, "Letter to the Editor," *Psychiatric Services* 59 (2008): 330. See also, letter to the editor, *Psychiatric Services* 59 (2008): 576–577.

48. Some within health policy have pointed out that socioeconomic status is more important than individual risk factors for disease and for health behavior. See Bruce G. Link and Jo C. Phelan, "Fundamental Sources of Health Inequalities," in Mechanic et al., *Policy Challenges in Modern Health Care,* 71–84.

49. Denise L. Duranleau to R. J. Reynolds, 12 November 1985, LTDL (Bates 505438082/8084), http://legacy.library.ucsf.edu/tid/fon13a00.

50. See for example, Lawn, Pols, and Barber, "Smoking and Quitting."

51. David Mechanic, "Correcting Misconceptions in Mental Health Policy: Strategies for Improved Care of the Seriously Mentally Ill," *Milbank Quarterly* 65 (1987): 203–230; David Mechanic, "Mental Health Services Then And Now," *Health Affairs* 26 (2007): 1548–1550.

52. Mechanisms for public commentary on federal policy, for example, are open in general but the particular concerns of the mentally ill may be absent. They are missing in the public commentary that followed the proposed FDA rule to regulate tobacco products in 1995. Andrew L. Roth, Joshua Dunsby, and Lisa A. Bero, "Framing Processes in Public Commentary on US Federal Tobacco Control Regulation," *Social Studies of Science* 33 (2003): 7–44.

53. For issues around self-control and reducing health risk, see Allan M. Brandt, "Behavior, Disease, and Health in the Twentieth-Century United States: The Moral Valence of Individual Risk," in *Morality and Health,* ed. Allan M. Brandt and Paul Rozin (New York: Routledge, 1997), 53–77.

54. See for example, Whitaker, *Anatomy of an Epidemic.*

55. There are programs that are working more on incorporating consumer groups, but they are still focused primarily on smoking rather than engaging on a broader, consumer-driven agenda. See for example, "A Hidden Epidemic: Tobacco Use and Mental Illness," June 2011, Legacy For Health, http://www.legacyforhealth.org/content/download/608/7232/file/A_Hidden_Epidemic.pdf, accessed 2 August 2013.

56. British scholars who described the importance of social inclusion for individuals with mental illness identified the need for cigarette breaks in order to make sure that these individuals were able to participate in policy discussions that affected them. Julie Repper and Rachel Perkins, *Social Inclusion and Recovery: A Model for Mental Health Practice* (New York: Bailliere Tindall, 2003), 198.

57. Patricia E. Deegan, "Recovery and the Conspiracy of Hope," Presented at the Sixth Annual Mental Health Services Conference of Australia and New Zealand, Brisbane, Australia, 1996, https://www.patdeegan.com/pat-deegan/lectures/conspiracy-of-hope, accessed 2 August 2013.

58. For an analysis of power issues between traditional approaches and a more client-centered approach, see for example Kristin M. Novotny, "Experts in Their Own Lives: Emphasizing Client-Centeredness in a Homeless Program," *Policy Studies Journal* 28 (2000): 382–401.

59. In Michigan, the Medicaid benefit for prescription nicotine is only available for three months in a calendar year.

60. Nancy Tomes, "From Outsiders to Insiders: The Consumer-Survivor Movement and Its Impact on U.S. Mental Health Policy," in *Patients as Policy Actors,* ed. Beatrix Hoffman et al. (New Brunswick, NJ: Rutgers University Press, 2011), 113–131.
61. One of the most effective treatments for self-injurious behaviors, dialectical behavior therapy, was created by a mental-health professional who recently revealed that she had struggled with this behavior herself in the past. Benedict Carey, "Expert on Mental Illness Reveals Her Own Fight," *New York Times,* 23 June 2011.
62. Sarah Elizabeth Gordon, "Recovery Constructs and the Continued Debate That Limits Consumer Recovery," *Psychiatric Services* 64 (2013): 270–271.
63. For an early first-person account that blames smoking for his diagnosis of schizophrenia, see Gilbert Daze, "Nicotine Addiction and Schizophrenia," *Journal of Orthomolecular Medicine* 5 (1990): 179–181.
64. See for example, Repper and Perkins, *Social Inclusion and Recovery;* Sally Zinman, Howie the Harp, and Su Budd, eds., *Reaching Across: Mental Health Clients Helping Each Other* (Boston: Center for Psychiatric Rehabilitation, 1987).

Index

About the Author

Laura D. Hirshbein is a psychiatrist and medical historian at the University of Michigan. Her first book, *American Melancholy: Constructions of Depression in the Twentieth Century*, was published by Rutgers University Press in 2009.

Available titles in the Critical Issues in Health and Medicine series:

CPSIA information can be obtained at www.ICGtesting.com
Printed in the USA
BVOW04s1002120115

382757BV00001B/5/P